Life Rhymes

For the Passion-Centered Life

Walt F.J. Goodridge

LIFE RHYMES
For the Passion-Centered Life

Published and distributed by:
The Passion Profit Company,
an imprint of a company called W
P.O. Box 618
Church Street Station
New York, NY 10008-0618
email: orders@passionprofit.com

Educational institutions, government agencies, libraries and corporations are invited to inquire about quantity discounts.

Retail Cost: $34.95
ISBN-10: 0-9745313-1-6
ISBN-13: 978-0-9745313-1-1
Printed in the United States of America

Library of Congress Cataloging-in-Publication Data

Goodridge, Walt F. J.
Life rhymes : for the passion-centered life / Walt Goodridge.
p. cm.
ISBN-13: 978-0-9745313-1-1 (pbk. : alk. paper)
1. Conduct of life--Miscellanea. 2. Affirmations. 3. Conduct of life--Quotations, maxims, etc. 4. Maxims, American. I. Title.

BJ1581.2.G665 2005
158.1--dc22

2004029906

The History of Walt's Life Rhymes

There seems to be some interest
in these thoughts I have to share
it's nothing more than encouraging words
we all do need to hear
--From Life Rhyme #100

My name is Walt F.J. Goodridge. On August 29, 1997, shortly after my introduction to the world of the Internet, I started a weekly email called *Walt's Friday Inspirations*. It was a creation born of my desire to share words of motivation and inspiration with my email list of friends, family, customers and business partners. Every Thursday night, I would peruse different motivational books, poems, and the like in search of profound and uplifting thoughts that I could pass on to the then 800 contacts on my list.

By the end of December, 1997, however, the ritual Thursday night motivation hunt was becoming a bit of a drag. And then I had an idea: Why not, I asked myself, write these inspirations myself and save myself the hassle of the usual search? After all, by that time I had already written a few books and even a few poems of my own, and felt that I could do just as good a job communicating positive thoughts as anybody else.

So beginning on Friday, January 2, 1998 with Inspiration #19, I took the chance that my self-authored inspirational thoughts would be appreciated just as much, if not more, than the tried and true words from the masters. I was right! Walt's Life Rhymes started to catch on. I started getting email requests from people wanting to be put on my list. I received support from newspapers and others who wanted to include them in their publications and websites and even read them at weddings.

So today, I proudly present to you the result of 365 *consecutive weeks of inspiration in this first-ever anthology of Walt's Life Rhymes. Enjoy them, be inspired, make the words part of your own silent inner performance, and let your greatness be expressed through them...and always remember....

...success is a journey,
not a destination!

Walt Goodridge
"I share what I know,
so that others may grow!"

**During a particularly turbulent and nomadic period of my life in early 1998 (the full story of my pursuit of entrepreneurial success can be found in Turn Your Passion Into Profit), I found myself composing my weekly emails on a friend's computer. When I eventually moved to my own space, these files got corrupted and lost forever. Life Rhymes 27-31, therefore, are not originals, but replacements of these fabled Lost Life Rhymes!*

Walt's Life Rhymes are presented
in descending order from 365 to 1
suggesting their use as daily guide for any
365-day period of your life.

Walt's Life Rhyme #365: An Easy Roll

Sometimes when you're lost
and you start giving in to fear
All you really need to know
is yes, the road's still there

Sometimes when the engine's on
but wheels just seem to spin
A touch is all it takes
to free you from the mess you're in

Sometimes when your vision's blocked
beyond the crests and turns
Reminders of your goal appear
and clarity returns

Yes, sometimes on this road called life
the easy role you play
Is giving hope by meeting those
who've yet to make their way

Just knowing those who traveled
who're alive to tell the tale
Makes possible the dream
you too can prosper and prevail!

An Easy Roll
Walt's Life Rhyme #365

"I share what I know,
so that others may grow!"
www.LifeRhymes.com

Commentary for Walt's Life Rhyme #365

A Fan Writes:

Hi Walt,

My name is Rhonda. I attended your seminar at the Learning Annex last night (I'm the woman who sang "I Feel Good" during the break) and just wanted to drop you a note to say thank you. It has taken some time for me to understand that there are no coincidences in life...you see, every time I ask myself if I am moving in the right direction I am answered with blessings like your seminar.

Fear (fear of failure or perhaps fear of success) has been such a paralyzing factor in my life and I have committed myself to change and overcoming that challenge. There are two passions that I have been drawn to pursue and I have been blessed with souls who have dedicated love and time to my efforts.

The first is my love of music and my strong desire to use my voice to help people feel good about the lives we live. In the quest of celebrating life in my own way, I seek the wisdom of others, through song and through other artistic expression...which led to the creation of "woven paper wonders" [my own] decorative keepsakes and gift boxes). I have given myself a deadline to develop and launch the full website, produce a Rhonda Denet LIVE! CD and DVD, and line up a gig with local dinner cruises as well as more playing opportunities throughout the city. With regards to woven paper wonders, I have a partner, and our goal is to develop a full line of themed and quote boxes as well as a substantial custom order clientele. (You're probably thinking...get to the point).

Well the point is that every day gets better, every moment and interaction lets me know this is the right thing for me. I have been more focused than ever before, but from time to time that old habit of succumbing to fear grabs me by the throat. Last night that changed, I know I am no longer alone! Reading books is one thing, but being in the presence of one who has achieved despite that same fear stirs my soul (I was so filled with joy and excitement last night I can't even explain).

Thank you so much for sharing your story and your inspiration. I will definitely keep an eye out and take as many of your classes that fit my schedule. I am buying your book from St. Marks books in New York today (pay day)!

Be well, Rhonda Lipscomb

Walt Replies:

Yes, Rhonda. I've found that sometimes my role is quite simply to show up to let others know I leapt, I lost, licked it, and I lived to tell the tale. It's a little push that can serve to get others rolling again. Thanks for contributing your song during the "massage break" at the workshop (see what the rest of you missed?), and for letting me share your email!--Walt

Walt's Life Rhyme #364: There's Something About Money

This thing about money and seeking it
Just look closely I'm sure that you'll find
Those who have it in spades are still searching for joy
those in lack think it's how life is defined

This thing about money and having it
this we learn from the day of our birth
Simply having a lot can't give life meaning at all
but the absence speaks about your self worth

This thing about money and happiness
This both pauper and king know for sure
While it's true wealth won't buy you the joy that you seek
you're served no better at all being poor!

This thing about money and evil
all who get it know this to be true
The money you have doesn't change you at all
it just brings out the real inner you

This thing about money and needing it
truth will out despite all that you do
Yes reject and refuse it as much as you like
money matters for rent is still due

So please once and for all just admit it
Face the facts. Things will change. Guaranteed.
Accept that you're trapped in a money-mad world
and from the clutches of money you'll be freed!

No sir, money's not the answer to happiness
Those who have it attest beyond doubt
So if it's true once I'm rich I'll be seeking it still
Then I'd rather seek with than without

There's Something About Money
Walt's Life Rhyme #364

"I share what I know,
so that others may grow!"
www.LifeRhymes.com

"The poor mistake the struggle for the seeking
and never get beyond simply how to survive
The rich may win the game of the getting
but learn too late there's more to being alive."
--Walt Goodridge

Commentary for Walt's Life Rhyme #364

Do you mean less to yourself than the money you need?

Despite your protestations that money doesn't buy happiness; Despite your belief that it's the root of all evil; despite your unwillingness to attribute more meaning to it in your life; the fact still remains you've got rent to pay. So why do you run from money? Why do you allow your talents to go unrewarded? Why do you allow money to be absent in your life and suffer the indignity of borrowing from friends and family? Why do you struggle when it's just as easy to thrive?

At the risk of oversimplifying a complex issue, I suggest to you that the amount of money you allow into your life is a direct reflection of and in direct proportion to the amount of value you place on yourself--i.e. your self worth. One could argue, in other words, that there's a direct correlation between how much you love yourself and how much joy you allow yourself to experience in life in a dollar-driven world, where money is the vehicle for the journey to peace of mind and happiness. How serene can you be with the landlord knocking at your door?

So is the possession and presence of money in your life always an indication of self-love? Absolutely not. We know many wealthy people for whom happiness is still an elusive dream. But we also know that for others, the absence of money, and the resulting struggle that many accept in their lives, reflects a reluctance to feel worthy of and embrace all the joy that life in our society offers; and it distracts you from the real search. I meet many people in my workshops who are conflicted about charging appropriately for their services, making more money than their parents, or simply pursuing wealth all because they undervalue their creations, and thus, themselves.

So do yourself a favor. Accept that it's part of a game that everyone born into a capitalistic society has to play to some degree. Whether wealthy or wanting, we all become trapped in the same race. Some get stuck at amateur. Some go on to Pro. In a dollar-driven world, every road leads to money. The journey only stops being about money once you get there! The real quest is for a happiness that money can't buy. The seeking never stops even when you have money, so you may as well have it while you search. Go for it!!!

Walt's Life Rhyme #363: Life Without Walls

The walls came down around me
and at first I was really quite shocked
For you never know quite how much you have missed
when your vision has always been blocked

The walls came down around me
and for a time all the world could then see
That it matters not much what side of the wall you live on
for it stops each one and all from being free

The walls came down around me
and when a new day began to dawn
We all got excited for what life could become
once all the walls built around us were gone

The walls came down around me
but then someone gave in to the fear
For some can't imagine a life without walls
so they rebel when real freedom is near

The walls came down around me
and what I've learned now makes me frown
That the hardest thing to achieve when you're pursuing your dreams
is keeping those darned walls down!

Life Without Walls
Walt's Life Rhyme #363

*"I share what I know,
so that others may grow!"*
www.LifeRhymes.com

Commentary:

Freedom has a price. Whether it's the freedom of being a full-time entrepreneur, the freedom of vulnerability in a relationship, the freedom of pursuing and achieving your dreams, or the freedom of living in a free society, all freedom comes with a price.

Taking risks as you venture into the unknown, changing old habits, redefining yourself and your views of others are the challenges we must face as we endeavor to enjoy the freedom life offers. If you're accustomed to seeing life through the narrow openings in the walls that society has built up around you, then the hardest part of growing into your new-found freedom, is keeping the old habits at bay while you establish new ones. Stay strong, and don't let your fears be manipulated by others who profit from them.

Passionpreneur and coaching client Ken Greene has written a new book entitled *When the Walls Came Down* about his first-hand, survivor experience inside the World Trade Center complex when the walls fell. Ken recalls the fall of those physical walls, but also the walls that some segments of our society seek to rebuild despite the optimism and opportunity for healing that existed after Sept 11, 2001.

*To commemorate the publication of
When the Walls Came Down by Ken Greene*

Walt's Life Rhyme #362: Like Wishes And Water

What good are all your wishes
when your words serve to negate?
What good are aspirations
when their power you debate?

For even without water
planted dreams might just take hold
But water from the wells of woe
on dreams will take its toll

Such words can dowse the flame
and kill your own will to succeed
Or words can be the water
that might save the starving seed

So speak your dreams aloud
and let them find a place to grow
Then water them with words
and all the power they bestow!

Like Wishes and Water
Walt's Life Rhyme #362

*"I share what I know,
so that others may grow!"*
www.LifeRhymes.com

Commentary:

We talked about trust. You felt it didn't exist. I offered a view of an alternate reality where love exists based on trust, and suggested that you can find it, and others who live it, if you simply looked.

You could fathom, but had no faith. So you countered my words with disbelief. So, I said the words again, and you parried with the only reality you know.

I said the words yet again. But this time, a moment of silence was what I asked of you. For there's power in letting the sound, scent, sight and substance of your secret dreams linger in the air without contest, without debate, and untainted by the water from the well of a jaded past.

I wanted the words to take root somewhere in a quiet, unprotesting part of your heart. And when we speak again, we can water your wishes with only those words and actions that support the realization of your dreams, no matter how unfathomable they may seem to you right now!

Dedicated to EJB

Walt's Life Rhyme #361: The Eternal Optimist

I've fallen and I can't get up, but wow check out the view!
The walls have crashed, but now I see the sunshine's coming through

The pain's intense, but now I know for sure what I can stand
I'm scared as heck, but doing this means comfort zones expand

Things didn't work the way I planned, but hey it's just one step
And failures are the lessons learned that make me more adept

It's really not so bad, I fall, I bounce back like elastic
Convinced I am beyond all doubt that life's always faaaaaantastic!

The Eternal Optimist
Walt's Life Rhyme #361

"I share what I know,
so that others may grow!"
www.LifeRhymes.com

Walt's Life Rhyme #360: Maximize the Moment
aka A Game Called Feed the Seed

We are gathered here today
for deeper reasons yet unknown
To pose to each a question
for some purpose to be shown

Yes someone holds a message
that is meant here to be shared
To help another cure a hurt
or face a challenge feared

Your presence is the proof
there's more beyond your mere arrival
For life never shows up
without the means for its survival

We all comprise the soil
that helps to nourish and to grow
So help another budding seed:
share something that you know!

Maximize the Moment
A Game Called "Feed The Seed"
Walt's Life Rhyme #360

"I share what I know,
so that others may grow!"
www.LifeRhymes.com

Commentary for Walt's Life Rhyme #360

Next time you get together with family or friends, play "Feed the Seed." It's sort of like a "Truth or Dare", but without the dare. The object of the game is to delve deeper into the potential and nourishing power that your family, friends and intimate relationships have in your life.

"Feed the Seed" is based on the belief that at any given moment, everything you need in your life is *always* there through the people and situations that show up. Proof of this is readily available in nature. No seed ever buds where life is not supported. And birds migrate by instinct to where conditions support their survival. In other words, life won't appear unless the conditions are right. Similarly, your very presence here today, and for that matter *any* place you show up, is the proof that there's food there for you to grow. Your mission, like the seeking roots of a tree, is to delve ever deeper into your environment in search of that food.

The reason some of those invited to an event don't show up; the reason why some people are not here today while others are is because they are someplace else that supports their growth at that specific moment. Their roots are someplace else. You, however, are always *exactly* where you need to be. Where you are now, is right where your seeking has gotten you. You are always in your *best* environment for the moment. Your "environment" is comprised of people and conditions. The fact you're here means there's food to grow.

Furthermore, we stagnate and get stuck in life because we don't maximize the moments with these people, or glean the most from our situations. Why is this person in my life? Why has this particular group convened tonight? Obviously there is an attraction of some sort, a hoped-for outcome, a seeking that has brought us here. So, let's maximize the moments in our lives, and play Feed the Seed! Here are the rules:

1. First, each person reveals his or her greatest personal fear, failure or feeling and why they feel that way. It must be something that they've never revealed before to the majority of the participants. (i.e. I fear I'll disappoint my kids because...", "I always feel out of control, because..." "I failed at my first marriage because...." I feel I'll fail in my business, because...)
2. Then, one by one, without interrupting anyone else, every person offers a comment or insight starting with "In my own experience, I've found..." The goal is to offer supportive spiritual, mental and strategic food to encourage growth, by discovering another person's perspective.
3. Always speak from your own experience only. Never tell a person what they *should or shouldn't* do. Never tell a person they shouldn't feel that way. To help, you might start your comments with "I know how you feel, I felt the same way, Here's what I found...etc.")
4. Remember, the game is its own reward. The object is simply to support one-another in a non-threatening, non-judgmental environment. The very act of sharing a deeper aspect of your thoughts and feelings, and of getting feedback at that deeper level is akin to a deepening of the roots that then soak up the nourishment that exists at that level--nourishment you could never find at a shallower level.
5. Repeat or simply do one round until everyone feels they got as deep as they want or need to.

Remember:

The food you need is always there
delve deeper and you'll find
You're nourished through the people
with whose lives you're intertwined--Walt

Walt's Life Rhyme #359: The Handwriting On The Wall

Part 1: For Others

It's not hard to tell the future
and in time you will agree
That everyone is well equipped
to see what prophets see

For all you need's a memory
and a working pair of eyes
To see beyond what's plain
and through most anyone's disguise

For actions not announcements
show what's really in one's heart
And feelings become clues to read
the future they impart

The way we do the single thing
is how all else is done
And odds of change unless compelled
go fast from bad to none

And most will do the very thing
that manifests their fears
Despite accumulated wisdom
woes or intervening years

Yes everyone's a prophet
it's not difficult at all
It's easy once you're fluent
in handwritings on the wall

Part 2: For Yourself

I knew it all along!
I wasn't shocked when it appeared
The thing that came to pass?
Yep, the very thing I truly feared

The most uncanny thing I've found
from younger years to old
I've got this knack for knowing
how things are likely to unfold

Sometimes things turn out wonderful
sometimes they go awry
But either way I'll sense it first
on this I can rely

When worry fills my day
the thing I fear will soon show up
On days my dreams excite me
blessings overflow my cup

The one thing that I can't predict
though, much to my dismay
Is whether fears or dreams
will rule my waking thoughts this day

With just that extra knowledge
Think of riches that could flow
I dream one day I'll get there
but, fear more I'll never know

The Handwriting On The Wall
Walt's Life Rhyme #359

"I share what I know,
so that others may grow!"
www.LifeRhymes.com

Commentary for Walt's Life Rhyme #359

As you read today's double-dose of Life Rhyme, think about how it applies to your relationships, your business affairs or dealings with coworkers on your job. Use it to reinforce the use of intuition as a guide in your life, and to help you prepare for life's seemingly unpredictable situations. Nothing happens by accident, or just out of the blue, you know.--Walt

Ever had something occur that you predicted would come true? Do you often notice the evidence and clues of something about to happen that others seem oblivious to? When that happens, it's said you've seen "the handwriting on the wall."

Whether in our own lives, or in relation to how others will act, we all have this ability. The truth is, however, your ability to read this familiar handwriting may be more than your knack for *predicting* the future. It could be, in fact, evidence of your success in *creating* it.

The handwriting on the wall reveals nothing less than the sum of all your fears and nothing more than your faith in all your dreams. And people will ascend by faith to the equivalent height of their dreams and descend through fear to the depths of their despair. And those who seem to have the power of prophecy simply know this to be so.

In other words, the sequence of steps that precede the outcomes in your life, as well as those intuitive glimpses, gut reactions, and prophetic insights that you experience right before life's seemingly unpredictable situations are not prophecy, they may, in fact, be plan. Things happen because of the attractive force of your fears, coupled with the creative power of your dreams. You've been attracting and creating these things all your life. You've also been noticing how other people attract and create in their own lives. So it's only natural that you get better and better at "predicting" the future.

To get better at prophecy, it helps to know these and other truths about yourself and other people:

1. A person's actions and feelings speak louder than words. Observe closely, and trust your instincts.

2. If it hatched from a duck egg, and was a duck yesterday and the day before, chances are it will be a duck today and tomorrow too. So accept that people will probably repeat tomorrow what they've been known to do today. (Yes, people *can and do* change. But in the absence of compelling reasons and the resulting effort on their part, you can predict what people will do)

3. The way we do anything is the way we do everything. One's habits and personality show up everywhere in life.

And always remember, the power of prophecy is in your thoughts. Therefore *you* decide whether fears or dreams will rule your day!

Walt's Life Rhyme #358: Dreamsicle
Enjoy Life's Frozen Treats

Time to make a Dreamsicle!
What's that??? I hear you say
A Dreamsicle's a treat you get
When life is going your way

A dream's just like a hot idea
like steam that's hard to touch
And just like steaming water
will evaporate as such

But cool the steam a bit
and liquid water's how it's known
And cooled ideas are actions
that like streams can wear through stone

Cool further, add some flavor
and like water when it's cold
Your actions yield results
like tasty treats to touch and hold

So make your life a Dreamsicle!
And as silly as it may seem
Know that nothing's ever sweeter
than to live the life you dream!

Dreamsicle
Walt's Life Rhyme #358

"I share what I know,
so that others may grow!"
www.LifeRhymes.com

Commentary:

Think about this. Everything in our reality in its most basic form is simply the same energy vibrating at different rates. Steam, water and ice are all the same H_2O. A glass of water is nothing more than gaseous steam (high rate of vibration, invisible) that has cooled down to liquid form. And when cooled even further becomes solid ice (low rate of vibration, visible).

Similarly, your thoughts are nothing more than ideas (high rate of vibration, invisible) that have cooled down to become objects or results in your life (low rate of vibration, visible).

So, just as popsicles are frozen, flavored soda pop on a stick, *Dreamsicles* are what your dreams become when they cool down and take on solid form. (Work with me here!)

Yes, your dreams start out as steaming hot thoughts or ideas that, if cooled, flavored and prepared correctly, can yield one of life's tastiest treats! But be careful. *Any* thought can become solid. (Thoughtsicle, anyone?) But not all thoughtsicles are dreamsicles. Negative, fearful thoughts can solidify into something real in your life, but don't taste nearly as sweet. You've got to add the right flavor to all your thoughts so you get the taste you want out of life. So dream the dreams, set some goals, take the necessary actions, and enjoy all the flavor that life has to offer! Make your life a dreamsicle!

Walt's Life Rhyme #357: Miss Fortune

I can sigh with deep frustration
at those times we disagree
I can wonder how it is
you just don't see the things I see

I can whine and tell my friends
that this was never meant to be
I can plot revenge and spite
so you can share my misery

I can contemplate departure
and the things I'll do once free
I can blame you if things fail
so that the spotlight's not on me

Yes, I can rail against misfortune
cursing fate and destiny
Or I can let you be just who you are
and work on changing me!

Miss Fortune
Walt's Life Rhyme #357

*"I share what I know,
so that others may grow!"*
www.LifeRhymes.com

Commentary:

When Miss Fortune enters your life, welcome her with open arms. She has come to teach you something. She is here to help you focus on those areas of yourself that need adjustment. She has not come to be changed by you. She is who she is, and is but a mirror to help you see yourself so you can accept, then love who you are.

Once you love who you are, then Miss Fortune's ways and woes won't sway your even keel. Her ways will simply remind you that you need to improve your patience, understanding, forgiveness, faith and courage. That is always her lesson.

Miss Fortune may appear as an actual person in your life. Or she may be a situation or circumstance that has come to visit. You won't always recognize her divine beauty and perfection, but, true to her name, Miss Fortune is a treasure to behold...once you see her for who she is.

So, if you're in a relationship with Miss Fortune, spend your time together wisely. For Miss Fortune holds a fickle flame, and will seek new suitors to play her game. And this test too shall you pass.

Walt's Life Rhyme #356: How Long? aka "Just You Wait"

The depth of your dreams
are unfathomable
to those who have none--Walt

How Long?
Walt's Life Rhyme #356
© Walt F.J. Goodridge
"I share what I know,
so that others may grow!'
www.LifeRhymes.com

How long should I keep asking
if I'm not getting a reply?
Perhaps I'll set a limit
and then no more Mr. Nice Guy!

How long should I expect
that "things will simply all work out"?
I've lived by that philosophy
But now I'm having doubt

How long should I persist
and follow those who do believe
You knock and doors will open
You ask and you'll receive?

How long should I keep waiting
for results to manifest?
I know the key is patience
And this is just a cosmic test

For time does not exist
'cause NOW is all we ever know
And measured dreams won't feed the soul
(like seeds we never sow)

I am, therefore I dream
of that there's nothing to debate
So as long as I keep dreaming,
as long, too, so will I wait!

Commentary:

I have a friend who, being the more traditional/practical member of a marriage to an entrepreneurial dreamer, asked me, "How long do you pursue your entrepreneurial dreams before you give up and get a real job?" She wanted to understand her husband's way of thinking, as well as how much time she should allow before asking him to change course.

"You don't understand," I told her. "Real dreamers don't set time limits on their dreams. They don't say, 'I'll work at this for 5 years, and if I don't make it, I'll abandon the dream'. Real dreamers commit to the journey once, and then go for it. For the journey's the thing, however long it takes. Dreamers can't stop themselves from dreaming. And when they dream, they dream with no end in sight save the living of the dream."

Walt's Life Rhyme #355: I Asked The Skies a Question

I asked the skies a question
as my goals I did pursue
I asked what will it take of me
to make my dreams come true

I asked what skills I needed
and what talents I should hone
I asked what education
and what textbooks I should own

I asked what royal lineage
would unblock my path to fame
I asked how much inheritance
would win me world acclaim

I asked for just one secret
I could use to turn life's tide
I asked for just one clue
and then, alas, the skies replied:

Truth be told the answer's
much more plain than you could know
For all it takes to change the world's
the will to make it so!

I Asked The Skies a Question
Walt's Life Rhyme #355

"I share what I know,
so that others may grow!"
www.LifeRhymes.com

Walt's Life Rhyme #354: Acorn

See the stream of circumstances
sailing through the air
Pulled in like a magnet
by the thoughts that brought them here

Mark the march of mortals
who meander through your life
Harmonize with lovers
and repel lovers of strife

Draw upon the genius
that you'll find within your hand
Turn this tide of talent
to create what you have planned

And like the acorn's patterned plan
attracts what's in the ground
Everything you need to grow
is already all around

And growth, just like the planted seed
can happen right on cue
But only what's in harmony
will find its way to you!

Acorn
Walt's Life Rhyme #354
©Walt F.J. Goodridge
"I share what I know,
so that others may grow!"
www.LifeRhymes.com

Commentary:

"Within the acorn, there is a nucleus or patterned plan that dictates the vibratory rate at which [its] molecules move. ...as soon as you plant the acorn in the earth, the patterned plan or the vibratory rate of the acorn sets up an attractive force and the acorn begins to attract everything that vibrates in harmony with it. If you were able to observe with the naked eye exactly what is taking place, you would see a "parade" of particles of energy--a never-ending stream of them--marching in a very orderly manner toward the acorn. As they come in contact with the molecules making up the acorn, they would join, marry, become one, and of course, the acorn would expand, become larger, grow."-- from *You Were Born Rich* by Bob Proctor:

All matter (solid, liquid and gas) is composed of atoms that are always moving (vibrating). Even our thoughts are nothing more than energy vibrating at a very high rate. So everything, including our thoughts, by virtue of their rate of vibration will, like the seed, and like the tuning fork which starts to vibrate when a similarly tuned fork is struck (remember that demonstration?), resonate with certain other thoughts, circumstances and people, which are inexorably drawn to them by the law of nature.

So think of your thoughts, attitudes, ideas, and the images you hold in your mind, therefore, as similar to the "patterned plan" of a seed which automatically attracts the elements from the environment that it needs to grow. Remember that successful, healthy and kind individuals vibrate differently than those who are not, and so will always attract circumstances consistent with their thoughts. Remember this affirmation as you grow through life: "My thoughts set about vibrations that automatically attract the corresponding people and circumstances I require for the manifestation of my dreams. I simply need to continue to resonate from the programmed plan at all times, and all the synchronous elements I require will be attracted through the ether, combine with me and facilitate the growth and expansion that will result in the full expression of my dreams."

Walt's Life Rhyme #353: Stone Juice

Life should be getting easier
If it's not then you haven't quite learned
That expectations alone cause you pleasure and pain
and you get from life that which you've earned

Fruits and seeds will yield to your pressure
And flowers give their nectar to bees
And if you tap them just right and are willing to wait
Even sap will start flowing from trees

But in due time you will come to discover
what the wise and the prudent have known
That no matter how much you may press it or plead
you just can't get juice from a stone

Stone Juice
Walt's Life Rhyme #353

*"I share what I know,
so that others may grow!"*
www.LifeRhymes.com

Commentary:

Happiness is an unmet expectation. Therefore, happiness is under your control.

What are you feeling sad about? What are you disappointed with? Who is not bending to your will, doing what you want them to do, or acting how you think they should act?

Chances are whatever you're unhappy about at this precise moment involves an expectation that you had that was not met. Instead of allowing people or situations to be as they are, you've decided to use this as an occasion to make yourself unhappy. You should realize, however, that people and situations don't make you unhappy, your attachment to specific expectations does. Once you accept this, you'll be able to control your unhappiness.

So how do you think positively while allowing for unmet expectations at the same time? Here's the trick. In life you should expect the best outcome. For it's the vibrations of your positive expectations that will attract the good into your life. But, if your dreams don't come true right away, renew the expectations, but detach them from your disappointment.

In other words, attach your positive emotions to the dream. But separate your negative emotions from the outcome. And most importantly, remember that people will be who they've come here to be. You can't expect something for or from someone that they don't see and expect for themselves. In other words, you can't get juice from a stone.

Walt's Life Rhyme #352: The Answer To Everything

"The toppled tree is silent
without you to hear it fall
The world without YOU in it
isn't really there at all"--Walt

I finally found the answer
to any question you could pose!
Before you say I'm crazy
here's the scoop from one who knows

The world's a simple place
it's not as complex as you thought
The answer's yours already, friend
and never need be bought

Whenever you ask where, or who
or why or what to do
Whenever there's a doubt, my friend
the answer's always you

For YOU will take the actions
that bring changes to your life
And YOU will bring the healing
that will calm and end the strife

And YOU will think the thoughts
that will attract the wealth you seek
And YOU will be creator
by the words you choose to speak

And YOU attract your friends and foes
by who you choose to be
And YOU will make things good or bad
by what you choose to see

And YOU confine or free you
through opinions you believe
And YOU plot your own path
through the horizons you perceive

For life's your own perception
expectations and demands...
So truth is every answer
is already in your hands!

Commentary:

As I always say, there's only one of us here!

The Answer to Everything
Walt's Life Rhyme #352

"I share what I know
so that others may grow!"
www.LifeRhymes.com

Walt's Life Rhyme #351: Reverse, Then Make A Right

It's not a sign of weakness to admit you might be wrong
In fact some say you'll access strength that's been there all along

It's not the end of greatness to admit you might be lost
It's greater to save time than to save face at any cost

It won't invite disaster to admit when you don't know
For only to the emptied cup will wisdom ever flow

It's not the road to ruin to go back and start again
The options on the retraced path elude most average men

It's not through compensation that you heal a victim's heart
To listen and seek justice...that's the best way you can start

And it's not by way of vengeance that true justice you invite
But actions that reverse your course, and serve to make things right.

Reverse, Then Make a Right
Walt's Life Rhyme #351

"I share what I know,
so that others may grow!"
www.LifeRhymes.com

Commentary:

A coaching client of mine once commented that she could never see herself conducting workshops about her passion because she didn't feel smart enough, and that there were things she didn't know. "What would I do if someone asked me something I didn't know?" she asked.

"Tell them you don't know," I replied. I suggested she practice saying: "That's a great question. I'm sorry, but honestly, I don't have an answer to that, but if you give me your information, I'll do some research and get back to you." Once I gave her that freedom, a whole new world of opportunities opened up! She became more confident to do speaking engagements and follow her passion.

While it may be true, as Shakespeare said (through Lady MacBeth), that "what's done cannot be undone," I believe the effects of our actions can often be reversed. Embarrassment, failure, mistakes, hurts and the effects of our actions can be reversed if we're willing to add a few words to our vocabularies.

How would your life be affected if you added *"I don't know, I apologize, I was wrong, I need help, and How can I make it right?"* to your life?

Once I added those phrases to my own life, my own fear of speaking engagements subsided, relationships improved, sales increased, and customer approval ratings increased! As a result, the freedom, to follow my passion full-time, and see movies in the middle of the day, became reality!

While listening to an interview with the author of a book entitled *The Myth of Moral Justice: Why Our Legal System Fails to do What's Right*, it occurred to me that those phrases and the ideas behind them would also come in handy in seeking justice for the families of victims of certain crimes. As the author suggested, we've mistaken compensation and retribution for remedy. Money and vengeance don't soothe the victim. It might make our justice system more effective if, instead of reducing pain and suffering to monetary terms, we develop ways to reverse and make a right! Try it in your own life!

Walt's Life Rhyme #350: Far From Shore

New winds have blown your ship off course
and caused it now to stray
And things you thought were forged in stone
have since been washed away

Who'd think that now you'd find yourself
adrift and lost at sea
Unsure of your direction now
unsure of what will be

But heed the great explorers
who leave land and love behind
Empowered by their dreams of wealth
and hopes of what they'll find

Though battered, bruised and buffeted
they held on for the ride
In time they found another star
to be their saving guide

And when their searched-for land appeared
and drift turned into drive
They took triumphant steps ashore
both thankful and alive

You too shall find a brave new world
despite all you'll endure
Just chart your course by faith
whenever lost and far from sure!

Far from Shore
Walt's Life Rhyme #350

*"I share what I know,
so that others may grow!"*
www.LifeRhymes.com

Commentary:

This is an exciting time. You're blazing a new trail, setting a new course and direction for yourself. Navigating these uncharted seas will cause a certain amount of uncertainty. This is normal. You may feel lost. You may feel that you're the farthest away from familiar land as you've ever been. But fear not. Whether in new relationships, jobs, or business ventures, there's always new land to reach. But the only way to get there is to keep a faithful watch on the horizon. Your new world always appears when you feel the farthest from familiar sures and shores.

Walt's Life Rhyme #349: Greener Fruit

The sheltered tree won't bear its fruit
and sheltered fruit won't turn
Exposure to the sun and rain
is how we grow and learn

Greener Fruit
Walt's Life Rhyme #349

*"I share what I know,
so that others may grow!"*
www.LifeRhymes.com

Commentary:

You will only be happy when your expectations are in alignment with reality. If you are expecting fruit from a sheltered tree, or sweetness from green fruit, you're bound to be unhappy. Trees need to be exposed to sun and rain in order to mature and bear sweet fruit.

People, too, need to go through certain experiences, exposure, and stages of growth in order to function effectively within the realm of expectations we call life. Your children, your mate, your business partner, and yes, you too need to feel the pressure of the soil, the heat of the sun, and the beat of the rain over time. This is the simple secret nature uses to create the sweetest fruit. It might work for you too.

Walt's Life Rhyme #348: The Rising Price of Greatness

Don't let their doubts derail you
Don't let their walls confine
Don't occupy the world
their narrow thoughts and words define

Don't give up on your vision
Don't sell your soul or heart
Don't walk away from dreams
for what you dream sets you apart

Don't live below your magic
Don't settle for life's crumbs
Don't let the taste for less
be the main course your life becomes

Don't ever doubt your value
Don't fear that they won't buy
The world will always pay the price
when great's in short supply!

The Rising Price of Greatness
Walt's Life Rhyme #348

"I share what I know,
so that others may grow!"
www.LifeRhymes.com

Commentary:

During a recent stroll through a bookstore, I came upon the preview edition of a book entitled *GOAT (Greatest of All Time),* a 75 lb, almost 2-foot high, 800 page book chronicling the life of Muhammad Ali. The price tag for this tribute to a life of greatness is $3,000, or $7,500 for the "Champ's Edition."

Wow. Think about that. There will be those, (and I may be one of them), who will pay up to $7,500 for a single gargantuan book that tells the story of one man's trials and triumphs. A testament to a living legend who transcended sports to become an icon of greatness for generations to come. A man who never forgot his own greatness nor where it came from.

According to the publisher, *"This is not a book. This is a monument on paper, the most megalomaniacal book in the history of civilization, the biggest, heaviest, most radiant thing ever printed - Ali's last victory." - Der Spiegel, Hamburg*

It is a reminder of what one can accomplish when committed to the passionate pursuit of a dream and one's purpose. It is also a reminder that the basic economic law of supply and demand is alive and well. In our world, the truly great are in short supply, and the world pays the price.

Walt's Life Rhyme #347: A Race Where Quitters Win

Ljubo quit his job today
no more is he confined
He bid his boss goodbye
then left the rat race far behind

Ljubo quit his job today
and took charge of his life
Encouraged by good fortune
and a sweet supportive wife

Ljubo quit his job today
and some think him insane
But mad are those who curse their lot
then still choose to remain

Yes, Ljubo quit his job
and learned a truth that's always been:
That life rewards the "losers"
in a race where quitters win!

A Race Where Quitters Win
Walt's Life Rhyme #347

*"I share what I know,
so that others may grow!"*
www.LifeRhymes.com

Commentary:

Hello Mr. Goodridge,

I've been on your list for a long time now, counting in years. I've read some of your books, and I love getting your Friday inspirations, but I've never really followed up on anything. It's always been like a seed waiting to sprout.

A few years ago I got a degree in audio recording from OIART (Ontario Institute of Audio Recording Technology). It's been real busy for me, studying, practicing, and working to pay my rent and bills etc. Lately, I'd had this burning feeling that I should quit my job, and plunge into my studio work. In the past 3 months I've had [several paid gigs].

In the past few days this itch to quit my job came to a boiling point, even haunting me in my dreams. Tonight I just snapped and did it. As soon as I got off the phone with my EX-boss, I felt almost drunk with excitement. My head was full of ideas for my portfolio. AND... not even a half hour after I quit, I got a call from one of my teachers at school asking me to record his band! What timing! Could that be a sign? I'll admit that I'm a little scared. I just got married a few months ago, and I currently have just enough money saved to last about two months. My wife has been very encouraging though. I'm very lucky to have her support.

Mr. Goodridge, I've been reading your Friday poems for years, and I feel like I'm finally starting to believe you. I don't expect a reply. I know that you must hear stories like this a lot. I just wanted to share my happiness with you.

Thanks for sharing YOUR PASSION so consistently for so long. Peace,
Ljubo* (**Pronounced LYOO-bo.*)

WALT'S REPLY: Hey Ljubo,

I can totally relate to the euphoria you feel. A decade after I quit my own job, I'm still reeling and enjoying the freedom of being able to go see movies in the middle of the day! Be ready to maintain the commitment through both the lean and lush times, and please accept this week's Life Rhyme as a token of support for your journey.

Walt's Life Rhyme #346: Beyond the Verbiage

I chose my friends from those
who matched my introspective bent
Convinced our thoughts were higher grade
the deeper that they went

But now I seek connection
through the heavy AND the light
And mine beneath the verbiage
for neither's wrong nor right

Beyond The Verbiage
Walt's Life Rhyme #346

"I share what I know,
so that others may grow!"
www.LifeRhymes.com

Commentary:

I was reminded by Positive Mind guru Armand Dimele, that there are two types of people in the world: those who like deep philosophical, introspective conversations, and those who like the superficial, light and airy ones. I was also reminded that those of us who profess to like the heavy, need to be wary not to judge as inferior those who choose the light. It's just a different way of being. There's no right or wrong. And so, I pass the reminder on to you. You can still find what most of us are looking for—connection and clarity—while engaged in heavy as well as light conversations.

Let others be who they are.

Walt's Life Rhyme #345: Fixing Birds

"Want to know how to REALLY help others? Help yourself first! Once you help yourself you become such a beacon of light that shines so brightly, that others will automatically be helped without you doing one blessed thing!"
--Gladys Edmunds

The clueless solve the mysteries
while the sightless guide the blind
And those without direction
lead the lost to peace of mind

The utmost height of folly:
ego's fed but you're defeated
You strive to cure the world its woes
while your ills go untreated

So climb the ladder first
and show you practice what you preached
Then throw a life line back
to help the world to where you've reached

Don't give away your map
before your own gold has been found
For you can't coach wounded birds to fly
while stranded on the ground!

Fixing Birds
Walt's Life Rhyme #345

"I share what I know,
so that others may grow!"
www.LifeRhymes.com

Commentary:

Last night, I had an insightful, inspiring 3-hour talk with Gladys Edmunds, entrepreneur, author and *USA Today* columnist with a long list of stellar achievements, who was the "16 year old who took 9 dollars and built a 9 million dollar business!"

During our talk, Gladys reminded me of some simple traveler's wisdom that she included in her *There's No Business Like Your Own Business* audio series.

Anyone who's traveled by plane, has no doubt heard "in the event of a loss of cabin pressure, place *your* mask on *first* before helping those around you." This simple wisdom works well on the ground too, and in many areas of life. What good can you be to others if your own life is in chaos? Can you really raise passion-centered children if you yourself live a passionless life? Can you really speak from a place of certainty, truth and conviction about anything which you yourself have not experienced? Well, many try. Many of these people are seeking the ego gratification of being the "give till hit hurts" sacrificing Samaritan who helps others while neglecting his or her own needs.

Noble, yes. Effective? Maybe. Gladys suggest that for the next week, resolve to do the things that benefit *you*. Ask, "what can I do for me today? What will I do to help myself up the ladder that is just about me?"

No it's not about being selfish. It's not about doing for yourself to the exclusion of others. It's not about winning so others lose. It's simply about making the time to do things that benefit you first and foremost. In fact, you want to know what's really selfish? Helping others to feed your ego-driven image of yourself without really having the means to truly help them--that's selfish!

Walt's Life Rhyme #344: Without Honey

I've learned a few things on this journey
Opportunities knock once then are gone
And the world's not a train that comes screeching to stop
just because you now want to get on

Realize that the world owes you nothing
But there's nothing you need ever want
Kind words and a smile make you rich, high and wise
as any millionaire, king or savant

We climb up on the shoulders of others
Tear me down and you've no place to go
For the one way to rise above others around
is to lift everyone whom you know

In your quest and pursuit of true greatness
share this truth with everyone you shall meet:
You'll still catch more bees using honey, it's true
And you'll find that your life's twice as sweet!

Without Honey
Walt's Life Rhyme #344

"I share what I know,
so that others may grow!"
www.LifeRhymes.com

Commentary for Walt's Life Rhyme #344

I received an interesting voicemail message a few days ago. An individual I met briefly a while back called me in search of a contact number of his former business partner--a mutual friend. If I had the number, he asked, I should call back and provide it. (A fair enough request, I thought.)

By the next day, however, I received a quite lengthy (almost 3-minute) message berating me for not being quick on the call-back. Among other admonitions, I heard affronts to my character, attacks on my credibility, and doubts about my talents. I heard, "practice what you preach", "show some respect for those who call you" and "return calls promptly", he even added, "I can probably teach *you* more than you can teach me about profit," and on and on...

I was saddened by my realization that this person who had gone through (I estimate about 60 years of) life, and the only strategy he knew to get people to help him was to berate them and shame them into it.

I recalled some of the lessons I had learned from my sales training in network marketing, *The Psychology of Achievement* by Brian Tracy, as well as the book *How to Win Friends and Influence People* by Dale Carnegie. Among those that stood out was that there are proven techniques for relating to others and getting people to help you. It's a fact, as well, that the only way to feel good about yourself is to boost the self esteem of others. Think about it. Think what a dismal reality life would be if the only way to move up in life was to tear others down. (Some people practice this technique but pay for it later).

The truth is that the best way to get what you want in life is to help others get what they want. The way to feel good about yourself is to say and do things to make others feel good about themselves. And the best way to get people to help you is to make sure they like you first. It's a simple lesson. But one that many people never truly get. It is true. You catch more bees with honey than with vinegar.

Don't make the same mistake this caller made! Get some honey!

Epilogue:

So what did I do, you ask? Some might say I should call and explain to the caller why such a message was inappropriate. But, I'm not sure that would work. If that individual felt within his rights and the realm of appropriate behavior, justified in leaving such a message, (people never do anything they *know* is wrong), then I'm not sure he could really grasp the concept of inappropriate, and I'd end up in a fruitless, irresolvable debate. So, I erased the call and moved on with my day.

Walt's Life Rhyme #343: I Can't See Beyond These Boxes
aka The Clutterer's Chant
aka A Paean to Packrats
aka The Hoarder's Hymn

(Hmmm, perhaps I need to throw some of these titles out)

I can't see beyond these boxes!
Can't see anything 'tall
And carrying this weight
my journey slows down to a crawl

Like snapshots of a life I've lived
I can't toss them aside
But now they're just a burden
in each new space I reside

But if I opened up
and looked inside what would I see?
Accumulated fears and foes
and frightened, fearful me

The payoff's the possession
how they're seen through others' eyes
And knowing I can reach them
anytime the needs arise

But the REALLY rich own nothing
And this truth I've come to know
That the REAL secure feel free*
to touch things once then let them go

When I conquer all the clutter
and move without this box I'm in
That's the day my world will change
and then my new life will begin!

I Can't See Beyond These Boxes
Walt's Life Rhyme #343

"I share what I know,
so that others may grow!"
www.LifeRhymes.com

**Note: Despite what people may suggest to you, my friends, security is the OPPOSITE of freedom.*

Commentary for Walt's Life Rhyme #343

It is one of the great, unanswered questions of our time. It is a quandary that has haunted the minds of men and women since time immemorial. It is a dilemma the answers for which truth seekers have embarked in their quests to understand the inner machinations of the universe. Nobel prize winners have contemplated it. Rhode Scholars have pitted wits to unravel its mystery. The eternal gratitude of humanity, as well as untold wealth and recognition awaits anyone whose ingenuity, creativity and personal connection with divine intelligence allows them to decipher what pundits, preachers and paupers have failed to see. Yes, my friends, as I prepare this month to move to a new place, I too am faced with the ages-old question:

"What the heck do I do with all these magazines?!!!?

Yes, I'm a self-proclaimed minimalist. But, I confess, this is my dirty little secret. I can't part with these darned magazines! I have issues of the now defunct *Success* that have followed me through two states and five apartments. I have *Ebony* magazines from the 1970s. I've got practically the entire collection of *The Source Magazine* (the magazine of Hip Hop Culture and Politics), the now departed *Reggae Report*, plus numerous one-hit wonders and short-lived excursions into editorial expression! The boxes are getting more abundant and heavier too! Like comedian Robin Harris' infamous BeBe's Kids, these magazines they "don't die, they multiply!" A friend suggested that I sell some of the collections, suggesting that money may soothe the pain of separation. But, as any collector will tell you, it's not about the money. It's about the pride of ownership and that special feeling that comes from hearing the oohs and aaahs of envious friends and strangers who marvel at my collections. Even if a collection *is* valuable, it's wealth I'll never realize since I don't plan to part with them for money.

I'll spare you the entire story of my bitter battle with the boxes of magazines, and simply say that I've forced myself to part with most of them. I've allowed myself *one* box of classic issues, and donated others to friends. The rest I'll give to the used book and magazine vendors on the streets of Manhattan.

But as you've come to expect from me, this life rhyme isn't about magazines. Yes, the magazines are a metaphor for a more profound question: How can I get rid of the clutter in my life without feeling like I'm losing myself or something valuable I might need in the future? Magazines, and clutter are representations of ideas, beliefs, and the effects of personal experiences that we take from one "mental living space" to another.

The trick is to part amicably with them, and thus remove the potential blockages of your new view of the world around you. Once removed, you open up the path for the light of new experiences and abundance to reach you. Here then, is my personal philosophy for the conquest of clutter applicable to books, furniture and other stuff. If you haven't touched it in 12 or more months, you probably don't and won't need it.

-News Articles? Scan it, or fax it to your PC's fax modem, and save it digitally
-Business Magazines? Get rid of them. Information changes rapidly. Current info exists online.
-Magazines & Books? That's what libraries, used bookstores, and guys on the street are for
-Valuable Junk? Give to charities to avoid the guilt of discarding.
-Memorabilia? Your future kids will likely not be interested in your life's minutiae.
I think the only thing worth keeping are my comic books, photographs and records!

And finally, learn how to live in the moment and seek your identity from things internal.

Walt's Life Rhyme #342: Higher Learning
Where Passion Rules

"While graduation rates in traditional high schools are reaching dismal lows of 5%, the percentage of kids graduating from a school like the Bronx Guild utilizing passion-centered learning are at 90% and above!"

Imagine if you would a world
where students yearn for class
Inspired to achieve much more
than just get by and pass

Their teachers get to know them
and what makes it all worthwhile
They learn about the world in ways
that honor their true style

Imagine just how far they'll be
the difference that they'll make
When energy and interests guide
the courses that they take

Their families' and teams' support
hone character AND mind
And yes they read and write well too
They won't get left behind

And mentored by adults
while they engage the world around
They'll gain some real life smarts
as they grow up and outward bound

Eventually they'll graduate
with life's best skills and tools
For learning's an adventure
in a school where passion rules!

Where Passion Rules
Walt's Life Rhyme #342

*"I share what I know,
so that others may grow!"*
www.LifeRhymes.com

Inspired by and dedicated to the Bronx Guild

Commentary for Walt's Life Rhyme #342

A few days ago, an administrator at a unique new school in the Bronx, New York, called and told me an intriguing story:

Alex, a tenth-grader attending The Bronx Guild, was searching online for a music industry internship, as part of the school's Apprenticeship Program. He found my hiphopentrepreneur.com website, downloaded my bio, and submitted it to the program coordinator as a possible lead.

On her invitation, I visited this unique school yesterday and was blown away! I met Rhonda (the program coordinator) and Al, Alex's teacher, who introduced me to a curriculum which featured, in addition to the standard focus on math, science, social studies and English, independent projects based on students' interests and an apprenticeship program which gives them real-world experience. During my short visit, I spoke to several students, including one who was interning in the mayor's office, another whose passion for horses had her doing research comparing equine and human immunity, and saw others actively engaged on computers in a variety of passion-centered pursuits. And, to top it all off, they end each day with ten minutes of positive affirmations!

This was all new to me! It was like seeing the type of school and educational environment I wished existed during my school years! Better still, being an advocate of the pursuit of one's passion, it was just the type of school I would start myself!

The most impressive thing I learned was that while graduation rates in traditional high schools are reaching dismal lows of 5%, the percentage of kids graduating from a school like the Bronx Guild, utilizing what I call passion-centered learning, are at 90% and above!"

The Bronx Guild is one of the new menu of educational options available to families, and that are using experiential learning (learning by being and doing), and using the *Big Picture*™ philosophy and model to engage students. They've realized that different individuals respond to different learning environments, as described by an excerpt from their mission statement:

"The development of Individualized Learning Plans for each student ensures that we are meeting the needs of all learners, that the curriculum is designed around how people learn, and that a student's engagement is based on his or her passion."--Excerpt from Bronx Guild Mission Statement

I met Alex, a bright and curious young man, and got a chance to learn more about him. Like his idol, Damon Dash of Roc-A-Fella Records, Alex is inspired to pursue his passion in order to give back to his community in meaningful ways. I promised Alex and Rhonda and Al that we would make something happen. What better way to start your life's pursuits than to be educated in a school where passion rules?

Walt's Life Rhyme #341: The Regime Change

Have you checked the captain's cabin?
Do we know who's at the helm?
Seems we're led by fear to folly
headed for a rocky realm

Check the laundry list of blunders
lies and chases for wild geese
Motives made by mass deception
never lead to inner peace

Lest we lead the charge for change
and search and find the smoking gun
First amuck, aground, then out of town
is how we'll soon be run!

Matters not the method chosen
coup, impeachment or votes won
Anything to stop the madness
get this over with and done

Don't expect a graceful exit
for kings and captains when deposed
Often kick and scream in protest
'til new order is imposed

Thoughts like leaders are selected
but be warned: they might be fools
If you don't like where they take you
Time to change who makes the rules!

Regime Change
Walt's Life Rhyme #341

"I share what I know,
so that others may grow!"
www.LifeRhymes.com

Commentary:

Who's making the rules in your life? Who or what is dictating what you aspire to, what you attempt and what you believe is possible for you? Who's controlling how you live your life? Is it your fear? Is it your history? Maybe it's someone else's fears and history. Whoever's in charge is in power because you've allowed their thoughts and ideas to assume power. You've elected (or selected) to give them free reign over your direction in life. Through the thoughts you entertain—thoughts of failure, thoughts of scarcity, thoughts of inadequacy—you have created certain results.

But, take heart, there are no effects that aren't within your power to reverse or change. Whether you stage a new election, an inner revolt (see Life Rhyme #153: Mental Coup d'etat), or request outside help (self help books, tapes, workshops, counseling/coaching, etc.), there are effective means of replacing the current "law makers" in your mind and installing new ones!

As you make these changes, however, be prepared that the old thoughts will invariably resurface to assert their dominance in your life. Watch out for those moments of doubt, and don't allow the old regime to retake the helm or seize the throne!

Walt's Life Rhyme #340: The Charge for Change

"Wherever man has the scent of the eternal unity in his spirit, he hunts for it in his home, in his work, among his friends, in his pleasures and in all the levels of his function. It is my simple faith that this is the kind of universe that sustains that kind of adventure. And what we are fumbling towards now . . . tomorrow will be the way of life for everybody!"—Howard Thurman

In every field and function
naught but change can be assured
But lest you lead the charge
your fancied future is obscured

For change can be a thing decreed
by rulers from afar
Or change can be a bubbling spring
that starts right where you are

Unless you lead the charge for change
there's little you'll command
You'll walk the roads that others pave
and pay what they demand

The charge for change is action
for no future's ever free
And never fear the fumble
as you strive for what might be!

The Charge for Change
Walt's Life Rhyme #340

"I share what I know,
so that others may grow!"
www.LifeRhymes.com

Commentary:

Today's Life Rhyme is inspired by a quote from Howard Thurman, poet, preacher, and political activist (1900-1981). Thurman, who had great influence on the US civil rights struggle of the 1960s, was referring to the changes that American society was fumbling towards through the efforts of people like Martin Luther King, Jr. In time, he intoned, what we now see as struggle will one day be the normal way of life for those who follow.

Yes, we do live in a world and a universe of change. Whether in the global spheres of politics, education, health, or the personal sphere of influence within your family or the pursuit of your passion, I encourage you to ask yourself, "Am I leading a charge, or am I paying a charge?

What are you doing to effect the changes you want to see in our world? Are you taking steps to improve life for your community, your world, its children and yourself? Or are you simply waiting to see what price you'll have to pay because of changes others have made? Are you leading a charge, or are you paying it?

Walt's Life Rhyme #339: Without Question aka Seeker Makes the Move

"She's always been saying yes, Walt.
You just haven't been asking the questions."--CK

You've not yet asked the question
But the world's been saying yes
No journey's undertaken
'til the question starts the quest

But once you ask the question
then all forces mobilize
And life's magic and mystery
will unfold before your eyes

Things tend toward fulfillment
without question this you'll prove
But no answer finds its question
'til the seeker makes the move

Without Question
Seeker Makes The Move
Walt's Life Rhyme #339

"I share what I know,
so that others may grow!"
www.LifeRhymes.com

Commentary:

Things tend toward fulfillment. In other words, I maintain (despite what others may see as evidence to the contrary), that we live in a creative and friendly universe that supports us in the fulfillment of our goals. First however, you've got to be able to recognize how that creativity functions. (See Life Rhyme #304: The Reconstruction Crisis)

In order to fully benefit from this creativity, you've got to be willing to frame your goals and ask the right questions. Once you do, however, new possibilities will open up for you.

For instance, if I told you how smooth it was (pun intended) to set up Sunday's interview on Smooth Jazz 101.9FM, you'd think I was lying. I had all sorts of reasons for not making that initial call: "I'm not ready yet, or perhaps there's a long waiting list," I thought. However, I eventually made the call to the station, spoke directly to Mark (the host), and within two minutes, he invited me to appear on his *Sunday Dialogue* program. Now that's both a testament to how supportive Mark is of his potential guests, as well as evidence of an answer that was always there simply waiting for me to ask the right question.

So today's Life Rhyme is a reminder that until you ask the right question, you may not recognize the answers and partake of the opportunities that life has waiting for you. Until you make that move and ask for, and then seek the fulfillment of your dreams, you might never experience the abundance life has in store. The seeker has to make the first move!

Walt's Life Rhyme #338: The Wool You Pull

The wool you pull may blind you
with excuses you believe
But rest assured, my friend
it's just yourself whom you deceive

For I know from experience
that when men commit to act
No mountain can obstruct them
and no detours will distract

To do the things that matter most
your schedule you'd revise
No lengthy list of reasons why
can make it otherwise

It's clear you simply made a choice
to do or not to do
This wool's for your eyes only, friend
For mine can see right through!

The Wool You Pull
Walt's Life Rhyme #338

"I share what I know,
so that others may grow!"
www.LifeRhymes.com

Commentary:

A coaching client of mine reminded me of something I told him that, he said, changed his perspective on accomplishing his goals. When he failed to accomplish a task we had agreed he would complete, I stopped him from listing his many reasons why he wasn't able to do the thing intended.

I told him that the reasons weren't important, and that only results mattered. I told him that I know that people find the time, energy, resources, ways and means to do what's important to them.

I encouraged him, therefore, to admit to me that he simply **chose** to do something else rather than the original task. I told him that he could choose to pull the wool over his own eyes if he wanted to, but that mine see perfectly clearly. I now incorporate that concept into my Ground Rules for the Journey when I coach anyone on turning their passion into profit!

Walt's Life Rhyme #337: If Oprah Calls, I'm Busy

If Oprah calls, I'm busy
Tell her I just couldn't wait any more
I had to do myself
the things I thought I'd need her for

If Oprah calls, I'm busy
And, no I'm not trying to be rude
I'm making the connections
between my world and attitude

If Oprah calls, I'm busy
Just say I'll have to get right back
I'm out here climbing walls
built by a mindset ruled by lack

If Oprah calls, I'm busy
sure I know "all the people I could reach"
But to best share what I know
I must first practice what I preach

If Oprah calls, I'm busy
Flattered. But, give her my regrets
Pursuing other options
'cause I had to hedge my bets

If Oprah calls--I'm--what's that?
you say she's holding on the line????! (gimme that!)
Busy? Ms Winfrey, don't be silly
For you? I'll always find the time!!!

Okay, so call me a wimp
But come on, I had to take the call
It's not the fame and fortune, mind you
I owe it to her audience, after all! :-)

If Oprah Calls, I'm Busy
Walt's Life Rhyme #337

"I share what I know,
so that others may grow!"
www.LifeRhymes.com

Commentary:

This one is dedicated to all those aspiring authors, speakers, self-help gurus and inventors with passion-centered dreams of success. As I always remind my clients and workshop attendees: no *one* person holds the key to all the doors that lead to your desired future. Any plan that hinges on the actions or participation of that one individual for its success is inherently flawed. Always have a plan B. And the truth is, whatever you believe you need from that one person may already be in your own power to achieve for yourself. Seek your own path. Become the thing you seek. Do for others that which you believe you need others to do for you.....But, if opportunity *does* open a door from your knocking, there's no need to get fanatic about it...step through and TAKE THE CALL, SILLY! :-)

Walt's Life Rhyme #336: No Need To Run

There's no need to run
for there's nothing to fear
But so much can be gained
by your presence right here

For people push buttons
yes, that's just what they do
But the buttons they push
are on the *inside* of you

Your emotions are clues
to what simmers below
And that pressure will build
'til you vent it or blow

Let the feelings arise
note the ways that you feel
For they point to the places
you need most to heal

And in time you'll be free
from the pain, fears and doubt
But they first must come up
as they make their way out!

No Need To Run
Walt's Life Rhyme #336

"I share what I know,
so that others may grow!"
www.LifeRhymes.com

Commentary:

Are you one of those people, like me, who just hates confrontation? When faced with a volatile situation or person, would you rather just walk away than bring things to a boil? Perhaps you're not accustomed to expressing emotion. Perhaps you fear you'll lose control. Perhaps your anger and pain are so close to the surface that you fear what you'll say or do, or what they (the emotions) will do to you. Perhaps the few times you've actually given in to your feelings, you became a puddle of watery emotion, or an explosive keg of anger and abuse that you'd rather not experience again.

Well, the bad news is that people will forever be pushing your buttons. That's just what people do. But, running won't help, because those buttons they push are on the inside of you. So no matter how far and fast you run, you take the buttons with you wherever you go. The good news is that you can be free of the fear that comes with having those buttons pushed! Having your buttons pushed hurts because they are connected to those sensitive places inside of you. The secret is to get to those suppressed emotions so you can do something about them. To be free of them, the memories, the pain, the anger and the fear all have to come back up on their way out!

Let the buttons be pushed. But know that nothing is required of you but a simple awareness of what's going on. No retaliation. No reaction.

Acknowledge. Admit. Accept. Grieve. Move on. Soon you'll be able to separate the buttons, from the pusher and from the past. There'll come a day when you won't simply react, but you'll have clarity and a peace from which you can choose life's best responses; responses that support your highest calling; responses that allow you to grow in your awareness of who you are: a you that you can't see clearly if you're too busy running! There's no need to run.

Walt's Life Rhyme #335A : Consolation Prize

Here's some dating advice for when you know!

What if I just tell him that I'd rather we be friends?
What if I just say "not now, but who knows, it depends?"
What if we have dinner so the words will not offend?
What if we just date a while, then simply let it end?

Every right is yours my friend to do what makes you smile
And choose the ones with whom you'll laugh and linger for a while
And just because another chooses you to fill their days
Does not in any way mean you'll return his loving gaze

And no you won't be crude or crass or crush his heart to pieces
But blame your own mixed signals if his jones for you increases
No need for dissertation, doubt, deception or disguise
For neither time nor love should be a consolation prize

Consolation Prize/But What if I'm Wrong?
Walt's Life Rhyme #335

"I share what I know,
so that others may grow!"
www.LifeRhymes.com

Commentary:

You're not required to give or be a consolation prize to someone simply because that person can't handle the truth of your lack of interest in them.

Walt's Life Rhyme #335B: But What If I'm Wrong?

More dating advice for when you don't know

What if he's the last man of my type who comes along?
What if it's just me, and I've been out the loop too long?
What if all the lyrics and the resume are strong?
What if I miss out and realize that I was wrong?

Your fancy for his flattery has dulled your usual senses
For love built just on data leads to days of false pretenses
If you don't know what you're feeling, then perhaps ask what you're not
For time spent in the desert will make everything seem hot

Consolation Prize/But What if I'm Wrong?
Walt's Life Rhyme #335

"I share what I know,
so that others may grow!"
www.LifeRhymes.com

Commentary:

It's more than just the stats and how he looks on paper. And yes, it is lonely sometimes. But, don't let your thirst for attention blind you to what your heart is telling you.

Walt's Life Rhyme #334: Beyond My Fence and Faces

Without the usual crutches
I stood nervous and unsure
Afraid without support
that I'd come crashing to the floor

Without a wall to lean on
didn't know quite where to stand
But now I'm feeling balanced
since you offered me your hand

Without the script I've memorized
didn't know what I would say
Somehow the words came easy
and it's never felt this way

Without the map I've mastered
will I know which road to choose?
We'll find our way together
even if at times confused

Beyond my fence and faces
you have found what's real in me
And proved once and for all
there's no one else I need to be!

Commentary:

Unconvinced of our greatness, we often build fences to keep the world from peering too deeply inside. Unaware of our beauty, we often don many faces to hide what's natural. Unaccustomed to letting things happen naturally, we often adopt a method of operation that keeps things safely under our control.

Here's an experiment: The next time you venture into a relationship, leave the crutches, the structure, the script, and the map behind. Step beyond the fence and leave the faces at home. Be open to doing things differently. There's an inner beauty that the world can see, even if you can't. There's greatness within you that needs no extra support or embellishment. Who knows, you might just find someone out there who can appreciate you just the way you are. Someone who can help you walk without crutches, live beyond fences, speak without a script and enjoy life's journey together without the old maps! And how cool would that be!?

Inspired by S-L.N. Encouraged by H.W.

Beyond My Fence and Faces
Walt's Life Rhyme #334

"I share what I know,
so that others may grow!"
www.LifeRhymes.com

Walt's Life Rhyme #333: The Settler's Wine

"Never settle for less
than your dreams at their best!"

Don't lose sight of the life you envision
Given time you can have what you want
You'll find bitter the taste of a glass poured in haste
with regrets that will linger and haunt

Don't give up on the journey you started
Stick it out through the rough and the slow
For what good is a trip or the sail of a ship
reaching places you don't wish to go?

You can have all you've ever imagined!
Persevere, stay the course, don't retreat!
For you'll learn this in time that the settler's wine
never does ever taste quite as sweet!

The Settler's Wine
Walt's Life Rhyme #333

"I share what I know,
so that others may grow!"
www.LifeRhymes.com

Commentary:

In many ways, I'm an "all or nothing" kind of person. If certain things are not the way I want them, then I'd rather do without. I'm flexible in many things, but in some regards, I don't want to settle for second.

Maybe you're the same way. Perhaps it's something as simple as the type of furniture in your home, or as important as the person with whom you spend the rest of your life. You know what you like, and you're willing to hold out until you get it. Go for it! Don't let other settlers convince you to join them in "a bitter glass of whine" toasting dreams that never were, or telling you to be "practical" or "realistic." Every sip of the settler's wine is a bitter reminder of the taste you really wanted!

Hold out for your best dreams. But, most importantly, do the inner emotional and spiritual work and take the necessary actions so you can grow and attract your best dreams quickly. Then you won't have to feel pressured to settle because "time is running out." Remember: the thing you seek is also seeking you! But *you* must become it first!

Walt's Life Rhyme #332: Unlike Before/Of Things To Come

Unlike Before

Unlike before, this time around
feels different to the touch
In many ways the same
but also new by just as much

Unlike before, we're closer
though this landscape is uncharted
Our quest will prove quite fruitful soon
despite how it was started

Unlike before, the music's ours
we'll dance to our own drum
And every step we take reveals
a sign Of Things To Come

Of Things To Come

Of things to come I'm hopeful
I'll reach goals that I pursue

Of things to come I'm faithful
that what works is what I do

Of things to come I'm thankful
just as if already true

Unlike Before b/w Of Things To Come
Walt's Life Rhyme #332

"I share what I know,
so that others may grow!"
www.LifeRhymes.com

Walt's Life Rhyme #331: One Day I'll Make a Movie

Those of you who've read Turn Your Passion Into Profit, *or who have ever attended my workshops, know I often make reference to wanting to go see movies in the middle of the day as one of my motivations for walking away from corporate employment. So, true to form, I've been treating myself to a few over the last two days.*

One day I'll make a movie
all the world will rush to see
An epic, yes, a classic too
a winner you'll agree

It'll pique your deep desires
of some riches to be won
It'll pose the sort of question
that makes conversation fun

It'll add a touch of mystery
so the future is in doubt
And tease you with an ending
that no one can figure out

Our hero's ways and walk
will make girls swoon and boys pretend
The search for pride or passion
adds some challenge to transcend

With drama, pain and struggle
and a world to save or fix
With victory over villains
you know, all the usual tricks

You'll laugh and cry and cheer
and hang on every word they say
Through settings and a climax
that just takes your breath away

And, then, the happy ending
(that's what all are rooting for)
Or one that gives you faith
to hope a sequel is in store

Perhaps I'll make a movie....yes
or maybe better still
I'll make my dreams the plot line
of the story I'LL fulfill!

One Day I'll Make A Movie
Walt's Life Rhyme #331

"I share what I know,
so that others may grow!"
www.LifeRhymes.com

Commentary:

The perfect movie sounds a lot like life, doesn't it? Don't wait for the director's shout of "action" or "cut" to take living your dream life and role seriously. Starting *now*, do something to make this a blockbuster year!

Walt's Life Rhyme #330: The Normal Rules Don't Apply

And the days apart creep by so slowly
while the moments engaged seem to fly
In the land called desire
and of this I am certain
The normal rules don't apply

And your thinking seems just a bit sharper
whilst much brighter things look to the eye
And the world appears crisp
like you've lifted a curtain
The normal rules don't apply

And it seems your energy is unending
food and sleep you will even deny
You'll find strength for the battle
even if things should worsen
The normal rules don't apply

If the clocks are suspended
and what's down is upended
You can bet there's a good reason why
When you're fixed on a passion
be it purpose or person
The normal rules don't apply!

The Normal Rules Don't Apply
Walt's Life Rhyme #330

"I share what I know,
so that others may grow!"
www.LifeRhymes.com

Commentary:

Love and desire can do that to you! And, you know *exactly* what I'm talking about! Whether it's in the pursuit of pleasure or profit; or whether it's that familiar zone of heightened awareness and timelessness into which you disappear during those moments of inspired creativity, the right motivation can make you do some otherwise extraordinary things! But, that's where life gets and reflects its best, most enjoyable and exquisite flavors and hues. Enjoy being in that strange new world, savor the moments, and experience the taste of passion! And don't question or over-analyze. Simply remind yourself: "The way I'm feeling today....the normal rules don't apply!"

A love poem Inspired by S-L.N.

Walt's Life Rhyme #329: Between You And Me

I'll share with you a secret
but be gentle once you hear
I'm guilty, yes, but selfish, no
The reason now is clear

It's not an act of selfishness
that's had me wait this long
But who am I to think (I thought)
the world would want my song?

Mandela said we fear our light
more strongly than the dark
Like many, I am one, too who
relates to that remark

But now I've heard some yeses
and I've even sold a few
I'm anxious now to share the gift
Performer? Me? Who knew??

Forgive me, then, the day's near when
you'll purchase and push play
And what you hear will justify
this seven-year delay!

Commentary:

"IT'S ABOUT TIME, WALT!! Sometimes humility or modesty may be perceived as selfishness, when it means denying others the gift given you to share, but which you choose not to."-**L.B.**

That was an email I received when I announced I was releasing an audio compilation of Life Rhymes. It gave me something to think about. I'd never thought about it that way before. I hastily sent my "apology" to LB and asked her not to judge me too harshly! But, I had to share some of my thoughts about the "accusation."

**And, for the sake of accuracy, the Mandela quote referred to is actually by Marianne Williamson, as quoted by Nelson Mandela. Here it is:*

Our deepest fear is not that we are inadequate. Our deepest fear is that we are powerful beyond measure. It is our Light, not our Darkness, that most frightens us. We ask ourselves, who am I to be brilliant, gorgeous, talented, fabulous? Actually, who are you NOT to be? You are a child of God. Your playing small does not serve the world. There is nothing enlightening about shrinking so that other people won't feel unsure around you. We were born to make manifest the glory of God that is within us. It is not just in some of us; it is in everyone. As we let our own Light shine, we unconsciously give other people permission to do the same. As we are liberated from our own fear, our presence automatically liberates others.-**Marianne Williamson**

Between You And Me
Walt's Life Rhyme #329
©Walt F.J. Goodridge
*"I share what I know,
so that others may grow!"*
www.LifeRhymes.com

Walt's Life Rhyme #328: The Trouble With Being Enlightened

The trouble with being enlightened
is I see all things as good
So poverty and pain
don't motivate me like they should

The trouble with being enlightened
is that nothing pulls my strings
'Cause it's all just an illusion
"y'know... in the cosmic scheme of things"

The trouble with being enlightened
is I hear a different drummer
I'll say things, and I'll get strange looks
Man, that can be a bummer

The trouble with being enlightened?
the in-betweens I often skip
I'm at the destination
before I even start the trip!

The trouble with being enlightened
is most people can't relate
They're all caught up in drama
trapped by lies of war and hate

But, what's GOOD with being enlightened
is I row gently down this stream
For merrily, merrily, merrily, merrily
life is but a dream!
(See? There's that strange look again!)

Commentary:

I shared a laugh recently with my good friend, Erroll.P., who always seems to provide the inspiration for some of my more off-the-beaten-path Life Rhymes (see Walt's Life Rhyme # 154: "I Ain't Goin' Out Like That!"). We were jokingly discussing the fact that if the Life Rhymes represent a path of spiritual growth, with the ultimate goal of eventual enlightenment, then what on earth's going to happen when we finally get there?

Think about it. At some point in the future, once we all complete the journey of enlightenment, the inspiration the life rhymes provide may be quite unnecessary. When you reach that state of perfect inner bliss, when you understand the universe's grand cosmic design, and when you're at peace with all, and at war with none, what on earth can you learn from a weekly email? The Life Rhymes may evolve to be quite short as they meet the needs of those whom they once served. Perhaps Life Rhyme #7,456 will need be nothing more than:

It's all good
and understood.

The end.

The Trouble With Being Enlightened
Walt's Life Rhyme #328

"I share what I know,
so that others may grow!"
www.LifeRhymes.com

Walt's Life Rhyme #327: Come Clean

You might as well just speak your mind
let consequence be damned
For sugar coats and tippy toes
will just dilute your brand

You might as well just play your hand
and jump into the fray
Let those who aren't prepared to deal
fold now and walk away

You might as well be true to you
and do the things you feel
An honest view of who you are?
Hey, might just close the deal

The ones who truly "get" you
are the ones who'll stick around
For lives built based on fantasy
aren't ever truly sound

Come Clean
Walt's Life Rhyme #327

"I share what I know,
so that others may grow!"
www.LifeRhymes.com

Commentary:

Come, come now....you know this one is for you!

Walt's Life Rhyme #326: The Clear Drive Forward

The clear drive forward frightens
when there's nothing in the way
If all the roads you took before
were filled with disarray

The path of plenty petrifies
when poor is all you've known
And skills for mere survival
are the only ones you've honed

You lose your balance standing
if you've always walked through wind
So give yourself some time to change
the way it's always been

Walt's Life Rhyme #326
The Clear Drive Forward

"I share what I know,
so that others may grow!"
www.LifeRhymes.com

Commentary:

Have you ever been walking against the wind, leaning forward to keep your footing, and then all of a sudden the wind stops? If you're not careful, you might lose your balance.

If for all your life you've steered through mine-filled, pothole-laden terrain, or if you've gotten so accustomed to chaos, noise, discord and struggle, then when a clear, peaceful path presents itself, you may not even recognize it at first. Worse, you may not know exactly how to move forward. But, rest assured, if you give yourself a little time to adjust to the new landscape, and perhaps seek the counsel of those who've traveled it before, you'll do just fine.

Walt's Life Rhyme #325: Tell Me How I'm Special

After a recent Passion Profit™ Workshop in Washington DC, I was approached by a gentleman who asked me a simple question. In the course of that dialogue, I was reminded that questions sometimes come with their own answers if you know how to hear them. Today's Life Rhyme is inspired by that exchange.

THE QUESTION

What's my gift and passion
that you say I should pursue?
Tell me how I'm special
'cause I haven't got a clue

I know it's not my brains
because I'm just your average sort
I know it's not my muscles
and I'm not too good at sport

I know it's not my talent
couldn't sing to save my soul
Can't dance or draw or paint
and don't quite know my earthly role

So help me any way you can
If what you say is true
I need to find my calling
there's some things I want to do

I've triumphed over obstacles
I've wished, then worked, then won
I've learned a thing or two
and faced some fears I've overcome

But many--even those most dear
are stuck in traps of doubt
And once I find my gift
then I can show them safe ways out!

THE ANSWER:

What I hear in your question is something quite powerful that you seem to have overlooked. You have a passion to succeed despite your obstacles. Although you think you were not endowed with obvious gifts, your accomplishments alone shine as valuable examples to those who believe, like you did, that they're just average. In addition, your heart-that burning desire to help others succeed-is as valuable an asset as any other more recognizable gift. Therefore, to do the most good for others, you may need to return and live among the very ones who understand you least, and simply be the you you've now become. For sometimes the best gift we have to offer the world is simply to be an example for them to follow. In other words:

Perhaps what makes you special
is not a single thing you do
But possibilities you represent
by simply being you

Tell Me How I'm Special
Walt's Life Rhyme #325

"I share what I know,
so that others may grow!"
www.LifeRhymes.com

Walt's Life Rhyme #324: A New Suit

Your wall of words and posture
keeps the ones you love at bay
Detached observer teacher
is the role you like to play

The distance keeps you safe
while observation feeds the myth
And teachers never take the tests
their students struggle with

The suit you wear most proudly
in your quest to self-define
Obscures the best of you from view
and dulls your inner shine

For if you knew the you WE know
the one that's sensed not seen
You'd realize the folly
of your trivial smoke screen

We all wear suits to shield us
from the blizzard in love's bliss
Reward and risk are one
so with each plunge remember this:

You can't control love's fire
it can warm but it may sear
But better to be scorched by love
than cold and dowsed by fear!

Commentary

There's only one of us here. Therefore, the people in your life are your reflection. Their challenges are the same ones you face. So the advice you find yourself dispensing to help another are the same words you need to hear to heal yourself. So, as I found myself helping a friend with the thoughts above, I also found myself in the same classroom benefiting from the lesson! Yikes!

So, to my friend who's kept that guard up for so long. I've been there, too. Let it down, my friend. Take the chances we all must if we are to pursue happiness. There's no guarantee there won't be pain, but you'll realize there's life beyond it, once you know that it's not a judgment upon you, but simply life playing itself out in ways that it inevitably must as we humans learn the same lesson over and over again.

You gain nothing real by maintaining the image that you think is keeping you safe. Those who truly love you see the real you anyway. It's not the facade that keeps us in your presence. It's the goodness behind it that shines through despite your best efforts to keep it cloaked. We know what's going on, and have decided to love you despite yourself. We'll all share a good laugh when you join us on this side of knowing, and throw that suit away for good.

Dedicated to D.O.

A New Suit
Walt's Life Rhyme #324

*"I share what I know,
so that others may grow!"*
www.LifeRhymes.com

Walt's Life Rhyme #323: Make It Matter

Enough with all that waxing
Put this baby on the road!
Construction time is over
Time to launch it, test and load

You've planted all the seeds
and tilled and toiled all that you can
This life was made for living
time to implement the plan

Unless you make it matter
Thoughts and things will stay the same
Indulge your other half
And bring some balance to your game

Make It Matter
Walt's Life Rhyme #323

"I share what I know,
so that others may grow!"
www.LifeRhymes.com

Commentary:

Energy and matter is all there is. Thought is energy. Action makes it matter. Convert your thoughts to action. Engage. It's time.

Dedicated to A.M.

Walt's Life Rhyme #322: Familiar Fears and Failures

PRELUDE:
For some there's pride in poverty
and luxury in lack
So powerful's the pull when freed
they often go right back

Just like a badge of honor
I wore suffering on my sleeve
My strength came from the triumph
Or at least, so I believed

Just like a rite of passage
I embraced the life that's dire
Quite proud of that which I became
when tempered by life's fire

But like all rites and medals
they're reminders of times passed
That tempt us to relive our wins
and make those moments last

I sought familiar fears and failures
rather than the new
To recreate the honors
of the hells I've made it through

It doesn't have to be like this!!
I now resolve today
To seek new fears to conquer
and let old ones pass away!

Commentary:

I know it's wrong, but I keep going back. I know better, but I always find myself in the same situation. Why is this happening to me again!!??? Perhaps because it makes a great story. Perhaps because it's a reminder of a moment of triumph you've had in the past. Perhaps because getting beyond this familiar fear would mean you'd have to face new ones.

Think about it. What better way to feel good about yourself than being able to tell a story of triumph over woe? What better way to win the sympathy and attention of friends than to wallow in the mire of a challenge that you see as character defining? The flaw, however, is that if you get too comfortable in defining your strength in terms of the chaos and deprivation you can endure, you may never have a good reason to really get beyond it. There's an even greater you beyond the current and comfortable chaos and catastrophes! Find it and move on!

Dedicated to A. Morrison

Familiar Fears and Failures
Walt's Life Rhyme #322

"I share what I know,
so that others may grow!"
www.LifeRhymes.com

Walt's Life Rhyme #321: Stripped Priceless

I know what really matters now
it's not what I had thought
It's not the fur and feathers
or the wings that I had bought

When stripped of all the wind
that I had used to fill my sail
I drifted, fell and faltered
but survived to tell the tale

Empowered by the insights
that life's turmoil often brings
I now live life much freer
way beyond the yoke of things

The Moral:

Some will fight too hard
to keep the walls from coming down
Some hang on for life
on sinking ships prepared to drown

Others see the light
and let the edifices crumble
They know they'll rise after the fall
so never fear the tumble

Stripped Priceless
Walt's Life Rhyme #321

*"I share what I know,
so that others may grow!"*
www.LifeRhymes.com

Commentary:

The losses, dear one, are all opportunities for rebirth. Each successive stripping away of the things you thought were so vital, are opportunities to see what's left after the non-essential stuff is gone. It's an opportunity to be reborn unencumbered by the attachments that have kept you imprisoned. You are only as valuable as the things you allow to control you. And it is only in the absence of these things that you will recognize the priceless worth and beauty within that shows you what you can do without.

Dedicated to S.A.K.

Walt's Life Rhyme #320: Just Us One

PREPARATION: Before you join me in the mental space of today's Life Rhyme, you'll have to shift gears. So stop whatever you're doing at the moment, take a deep breath, and think about this:

I'd like you to think for a moment that as far as reality is concerned, none of us have ever experienced *anything* outside of our own minds. In other words, there isn't any object, any perception, any disappointment, any thing we that we can know as real that we can ever prove really exists by a means that doesn't involve our own senses. How do you know this book you're holding is real? You have to use sight, hearing, touch, taste or smell to convince yourself. So the truth is, everything that you know is knowable only as a function of your mind. Since there's no really objective proof that doesn't involve your own perceptions, it could be that the entire world is nothing but an elaborate illusion taking place nowhere else but within the confines of your skull. There's just no way you can ever be sure that there's really anyone or anything else out there but you. Everyone is walking around alone in a world that exists in their minds. Therefore, everyone is really experiencing a world of a single me. Just one "I am." With that said, enjoy today's thoughts.

There's really no one else. No one else out there at all
Just one soul. With many different faces
And there's nowhere you can go. To escape or retreat
that you won't find me alive in all the same places

For if you look deep enough. Deep deep into my eyes
You'll see I'm right. You'll prove it fully beyond all doubt
For deep down within me past the illusion of separate selves
you'll find yourself inside me peering back out

And though you think that you hear me. Hear me talking to you
Listen closely and I trust that you'll find
That these words and the voice that seems to come from MY mouth
is the same one that echoes deep in your own mind

That's why you cannot hate another. Cannot blame or despise
You cannot hurt me, without feeling the same pain
That's why you cannot help your brother. Lift him up from despair
and avoid the very same experience of gain

This makes life so much easier. Makes it easy to connect.
And the reason why is that when all is said and done
There are no multitudes to master, none you ever need to know
No one at all. For there's really just us one...

Just Us One
Walt's Life Rhyme #320

"I share what I know, so that others may grow!"
www.LifeRhymes.com

Walt's Life Rhyme #319: The Power of the Re-Meet
aka "To Every Bee Who's Got Pollen To Share"

It's so odd that we keep meeting each other like this
What on earth do you think that it means?
It's as if some weird force has now linked both our paths
now we're destined by fate to convene

It's my ardent belief that there's something afoot
deeper reasons or kismet at work
That there's something, some thought we're supposed to now share
that it's NOT just a random life quirk

Yes, I've thought long and hard about meetings like this
Over time here's the secret I've found:
That the good that we seek comes through people we meet
and more so as we find common ground

For the cycle of life binds us tightly
And survival's a mutual affair
And every flower has nectar to give in return
to every bee who's got pollen to share!

The Power of the Re-Meet
Walt's Life Rhyme #319

"I share what I know,
so that others may grow!"
www.LifeRhymes.com

Commentary for Walt's Life Rhyme #319

I had a conversation earlier this week about the power of those seemingly random encounters, and those recurring ones that my friend refers to as "re-meets."

I believe that there's hidden power in the meet and the re-meet. It stems from a belief that we live in a friendly universe; a universe that supports our dreams and goals and aspirations at every moment; a belief that the thing we seek is also seeking us. A belief that life, nature, God, the universe wants us to grow and expand.

Nature's support of the imperative for growth and expansion is a universal constant that we see playing itself out everywhere in life. Plants supply the oxygen that animals need to breathe, and animals supply the carbon dioxide plants use for their own growth. The bees, birds and bugs support the flowers in their struggle to grow by carrying pollen that supports the flowers, and the flowers supply nectar that feeds the pollen-bringers. I believe that we, as humans, all have some pollen to share with each person we meet to help them blossom and grow. I believe that every good thing that occurs in our lives will come as a result of the thoughts, words or deeds of other people.

That's why I don't believe that any encounter is really random at all. A person's pollen (i.e. their contribution or blessing) may simply be a smile on an otherwise dreary day. Or they may provide a contact that results in a much desired career change. Or they may impart some information we've been seeking for things to make sense in our lives.

Whatever that gift is, if you search for it, you'll find it. And, if you miss the opportunity the first time, you may get the nugget of knowledge you need from another person further along your path. Or perhaps, in those cases where you seem to keep running into a particular person, the universe might be staging a "re-meet" to give you another chance to get to the common ground you share with that person. Be vigilant. Bees abound!

Dedicated to Connie. T. A.

Walt's Life Rhyme #318: Bad Here Days

You'd rather be someplace else I know
I've felt that way sometimes
The kind of day where decent folk
feel like committing crimes

You'd rather be doing something else
why ANYTHING else in fact
The work's hard AND you work
to keep your sanity intact

A Bad Here day is what it is:
"It's bad here. Got to go!
And find a place and people
who support my need to grow!"

The question asked on bad here days
is not "what am I doing here?"
But "what am I learning here
so I can go from here to there?"

Bad Here Days
Walt's Life Rhyme #318

"I share what I know,
so that others may grow!"
www.LifeRhymes.com

Commentary:

A "bad here" day is an experience in which you realize that "it's bad here" and you need to be someplace else. Whether it's a toxic relationship, a job that you hate, or a brief encounter with someone else who's acting out their own issues, your life will always have its share of "bad here" days. Be reminded, however, that each experience does, in fact, have something to teach you about yourself and others. But once you get it, there's no need to linger longer! Learn the lesson and leave!

Here's a helpful hint to help you get through those kinds of days: Remember, all unhappiness is caused by an attachment to an expectation. Ask yourself, "what expectation did I have in this situation that was not met? Is my attachment to that outcome helping or harming me?" In every journey from where you are to where you want to be, the goal of self awareness is what matters. Everything in between is merely ego. Unhappiness is what the unreal you needs to survive. Freedom comes when you can let it all go because you've found what's real about you. Now *there's* a bit of cryptic clarity for you! Enjoy!

Walt's Life Rhyme #317: On Principle or Posture

At a recent event, a participant asked a question: "You advocate taking risk. But, how do decide if by the choices you make you're being a risk taker or simply being foolish?"

On principle or posture, friend
is how you will decide
Is what you do for you
or to sustain your sense of pride?

Oh, sure, we all have bills to pay
and some have mouths to feed
But some dreams pay out dividends
whose risks they far exceed

The very things you fear you'll lose
are what keep you enslaved
But freedom comes from overcoming
challenges you've braved

Convenience or conscience? Hmmm
Which one will set your course?
When sails are filled with others' wind
you'll drown deep in remorse

There's one of two paths that you'll take
and one leads to your good
You'll do what feeds your passion
or what others think you should

To risk all you think matters
shapes your power to transcend
But know what's done on principle
will work out in the end!

On Principle or Posture
Walt's Life Rhyme #317

"I share what I know,
so that others may grow!"
www.LifeRhymes.com

Commentary:

There may be no safe way to cross the bridge. The risks are real. Unless you are prepared to give up the safety and security of standing (unhappily) on this side, you may not really be ready to cross over. So the question to ask is, "Which is more important to me? Do I follow my principle, take a chance, risk looking foolish, and take what may be the only path to my dream? Or do I remain where I think safety lies, and maintain the current image of myself that I have constructed, however unfulfilling it may be?

Walt's Life Rhyme #316: Excuses, Excuses

Decisions come from the desire to want the thing desired to be true...That's all you need. Anything else that comes into your mind and out of your mouth other than 'I want this to be true' are just excuses.

It's not about credentials
regulations or degrees
It's not about some board
that validates your expertise

It's not about the cash flow
or that "money's kinda tight"
It's not about your rent
or getting finances just right

It's not about you needing proof
and knowing this scheme works
It's not about your pension plan
job benefits or perks

It's not about your debts
or paying back the student loan
It's not about your age
or waiting 'til the kids are grown

And NO, it's not a time thing
so just stop THAT idle chatter
We all know people find the time
for things that really matter

So what is it that stops you?
Well, the truth is that you're scared
But rather than admit it
you just say you're unprepared

When children want they're fearless
for there's nothing they want more
But as adults choose safety
the predictable and sure

And skill and time and money?
You know what I'll say is true:
Some do more with less
and they're not half as bright as you!

Yes, all you need's desire
forget all that other stuff
And simply ask one question:
"Do I want this bad enough?"

Excuses, Excuses
Walt's Life Rhyme #316

"I share what I know,
so that others may grow!"
www.LifeRhymes.com

Commentary:

Are you ready to do this? When you answer, don't tell me why you think you can't before you even commit. Don't use your doubts and demons as the reasons why you won't try. The world's approval isn't a requirement for your commitment. Never has been. Never will be. If Martin Luther King, Jr. waited for this society's approval before committing to his dream, where would we as a society be now? Just tell me first you really, really, really want this now. We'll worry about the *how* later.

Inspired by Z.T.O.

Walt's Life Rhyme #315: Fear Not the Fanatic

I fear not the fanatic
Mediocre scares me more
It's those who fight fierce for a cause
who know what life is for

For anything the masses do
is suspect from the start
The world is trained to follow fashion
rarely gut or heart

Just try to change your thinking
try to go against the grain
Push hard the world starts pushing back
starts calling you insane

All things in moderation?
Yes, for some this may hold true
But victory goes to those
who go beyond and push on through

Sometimes to make great changes
you must go to some extremes
It's force of will that conquers
rigid thoughts and ways and means

So take the roads less traveled
seek new worlds and faster tracks
Burn bridges and leap out on faith
run forward, don't look back

And call me what you will
contrary, zealot, cracked or crazed
With zeal come revolutions
and through zeal new worlds are made!!!!!!

Fear Not The Fanatic
Walt's Life Rhyme #315

*"I share what I know,
so that others may grow!"*
www.LifeRhymes.com

Commentary for Walt's Life Rhyme #319

Much of who I am today and many of the life-changing discoveries and insights I've achieved in my life have come from my exposure to beliefs and institutions that some may call radical or extreme.

Whether it was the eye-opening Scientology courses I've taken, the New Age books I've read, my vegan lifestyle, which grew out of an association with a friend in the Nation of Islam, my stint in a network marketing company, (an industry often termed "cultlike" by observers), the LifeSpring™ weekend (a self-help workshop), I've grown and developed as a result of embracing the wisdom that often comes through those who challenge traditional ways of thinking.

If you're going against the grain, you're likely to pick up a few splinters. From the beginning, I inherently realized that if I wanted a different life than that of the masses, that the things I did and what I believed would have to be different as well, and that there would be consequences. I was prepared for the ridicule. I was prepared for the judgment. I was prepared for the slings and arrows of outrageous fortune that took me through two evictions, virtual homelessness, my own personal power grid failures and blackouts (that's what happens when you don't pay the bill), and everything else I've experienced in my journey. I sincerely believe that it is this embrace of things extreme that helped me create the lifestyle that I now enjoy.

The fact is, in some way, we're always fighting a battle to first discover and then maintain our true identity. Some of us lose the battle to what's familiar to us (i.e. giving up on your true calling in favor of what others want you to be, or what you think is "safe"). And some of us surrender willingly to that which we wish to become. (i.e. immersing yourself with zeal in a new belief system that gets you where you want to go).

So decide which you prefer. But don't fear the fanatic. It may be the only thing that saves you!

Inspired by Z.O.

Walt's Life Rhyme #314: Someone Lied

What do you tell a friend to have her truly recognize, accept and really believe in the inner greatness that's evident to everyone but her? What can you say to help her battle the demons of doubt and feelings of inadequacy? I'm not sure if words alone can do, but all I can say is

Someone lied
and told you that you had to save the world
And honestly that's too much pressure
for a little girl

Someone lied
and told you that you just weren't good enough
And burdened you with guilt
and weighed you down with all THEIR stuff

Someone lied
so now your actions lack a certain verve
The victim of a heart
that never got what it deserved

Someone lied
so now you seek to shoulder all life's blame
Despite the fact you've helped
to raise the level of our game

Someone lied
so now you're blind to truths that others see
And cast yourself as captive
when in fact you're really free

Someone lied
so now you feel inadequate some days
In spite of past performances
and accolades and praise

Someone lied
I wish I could undo those lies you've heard
And prove your false assumptions
are just patently absurd

Someone lied
but hold on, don't give up, please push on through
There's more to you than meets your eye
I swear to you that's true

Someone lied
and all I do is hope that someday too
You'll revel with us all
and know the glory that is you!

Someone Lied
Walt's Life Rhyme #314

"I share what I know,
so that others may grow!"
www.LifeRhymes.com

Commentary

Your presence here has not been in vain. You have not let us down. We love you just the way you are. And, in fact, many of us wish we had the beauty we see in you. You're a winner! You're a champion!

Walt's Life Rhyme #313: Comfortable Conclusions

We dream big dreams as children
but by the time that we're adults
We settle for conclusions
rather than life's best results

And those who curse their fate
who once aimed high but missed the mark
Believed their trip had ended
and thought they had to disembark

But no results should matter
save for those for which we strive
For the only goals we'll reach
are those each day we keep alive

Comfortable Conclusions
Walt's Life Rhyme #313

"I share what I know,
so that others may grow!"
www.LifeRhymes.com

Commentary:

There's a BIG difference between results and conclusions. In creating the life of your dreams, the worst mistake you can make is misinterpreting a particular result to determine your conclusions about your chances of future success. Make sure that when you strive for a particular goal, that you commit to achieving a specific outcome, and not simply to reaching a conclusion that you can use to justify not trying in the future. What many people really want is to justify their deep-down belief that "it's not possible" or "I'm not good enough" or "I'm not ready" or "this is difficult" or some other limiting idea. So they give only half their best effort, or sabotage their success so they can reach a comfortable conclusion rather than the intended result.

(Even worse, some people use other people's conclusions about the way things are to dictate what they believe is possible for themselves.)

In any journey you embark on, setbacks, disappointments, and the failures you encounter are all simply stations along the way, not final destinations. You don't have to leave the train unless you want to. So today's question is: "What conclusions about the way the world is have you drawn that you'd like to change?" The power to change the conclusion often lies simply in committing to a different result.

Walt's Life Rhyme #312: On Days When Darkness Falls

When darkness rules the day
how things will work out in the end
Depends on what you see
until the lights come on again

Some see as a disaster
what for some's a stroke of luck
Some hold it together well
while others run amuck

Some resolve to finger-point
while others simply cope
Some see worlds of options form
where others give up hope

Some wax philosophic
laugh and take it all in stride
Others fear for life and limb
and find some place to hide

Some plot their escape route
wishing that they had a plan
Some shine lights for others
helping any way they can

For based on your perspective
you'll adapt or climb the walls
You'll find out what you're made of
on the days when darkness falls!

On Days When Darkness Falls
Walt's Life Rhyme #312

*"I share what I know,
so that others may grow!"*
www.LifeRhymes.com

Commentary:

What's clear even on life's darkest days, is that you always have a choice between actions that empower and those that imprison. Hope you see clearly enough today to make the choice. Let there be light!

For The East Coast Blackout of 2003!

Walt's Life Rhyme #311: For Better or For Worse

For better or for worse I made a choice not long ago
to wish a different world and then pursue my present course
And some may think I'm cursed for choosing such a path of woe
with all its ups and downs yet through it all I've no remorse

This path that I traverse to some who watch seems quite unsure
no clear and present jackpot with a payoff much delayed
Though tempted to reverse I've since decided to endure
and simply based on faith I'll have the things for which I've prayed

Despite an empty purse my morals still remain unsold
I've stayed true to my standards of the things I just won't do
The pressures were adverse but soon I'll have my pot of gold
when riches of another kind come fully into view

One day as if rehearsed I'll reach the goal for which I strive
And everything once wished for at that time will then be mine
Investments reimbursed when I arrive alive to thrive
What's worse will then get better and better yet... all by design!

For Better or for Worse
Walt's Life Rhyme #311

"I share what I know,
so that others may grow!"
www.LifeRhymes.com

Commentary:

Sometimes words will not be adequate to explain your choice of actions. Sometimes you'll do things from an inner conviction that it's the right thing to do, with no justifiable, quantifiable, or logical explanation that would satisfy those who view your life from the outside. Sometimes you don't need to have the words, but simply the faith in your commitment to your ideals. Those sorts of decisions carry you forward on a path that may be obscure to eyes, but that your soul sees quite clearly. And you may only fully see the path, and make sense of it all once you've traveled it, and once you turn to look at whence and how far you've come.

Walt's Life Rhyme #310: Men of Vision. Men of Blindness

Men of vision see the world
in terms of what's to come
Men of blindness trust what's passed
and from the new they run

Men of vision practice hard
preparing to advance
Men of blindness laze
and leave their outcomes up to chance

Men of vision seek to be
right where the ball will land
Men of blindness watch the game
but don't quite understand

Men of vision make their move
and grab the ball and play
Men of blindness wait
and watch the moment slip away

Men of vision take the shot
and move to win the game
Men of blindness miss the chance
their scorecard stays the same

Men of vision act because
despite how things may seem
The future's what you do today
regardless of your dreams

....and by the way

Lest you think the game is won
by only what men do...
The things that men of vision do
applies to WOMEN too!

Commentary:

Success belongs to those who embrace change, prepare for opportunity, anticipate future trends, seize their chance when it appears, act decisively, and focus on doing *today* the things they want to see themselves doing *tomorrow*. What are you doing today to bring your dreams of tomorrow to life? Even when things were at their worst for me, I refused to spend time looking for a job since *that was not* what I wanted to see myself doing in the future. I refused to spend time doing it in the present. The truth is, unless you make some drastic changes in thoughts and behavior, what you continue doing today is most likely what you'll be doing tomorrow!

Inspired by Retire Young, Retire Rich by R. Kiyosaki

Men of Vision. Men of Blindness
Walt's Life Rhyme #310

*"I share what I know,
so that others may grow!"*
www.LifeRhymes.com

Walt's Life Rhyme #309: When Spinning Wheels Touch Ground

We'll bust out of the gate
and shock them all and win the race!
And all their doubts and digs
with awe we'll instantly replace!

They'll call our meteoric rise
an "overnight success"
They won't see all the sacrifice
or months and years of stress

The speeds that we'll attain
and yes, the distances we'll reach
Will leave observers guessing
and the critics without speech

With mikes and cameras rolling
and the spotlight in our eye
They'll say, "So what's your secret???"
and to this we will reply:

Been busy building assets
'stead of looking for a job
Not happy chasing paychecks
so our time no one can rob

Preferred pursuing passion
even if we worked for free
In time the time invested
will pay dividends, you see

While revving, others passed us
Felt like losers. But we found
We made up for it all in time
once spinning wheels touched ground!

When Spinning Wheels Touch Ground
Walt's Life Rhyme #309

"I share what I know,
so that others may grow!"
www.LifeRhymes.com

Commentary for Walt's Life Rhyme #309

In *Retire Young Retire Rich*, author Robert Kiyosaki outlines the ten-year plan he and his wife Kim followed to be able to retire with passive income in the tens and hundreds of thousands of dollars monthly. Their secret: rather than work for a paycheck, they spent their days building assets. Even when they had to live in their car for three weeks, they never gave in to the temptation to follow their friends' admonitions and "get a real job!" In their case, the assets they chose to focus on instead were business ventures and real estate in the form of rental property.

He states, *"The trouble with working at a job for money is that you have to start over selling your labor each and every morning. In most cases, your labor has no long-term residual value, if you are working for money. On top of that, if you are working for money, then your earning potential is limited. If you work slowly acquiring assets (businesses, products, paper assets, rental property, real estate), your income potential is infinite and that income can be passed on for generations to come. Your job or profession is not something you can pass on in your will to your children."*

Often, as you follow the passion path to freedom, there'll be times when you feel that you're just spinning your wheels because you don't immediately see the fruits of your labor. Once you're operating outside the box of conventional thinking, you'll find that few will understand the sacrifices you are making in the short term in order to have long term freedom and real security. There'll come a moment, however, when your revving car with its spinning wheels finally touches down on the road towards your envisioned future.

So, to all my passionpreneur friends and those pursuing their dreams who feel the same way: stay focused on the dream! The time you're spending in creation mode is an investment in your future. Don't give in to the pressure to conform and run someone else's race. You're on the right track. You'll soon kick up some dust when your wheels touch ground!

Walt's Life Rhyme #308: Oh, My Word!

So what's the word you bring to mind?
What concept do you own?
What attribute above all else
are you most widely known?

Do people think you gracious, great
or giddy, good or glad?
Perhaps they think you surly, spiteful
shallow, sick or sad

Perception is reality
know this, and if you're wise
You'll learn how others see you
for their truth lies in their eyes

And if the word's consistent
with the best you strive to be
Then count yourself among the few
who like what others see

But if that word reflects a you
of which you're not too proud
Then make the change your goal
so that in future all are wowed!

Oh! My Word!
Walt's Life Rhyme #308

"I share what I know,
so that others may grow!"
www.LifeRhymes.com

Commentary:

In reading *The 22 Immutable Laws of Branding* by Al Ries, I started thinking how to translate what I'm learning about brand-building in the business world, into building one's brand on a personal level.

Here's an exercise for the bold and daring. Ask your closest friends and family what one word they associate with you. (Tip: Don't do this if you can't handle the truth). Volvo™ owns the word "safety." (If you want a safe car, you look to Volvo.) Kleenex™ owns the word "tissue" ("Pass me the Kleenex!") Federal Express™ owns the word "overnight." ("Fedex this to our client in Seattle"). Xerox™ owns "copier." ("Xerox this for me, please.")

Similarly, as you endeavor to grow into the new you, like any entity seeking to make its mark in others' minds, know that there's probably a word that comes to mind when others see, think or hear of you. And the key to being all you can be, at least in others' minds, is knowing what that word is. That's your brand. That's the word that represents your brand attribute. And when it comes to branding, the reality of what you stand for is the perception others have of you. In other words, you are what people think you are. [Note I said "when it comes to branding" not in ultimate reality.]

What if you don't like what you hear? What if people think you whiny, rigid, bossy, difficult, boring, or offer some other colorful expression to describe what makes you special? The bad news is that, like a first impression, it might be hard to change current public perception. (That's why Coors' bottled water and Levi Strauss' shoe ventures both failed). The good news is, you can always change friends! Just kidding. But seriously, life gives you the chance to establish a new brand identity with each new person you meet. Use the feedback from those who know you, to help you grow into the person you want others to know! And don't worry, with enough patience and persistence, you can change any negative perception people have of you.

Walt's Life Rhyme #307: Connect The Dots

PROLOGUE:

With your world in pieces
life's a puzzle and pretense
Once the lines are drawn
the picture's clear and things make sense

Pick up all the pieces
that are strewn about the floor
They represent your talents
each with worlds yet to explore

Gather all the games you played
that used to make you smile
And know that in your joy
life gives you clues to what's worthwhile

Recollect the words of praise
of people whom you've met
The world can see your magic
although you yourself forget

Consider all the things you've done
that boosted your self worth
Chances are those very things
are why you're here on earth

Yes, life is like a picture game
with lines lost or concealed
Reconnect the dots
your hidden life can be revealed!

Commentary:

Remember playing "Connect the Dots" when you were young? By using your pencil to draw lines from one number to the next in sequence, you were able to draw a picture that was previously invisible to view. Well, life can be like that. Sometimes, discovering your passion is done by connecting the dots from one experience, idea, or awareness to another in a sequence that reveals a picture that's always been there. I've found that if you recall the things you enjoy, the talents that you've left undeveloped, the things others say about you, and those activities that give you your greatest sense of satisfaction, fulfillment and self-worth, you'll be closer to discovering your true passion! It's like compiling a collection of your greatest hits! (See The Discovery Exercises in *Turn Your Passion Into Profit*)

Furthermore, once you've found that thing that is your passion, you'll often find that there is an underlying thread connecting the seemingly random experiences and encounters throughout your life. You'll find that in some way, you've always been doing "that thing" in some form or another. Once that connection is made, you'll be more in alignment with your purpose!

Connect the Dots
Walt's Life Rhyme #307

"I share what I know,
so that others may grow!"
www.LifeRhymes.com

Walt's Life Rhyme #306: The Deer And The Hunter

"Be careful what you take for truth from news peddlers.
The antelope's report about the hunt is far different
from the story the hunter tells."--Padmore's Grandma

The hunter tells a story
And the deer she tells one too
But lo you'll find the teller
makes you doubt which one is true

For perspective alters plotline
and your purpose feeds your point
And advice on where to walk
to say the least may disappoint

For the one who tells the story
tells the tale to suit his kin
So before you praise the moral
know the story that YOU'RE in!

The Deer and the Hunter
Walt's Life Rhyme #306
© Walt F.J. Goodridge
"I share what I know,
so that others may grow!"
www.LifeRhymes.com

Commentary:

As with all advice and conclusions about life, it's important to know the perspective, personality, pre-disposition, and predilections of the person who offers them. Whose story do you want to live?

Today's offering was inspired by Padmore Agbemabiese, a professor at Ohio State University, and one of the international members of the poetsniche.com website, where you'll find links to Padmore's site with other great proverbs from his Grandma!

Walt's Life Rhyme #305: Why Do I Trust You?

My trust you'll never earn, my friend
by what you do and say
My trust is like a gift
you'll keep or lose along the way

My trust is automatic
yes, I'll trust you at first sight
I trust you first and what you do
will prove me wrong or right

My trust is what you need
to do your best, so why indeed
Would I withhold the very thing
you need most to succeed?

For trust is not a prize you win
from points that you accrue
No trust derives from what's inside
and THAT'S why I trust you!

Why Do I Trust You?
Walt's Life Rhyme #305

"I share what I know,
so that others may grow!"
www.LifeRhymes.com

Commentary for Walt's Life Rhyme #305

I recently recruited a new business associate to oversee several sensitive aspects of my growing company. I asked for no resume or referrals, but simply acted on a feeling I got upon first meeting her. Within 48 hours of her signing on, I had shared with her details of my business and personal life that apparently surprised her. She called today, to ask a simple question: "Why do you trust me?" she asked. "I've been with the company less than 48 hours officially, and already I know things about your operations and you personally, that indicate a deep level of trust. So, I ask, why do you trust me?"

The question was a fair one. So, I gave it some thought. These are some of the answers I gave her on the phone, which I'll now share with you.

Why Do I Trust You?

I trust you because with me, trust is a given. It's not something you have to earn, necessarily. It's something that we start off with, and you either keep it or lose it as time goes by. You either confirm the soundness of my decision, or you reveal that I made a mistake.

I trust you because trust is the basis of you meeting the expectations of our interaction. I trust you, therefore, because I want you to succeed, and my trust is what you need in order to do your job.

I trust you with and share the intimacies and secrets of my world because you cannot harm me. As a spiritual being, no one can harm me in any way that really matters. I am not my userid and password. I am not my credit rating. I am not my bank account. I am not the image and impression you may have of me once you know these things. And, passwords can be changed. I trust you, therefore, because I am fearless.

I trust you because it's efficient. I trust you because if I am wrong in giving you my trust, there really is nothing that I've lost except a little time. If I am right, however, we hit the ground running and conquer the world starting from day one. Whereas, if I wait for something you do to earn the trust, we may wait and waste days or weeks that might have been spent productively producing results.

I trust you because trust is a function of a vibe that I respond to. If I felt I could not trust you, I would not trust you. You need prove nothing, but simply be who you are.

In other words, I trust you because trust is a function of character, and your character is what it is from the day I meet you. It's not a gift I give you for something you do tomorrow, but a given *you* come with based on who you are today.

Inspired by S. Lewis

Walt's Life Rhyme #304: The Reconstruction Crisis

To build a better life, my friend
here's something that I've found
Things might just get a little worse
before they turn around

The reason is you've spent your life
constructing woes and troubles
In breaking down those structures
you'll find chaos often doubles

The fights increase, the tension mounts
close friends you may estrange
The world you've made is falling
so some things are bound to change

The thoughts you keep have shifted
and so too whom you attract
Let all the players clear the stage
make way for life's new act

You'll face this choice in life
each time you go against the grain:
Let go and risk it all,
or seek my comfort in the pain?

If better's what you seek
then face life's turmoil without fear
The reconstruction crisis
is a signal change is near!

The Reconstruction Crisis
Walt's Life Rhyme #304

"I share what I know,
so that others may grow!"
www.LifeRhymes.com

Commentary:

I've found that once a person decides to set upon a new course to better his or her life, a unique series of events—what I call the Reconstruction Crisis—is always precipitated by the nature of these new thoughts.

We live in a receptive universe that responds to our thoughts. When you say you want a better life, and visualize and set goals accordingly, things naturally start to happen to bring you the life you desire. (Really! It's true!) What typically happens, however, is that most people miss the clues, and interpret the ensuing chaos, tension, stress, turmoil, strained relationships, disagreements, disappointments, betrayals and lack of support from those we love as an indication that we've made a bad decision. Or worse, we fail to see the effects our new way of thinking is having on our relationships and environment, and get distracted putting out these seemingly unexpected, and unrelated fires in our lives.

What's *really* happening is that the *Reconstruction Crisis* is in effect. Our lives are being reconstructed, and the people and circumstances that have no place in our envisioned future start to feel the effects of the old world being dismantled and being prepared for reconstruction.

If you understand, therefore, what's going on, you'll welcome the potential for change and betterment that crisis always brings. Could the chaos you're currently experiencing be *change* knocking at your door?

Walt's Life Rhyme #303: The Game Believe

That's all it really is, you see
when broken down to core
It's just the game believe we play
not less and nothing more

And all things manifesting
also all things that elude
Will come and go to that degree
of faith that you exude

The struggles that you'll face
aren't simply puzzles you must solve
But also test commitment
and the strength of your resolve

So plan and play each game
but know the secret to achieve
Is found when you are master
of the game we call believe

The Game Believe
Walt's Life Rhyme #303

"I share what I know,
so that others may grow!"
www.LifeRhymes.com

Commentary:

Recently, in helping to launch a new product for a client, I encountered some negative consumer feedback that had me doubt the sanity and viability of the venture. I had the chance to mull over the feedback for a few hours while I reframed the experience and my interpretation of it. I applied many of the same perspectives I teach in my workshops and Life Rhymes. I had to remind myself that on a planet of over 6 Billion individuals, when one person's opinion can derail your plans, it may not be your plan that needs tweaking, but your faith in it.

Every idea is only as good as the belief behind it. Every outcome is only as sure as the commitment of the one who dreams it. The actions that you take are less important than the all-consuming passion that inspire them. For passion is the soil from which new creative solutions grow.

On a scale of 1% to100%, how much do you believe in the game you're playing? Do you think you have a 90% chance of winning? 70%? 50%? Well, when you play the game believe, there's no such thing as a partial win. Belief either is or isn't. Play to win.

Walt's Life Rhyme #302: All Roads

That which you fear becoming
that you flee from and despise
Is brought to life since fears
do not repel but magnetize

Your efforts to define yourself
as NOT this thing or that
Gives power to the very thing
you're seeking to combat

You'll often find in life it seems
no matter what you do
All choices based on fears
will bring those fears right back to you

A thing feared is empowered
then that thing assumes control
And all roads lead you there
because your fear becomes your goal

You never can outrun the fears
that live within your mind
Accept them first or else
by them you'll always be defined

Confront the very thing you feel
will be your great undoing
Beyond it you'll find freedom
and the one road worth pursuing!

All Roads
Walt's Life Rhyme #302

"I share what I know,
so that others may grow!"
www.LifeRhymes.com

Commentary:

Have you ever noticed that although you've made the best efforts to be exactly the opposite, say, of a person or type of person you despise, that one day you find that you've become the very thing you'd been trying hard *not* to be? Or, have you made efforts not to choose a particular type of person as a partner, and found that you've ended up in the same relationship yet again, with just a different face?

The reason is that while your *outward* choices and actions may have appeared different, what remained the same was the *inner* identification with the thing you feared.

Wen you say, "I don't want or want to be anything like 'this'," you have given 'this' the power. 'This' becomes the subject of your definition of yourself. Until you create an entirely new definition of yourself (I am "that"), then all your actions, no matter how seemingly different, will be merely elaborate, creative and ingeniously disguised ways to end up in the same place....by all roads.

The more we fear a thing, the greater is its power over us, and the more control we give to the very thing we fear. And every path based on fear knows only one destination. It will always lead to itself. All roads lead to the thing envisioned.

Our emotions give focus to our thoughts. Fear is nothing but an emotion that gives a charge to that upon which we dwell in our minds. The thing we focus on becomes the goal we subconsciously program ourselves to create and achieve. Every thought is bound by the laws of creation to attract unto itself the very circumstances and people which help it manifest.

The solution, therefore, is to run *towards* your fear. You've got to move in the very direction of the thing you fear. Once confronted, accepted and released your fear can be left behind. And then *beyond* it you will find the new definition of yourself that you truly seek. And then you can apply the same creative forces to create your new "I am" and travel on some different roads to get there!

Walt's Life Rhyme #301: A Mantra for My Mission
(A Prayer for My Passion)

When all is said and done today
I hope that what I say
Instills in me and others
truths that help to pave a way

When all is said and done today
I hope that what I hear
Ignites my heart with passion
and yet dowses all my fear

When all is said and done today
I hope that what I've learned
Equips me to achieve the goals
and dreams for which I've yearned

When all is said and done today
I hope that what remains
Are pathways to my purpose
and a will I will sustain

When all is said and done today
I hope what I attract
Will spark a sense of purpose
that inspires me to act

And after all is said and done
I hope more's done than said
For action's what it takes in life
to help me move ahead!

Commentary:

I can't emphasize that last point enough. So, again:

When all is said and done today
make sure your plans take wing
Many people analyze too much
then they never do the thing

A Mantra for My Mission
Walt's Life Rhyme #301

"I share what I know,
so that others may grow!"
www.LifeRhymes.com

Walt's Life Rhyme #300: The Second Power

One can play the game to win
and one can lead the cheer
One can draw what's yet to be
and one can engineer

One can paint the picture first
and one can sell the art
One can think first with the head
and one leads with the heart

One can fly to fantasy
and one can keep it real
One can set the policy
and one can close the deal

One can do the gathering
and one carries the load
One can read the map for both
and one can watch the road

One can ask the questions first
and one can then advise
Sometimes you'll see farther
with a second pair of eyes

One can do a lot of things
but this I'll share with you
"when two or more are gathered…"
there's no telling what you'll do!

The Second Power
Walt's Life Rhyme #300

"I share what I know,
so that others may grow!"
www.LifeRhymes.com

Commentary:

No matter what project or journey you're embarking on, you can go much further, see more clearly, fly much higher, and achieve greater things when the dream is shared with and aided by another. Sometimes all you need is that one extra set of eyes, or that one extra mind focused on your goal to make it come true. There's an exponential increase in the energy available for creation, and a greater hope of success when you harness other people's energy. (H.O.P.E.= Harness Other People's Energy)

Metaphysicians, spiritualists, motivational speakers, and all religions speak of this phenomenon, and much evidence supports the documented power of teams, networking, group prayer, mentoring, friendships and mastermind alliances as critical components of success, prosperity, healing and personal growth. So, in whatever you do, make it your first priority to find your second power!

Walt's Life Rhyme #299: Without a Clear Objective

Without a clear objective
there's no way for you to know
Whether what you choose has meaning
or is just a moment's show

Without a clear objective
there's no telling what you'll do
When you don't know where you're going
well then, any road will do

Without a clear objective
there'll be times you'll want to hide
You'll resent life's impositions
and feel taken for a ride

Without a clear objective
people make you part of theirs
Fighting all their battles
and swept up in their affairs

Without a clear objective
you can't know if you're off track
Life's one detour then another
no main road that calls you back

But with purpose you gain power
strength to do a world of good
For beyond all doubt and question
you'll be doing what you should

And with purpose you gain clarity
to choose what's right for you
"Does this help or does it hinder me?"
(And you'll know what you should do)

And with purpose you gain courage
to embrace life without fear
When you know where you are going
every road helps you get there

And with purpose you gain time
to handle all of life's concerns
For you know when this is over
you've got someplace to return

And with purpose you gain peace
and chaos leaves without a trace
For when you're clear about your calling
everything falls into place!

Without a Clear Objective
Walt's Life Rhyme #299

"I share what I know,
so that others may grow!"
www.LifeRhymes.com

Commentary for Walt's Life Rhyme #299

Are you feeling stressed? Do you feel confused by the many options and opportunities that are open to you. Don't know which to choose? Are you feeling stretched to the limit by the many obligations and expectations the world has of you? Well, it could simply be that you're not clear about your calling. When you have a clear idea of why you're here on the planet, then things tend to make a bit more sense.

If there was something that you absolutely knew was your purpose, then everything else would take its rightful place in the hierarchy of your mind. And when faced with opportunities, you wouldn't wonder, "Is this more important than what I'm currently doing? Is that a better opportunity than this?" And when the demands of being mother, wife, sister or friend get overwhelming, you wouldn't feel yourself frustrated or unduly distracted by those duties and responsibilities. For you would know that, while important, you'd have something to return to focus on once you'd taken care of them. And when required to make time management choices, you would simply measure them against your purpose and ask, "Does this help me to accomplish or hinder me from doing the "thing" I'm here to do?" "How can I help this person and their cause, without diverting myself from my core expertise and from accomplishing my clear objective?"

Suggested reading for finding your purpose: The Tao of Wow which includes an overview of life themes in "The 45 ways of Men (and Women)"

Walt's Life Rhyme #298: Change the Game

Your game is not like others'
for you don't think like they do
But you've known this fact forever
ball and chain games aren't for you

Even with their clear advantage
you do things that they can't name
Different field. Different rulebook
Different outcome. Different game

Works of art from hits and misses
risks they'll never understand
To the untrained eye observing
seem both exquisite and planned

Pulling outcomes from a place
where earthly rules just don't apply
Leave them doubting laws of physics
Seeing things their minds deny

In your hand you wield a power
all who've seen it will agree
In your other hand's more options
those who play will never see

So here's your mantra for the moment:
Do the thing for which you came
With deliberate intention
Make it happen. Change the game!

Change the Game
Walt's Life Rhyme #298

"I share what I know,
so that others may grow!"
www.LifeRhymes.com

Commentary for Walt's Life Rhyme #298

I had a few challenges on Friday that I almost allowed to prevent me from getting to Washington D.C. for the National Money League event at which I was scheduled to speak. At 2:30pm, I was still in New York, not yet on my way to the 6:30pm event. (From New York, Washington is a 4 to 5-hour road trip if traffic allows. You do the math!)

At the last moment, just as circumstances threatened to derail my train of intention, I remembered that whether I ended up in DC or not simply depended upon me making a single decision. It had nothing to do with car troubles, schedules, or anything else. I simply had to decide if I wanted to be there. Once I made that decision, I used the powers at my disposal to simply make it happen. I'd done this numerous times before during much more challenging situations. In such situations, the solution might require calling in favors, turning on the charm, thinking creatively, etc. I guess things had been going so smoothly for a while, that I'd been out of practice in my ability to "go deep down, pull out an intention, and make it happen."

Today's Life Rhyme is a reminder of *your* power—*your* ability to get things done. Your power is a function of your intelligence. We all have intelligence, and it's not always defined in scholastic and intellectual terms. Your ability to create art is a form of intelligence. Your skill at inspiring others and moving people to action is another. These are all forms of intelligence that we possess to varying degrees. This intelligence is sharpened by your desire, strengthened by your passion, and focused through the lens of your intention, that is, whatever goal you've set for yourself at a given moment. Unless you keep it honed, reminding yourself that it's there, you might let it atrophy. When you bring that talent to the things you want to achieve, you discover new and creative ways of getting those things done. When you use that intelligence, you find that the people and circumstances in your life playing by different rules. You find that the things others say can't be done come easily to you. It's at those moments that you "change the game" both for yourself and those around you.

Go forth today confident of your power and remind yourself that whatever you want to achieve stems from a single decision to make it happen. You have the power to change the game!

*Types of Intelligence.
1) Linguistic intelligence includes talent in using language and thinking symbolically.
2) Logical-mathematical intelligence--the ability to think logically, recognize patterns, work with abstract concepts.
3) Musical intelligence gives one the ability to distinguish sounds and create music.
4) Spatial intelligence deals with precise perception of things and the ability to recall visual patterns.
5) Bodily kinesthetic intelligence involves ability in physical movement as seen in both athletes and dancers.
6) Interpersonal intelligence is seen in a good teacher or salesman as they sense the needs and interests of others and use that knowledge to communicate.
7) Interpersonal intelligence can be found in introspective people who prefer exploring inner landscapes. They are often highly intuitive and have a clear sense of self.
8) Naturalist intelligence is displayed by those who are talented at observing, understanding and organizing patterns especially those found in nature.

Walt's Life Rhyme #297: Square Pegs

Like pieces of a puzzle
there's a space we all must fill
But honoring your calling
that's the part that takes some skill

I call it "square peg living"
where you force yourself to fit
While knowing in your heart
that there's no way that this is it

A noble effort, granted
Much respect, don't get me wrong
With all your quirks and edges
I'm surprised you stayed this long!

For some would stay for money
and still others out of fear
You've never bowed to either, so
what the heck are you doing there?!!!

When square pegs meet round holes
there'll be a gap that's not quite filled
Make room for who'll fit better
and go forth, with faith and build!

P.S. I guess this just confirms
a truth you've known down in your gut
You fit in fewer places
when you're intricately cut

Commentary:

A friend of mine just walked away from a position at a major clothing company (To protect his privacy, I can't reveal which one. You'll have to guess!). He did it to stay true to his creative standards and to pursue his passion.

Though personal, his situation can apply to many who've been there (like myself), and those currently struggling in a square peg environment while dreaming of their passion. Some pieces of the puzzle can fit just about anywhere. The more intricately cut pieces have to find the exact place in life where they belong..

Square Pegs (aka "Filling The Gap")
Walt's Life Rhyme #297

"I share what I know,
so that others may grow!"
www.LifeRhymes.com

Walt's Life Rhyme #296: Checkpoints

As you travel on life's highway
the key to faring well, my friend
Is to recognize the checkpoints
as they come around each bend

If you find yourself exclaiming,
"How could things have come to this?"
Chances are it's just a checkpoint
not that something is amiss

See, a checkpoint is a moment
that demands that you take stock
What most people see are obstacles
impassable road blocks

It's as if you're crossing borders
to another state of mind
And the border guard asks questions
so your answers must align

Checkpoints challenge your identity
and prepare you to compete
Necessary rites of passage
no avoidance or retreat

All that's needed is a picture
of the you you need to be
Once presented then you'll pass
how much simpler could life be?

When you're tested by life's challenges
and don't know what to do
Teat them like you would a checkpoint:
get beyond by going through

Commentary:

Checkpoint experiences are life's challenges that test your mettle. They present you with people, circumstances and situations that allow you to confirm your new identity. Don't avoid these experiences. Like the checkpoints along a highway, you get beyond them by going through them.

Border Instructions

Life is a journey.
Your choice of roads determines your checkpoints.
Checkpoints exist when you pass between states of mind
Do not avoid the checkpoint.
You are your own border guard.
To pass, ask yourself the right questions.
Determine your new identity.
Go THROUGH the checkpoint experience.
Proceed and fare well.

Checkpoints
Walt's Life Rhyme #296

"I share what I know,
so that others may grow!"
www.LifeRhymes.com

Walt's Life Rhyme #295: Find the Future

"The future is a frame of mind
achieved by a sequence of
present-time experiences."

The future's just a place to live
you haven't lived before
It's yours the day you really see YOU
stepping through the door

The future's just the things you'll own
you haven't bought as yet
You still believe that what you have
is all that you should get

The future's just a car you'll drive
that sits now in a show room
The more you see YOU in it
pretty soon...guess what? zoom zoom

The future's just some clothes you'll wear
that now sit on a shelf
They come by magic once you change
your image of yourself

The future's just the cash you'll have
you feel you don't deserve
Your money's a reflection
of the self-worth you preserve

The future's just the things you'll do
you've not made time for yet
And all that stands between you
are the goals you first must set

No law exists that says
the journey must in fact be long
The future's just what happens
once convinced that you belong!

Find the Future
Walt's Life Rhyme #295

"I share what I know,
so that others may grow!"
www.LifeRhymes.com

Commentary:

Here's the secret of Time Travel: No matter what future you can imagine for yourself, there's someone, somewhere who's living it right now. That means the car you'll drive, the house you'll live in, the clothes you'll wear, etc., all exist right now. They are not merely images in your mind. They are real. Find them. Walk around in them. Try them on. Test drive them. Associate with those people and objects who are living in your future, and convince yourself you belong there too!

Walt's Life Rhyme #294: there's more

more power we have access to
more knowledge than what's known
more options than those offered here
more views than what are shown

more questions than we ask each day
more answers than we're given
more journeys that we've yet to take
more roads than we have driven

there's more at work behind the scenes
more beauty than we see
more causes behind all effects
more ways for us to be

there's more to life than what we think
more wisdom not yet matched
there's more beyond the world we'll know
perhaps once we're detached

there's more
Walt's Life Rhyme #294

"I share what I know,
so that others may grow!"
www.LifeRhymes.com

Commentary: *(an excerpt from a recent interview)*

Nigel A: ***What do you know for sure?***
Walt G: About the only thing I know for sure, is that it would be foolish to claim to know anything with absolute certainty. In other words, I'm sure that we can never really be sure, and even then, I'm not so sure. :-)

Everything that we think we know could be rendered useless and found to be totally off the mark in the blink of an eye, i.e. the dawning of a new consciousness. Perhaps all the apparent injustice, chaos, and strife, could reflect some hidden purpose and meaning which could all become perfectly clear--or maybe not.

So what I believe is this: there's more. There's more power that we have. There's more that we know that we don't even know we know. More to the story. More to the questions. More to the answers. And, once you accept that there's "more", then nothing can be an absolute. Everything becomes a transition towards a greater understanding, and life becomes an unknown for which we seek answers.

And, applied to the more mundane "day to day" of life, realizing that 'there's more' can help you be patient in your relationships, more forgiving of the world and her people, more objective when it comes to forming opinions and making judgments about others, or even when making business deals.

Walt's Life Rhyme #293: The Art of Waste Management

So where is this train heading?
Am I going for the ride?
Two questions you should ask each day
and here's how to decide

First ask, "What number train is this?"
"Have I taken it before?"
If chances are the route's the same
don't board until you're sure

Next, find a high perspective
so you can see far down the track
If it's not a place you want to go
no need for you to pack

One day of pointless travel
and you can kiss your dreams farewell
Spend your time instead on trains
bound for the place you want to dwell

For the train called opportunity
oft departs with all due haste
Last call, non-stop, now all aboard!
no time for you to waste!!

The Art of Waste Management
Walt's Life Rhyme #293

"I share what I know,
so that others may grow!"
www.LifeRhymes.com

Commentary for Walt's Life Rhyme #293

Getting better at the art of "waste management" will help you foresee the likely outcomes of certain conversations, interactions, arguments, disputes, etc., so you can avoid having them intrude on the smooth flow of your life or business.

Once you start to see patterns in how certain situations typically unfold, then with just a few questions prior to engaging in any interaction or activity, you can predict where that "train" is heading. You'll then eliminate unnecessary wastes of your time, energy, thoughts, words and actions, while focusing instead on the routes that get you where you want to go.

That's one reason I rarely get into political or religious discussions (read: arguments) with others. If the participants of such a discussion can all "agree to disagree", and if they simply want the mental stimulation of conversation, that's one thing. If, on the other hand, they're not able to see the inevitable outcome of being too attached to their individual viewpoints, then emotional involvement, escalating tension, hurt feelings and deterioration of good will is sure to follow.

In such a situation, I always ask, "how likely is it that this conversation I'm about to have will result in this person completely abandoning their position, adopting another, and relinquishing a belief system to which their very identity and sense of self is most likely attached? Is this a train I've been on before with a destination I already know? Do I need to exercise some waste management techniques here?"

The same approach can save you time and energy in business and personal affairs. There are certain people, processes, etc., that always seem to produce the same outcomes. It's been said that the definition of insanity is "doing the same thing over and over, but expecting different results." Are you going down the same track day after day, year after year with the same people, situations and circumstances and expecting different results? That, my friend, in addition to being poor "waste management", is quite possibly insane!

Walt's Life Rhyme #292: This Life

Over the years, I've used many different Life Rhyme metaphors to make different points. Today's Life Rhyme is about choosing the right metaphor for life.

This life as road to travel
with much scenery to the side
With no real destination
just relax, enjoy the ride

This life as race for others
out in front they lead the pack
Ever watchful for who's gaining
so they're always looking back

This life as war some live
upon a constant battlefield
Ambushed at any moment
by new enemies revealed

This life as show for watching
keeps some always on the fringe
Observers, not involved
until the final act begins

This life as dream for some
all's just a fantasy they say
Merrily thinking what they do
won't matter anyway

This life as maze and mystery
sets some always on a quest
In constant search for answers
seeking truths not yet expressed

This life as nature's fury
for so many is the norm
And buffeted and battered
they're the victims of each storm

This life as mere existence
with no purpose or pursuit
Who knows, perhaps, not sure? Oh well
The question might be moot

This life as roller coaster ride
ah, now the games begin
A crazy, topsy turvy ride
Let's go! Have fun! Hop in!

This life as test, (my favorite)
yes, this view has served me well
A grade for every challenge faced
I pass it and excel

No right or wrong perhaps
what really matters most is this
Does how you see things make life bleak
or does it bring you bliss?

This Life
Walt's Life Rhyme #292

*"I share what I know,
so that others may grow!"*
www.LifeRhymes.com

Commentary for Walt's Life Rhyme #292

How do you decide if you're living your life according to the right metaphor? And if you're not, how can you change it?

Well, you first must believe that any metaphor you're presently living is simply a choice you made a long time ago. Here are some questions to ask to determine if you're living the right metaphor: *"Does the view I'm choosing get me what I say I really want, or does it simply keep me wedded to my fears? Does it help me respond in ways that empower me, or does it simply allow me to say, "See? I was right!" even if what I'm right about is something negative? Would a different belief help me act and react differently to the things that happen to me?*

Next, you need to realize that you can change life's day-to-day realities simply by making different choices in the metaphors you believe in. For example, ask yourself, "How would I respond to people's statements and actions towards me if I really believed that instead of being evil, that people are basically good and kind? How would I respond to this situation if I believed that the universe is friendly, ordered, predictable, supportive, and full of abundance rather than a hostile, random, free-for-all battlefield where anything goes?

Life is the answer to a question, my friend, so your life depends on which question you ask. Ask the right questions, and choose the right metaphor today.

Walt's Life Rhyme #291: From an Elevated Perspective

Too Big
With your head in the clouds
it's a whole different view
and you see like the eagle and hawk
While unseen at your feet
are those trampled below
who say simply, "Sir, watch where you walk!"

Right
When the world is against you
and don't see things your way
then perhaps that's the time for a fight
But don't make the mistake
and miss forest for trees
Just to say one to all "I was right!"

Left
All position is relative
The question to ask
must become first "Whose right?", and "Whose left?"
Opposition eliminated
The question to ask
now becomes not "Who's right?", but "Who's left?"

From an Elevated Perspective
Walt's Life Rhyme #291

"I share what I know,
so that others may grow!"
www.LifeRhymes.com

Commentary for Walt's Life Rhyme #291

When the world around us seems confusing and disappointing, it's usually because we are viewing it through the world's lenses. I've learned that the world is best viewed "from an elevated perspective." Not the elevated perspective of someone whose head is in the clouds, but from the perspective of someone who strives to see beyond the visible, the commonly accepted and the seemingly apparent and obvious. It's true that we're living a "material illusion" and that as far as earthly things go, we are affected by the material world and goings-on around us. But the basis of our internal coping mechanism (i.e. how we deal with things) must come from other realms that are not rooted in the illusion of the here and now.

So some of the best advice you'll hear, and much of what will keep you sane in the face of adversity, therefore, will often seem counterintuitive *(Buy when the market is low; look for success in every failure; see the glass as half-full; see the future as bright when the present seems dark; turn off the television; stay in control in the face of things you can't control, etc.)*. But that's the challenge for those who seek to become masters of their fate. The path to freedom is often exactly where the rest of the world fears to go.

Walt's Life Rhyme #290: And if Sharing Were Like Breathing

If I asked the price of wisdom
would you know just what I meant?
I'd be asking if you thought that it
was bought, borrowed or spent

For if bought then there's a price you pay
for all the things you know
And if borrowed then in time
you must give back like seeds you sow

But if spent, then by its giving
you believe its worth decreases
And you hold on tight to what you know
reluctant to release it

And if spent, then you believe as well
the wisdom that you get
Increases your own value
over those you've not yet met

Ah, but what if we believed instead
true wisdom were like air?
Available to all who breathe
and yours because you're here

And what if just like breathing
we receive, and then we give
And what we share is just the thing
that others need to live?

And of knowledge being power?
Well, that's only partly true
The power comes from sharing
and that's how it strengthens you

And if, in fact, it's more like air
this truth we all should know
For sharing then becomes
the only way we truly grow!

And if Sharing Were Like Breathing
Walt's Life Rhyme #290

"I share what I know,
so that others may grow!"

Commentary:

In nature, there is a symbiotic relationship between plants and animals. Carbon Dioxide, the very thing that we, as animals, give off when we breathe, is the very thing that plants need in order to do what they do. Plants, meanwhile give off Oxygen, the very thing that WE need to survive. How perfect!

Well, it's the same in life and business. I've found that the best, most profitable business partnerships and strategic alliances are those in which MY greatest immediate need (for sales support, marketing skills, etc.) is just what my new partner brings to the table. And similarly, what THEY are looking for, is just what I can offer. Look for the synergy, and know, too, that whether it's love, support, encouragement, happiness, or peace, sharing what you have is the only way to grow. And, just like breathing, what you share will give life to another, and indirectly help you to grow as well! With that, we can all breathe a collective sigh of relief!

Walt's Life Rhyme #289: A Process of Conversion *(aka "Yes, Tammy, You Can Make Money Doing What You Love")*

I never said that "easy"
would define the path you'd take
I'll say, though, your assumption
is perhaps your first mistake

For passion OR for profit?
as if both mutually exclude
As if in lieu of freedom
we choose shelter, clothes and food

Now, I'm not saying that your duties
will just up and disappear
What <u>will</u> change is your perception
of the skills you bring to bear

Yes, it seems from where you stand
this is a SINGLE choice you make
When, in fact it's MANY choices
in a journey that you take

There's no wand that I can wave
no incantation I can say
That can simply make it right
'cause this ol' world don't work that way

And if such "rock and hard-place" choices
represent all that you see
Then "the best of all known choices"
won't do much to set you free

For a job is just a job
no matter who's running the show
But a passion's something fluid
that you make up as you grow

So the answer to your question's
in your question, I've no doubt
It's a process of conversion
choose your path and "venture out"

A Process of Conversion
Walt's Life Rhyme #289

"I share what I know,
so that others may grow!"
www.LifeRhymes.com

Commentary for Walt's Life Rhyme #289

***Tammy wrote:**

"Walt, I have just recently discovered your website and have only received two of your Friday letters but, found both of them very interesting. I particularly enjoyed this past Friday's. I agree with it but am not so sure how to do just that when there is the house payment, daycare payments, insurance, etc. It seems like it would be so easy do just go out and enjoy life but unless you have a job that pays good money the travel and some of the other things are out of reach. I am in a predicament where I want to find a job that I enjoy but I also have the responsibility of paying for half of everything in our lives. How do I venture out and take care of my son and enjoy my life now?"

As promised, Tammy, here is my response:

What I offer in my books and workshops and often in these Friday Inspirations is simply the awareness that other choices exist for how to live your life. These options, however, often require a sustained effort and focused intention in order to first make them real, and then make them work. The way things are currently structured in your life, I'm sure the options appear limited. There's no "passion seekers wanted" section of your daily paper. There's no tried and true path for those looking to turn passion into profit. (until we came along, that is!) The only choices you'll likely see will seem to reinforce the stark contrast between the road the masses take--with the roadside littered with discarded dreams--and a road called "Passion Seeker Way", a road less traveled, and thus for which fewer maps exist.

The truth is, that "Yes, Tammy, you CAN make money doing what you love." But, it requires seeing that possibility as an ongoing process of conversion from one reality to another, not a "now or not at all" proposition. The first step is simply knowing that the future you desire exists as a road you can travel. It's not a single decision that either works or not, but a step-by-step journey in which you make successive choices that support the goal and keep you headed in the desired direction, not away from it. This doesn't always happen overnight. But, unless you see it as a possible and necessary process of conversion, rather than a "today only" choice, you'll never even take the first step to get there. Yes, there will come a day when you're doing what you love AND the food, clothing and shelter responsibilities are also being taken care of financially. And as that day approaches, every "now" will get a little more satisfying. So, take a step today by sharing the venture and the vision with your son, and ask yourself, "What do I love to do?"

Walt's Life Rhyme #288: The Worst That Can Happen

Well, it's clear that you're just apprehensive
and you're making excuses to stall
For the choice you've presented to me here today
Well, there's really no choice there at all

You can do something new with your talents
venture out into realms now unknown
Or instead stay at home with your mind wrapped in doubt
wondering, "Has another chance just been blown?"

And "So what?" if the outcome is "iffy"
Sure, your ego may suffer a bruise
There's no contract, no blood, and you keep your first born
What the heck, you've got nothing to lose!

When you look at the possible outcomes
This might work, though we're not quite sure how
But, the worst that can happen is "nothing at all"
And, hello? That's what's happening now!!

The Worst That Can Happen
Walt's Life Rhyme #288
© Walt F.J. Goodridge
"I share what I know,
so that others may grow!"
www.LifeRhymes.com

Commentary:

One of my coaching clients was considering entering a "Submit Your Ideas" contest/call for entries being hosted by a fairly reputable organization here in the city. While the prize (a full-time position with the company) was enticing, she feared that the contest organizers might simply take and use her marketing ideas without compensation. We weighed the pros and cons, and eventually, I encouraged her to enter the contest anyway, but to structure her ideas in such a way as to make herself an indispensable part of their success. I acknowledged her concern, but insisted she had nothing to lose when she considered the alternative. My exact words were, "Hey look, you might as well. 'Cause the worst that can happen, well, is already happening!" We shared a laugh, and then pondered the truth and profound implications of the statement.

Walt's Life Rhyme #287: Breathe as You Move

Do you feel you're "reaching" while moving through life…
but that somehow you've not yet "arrived?"

Friend, I know how you feel, but the peace that you seek
is here NOW not the end of the drive

If you really could just "get it" now this once and for all:
In the drive is where value resides

If you can just feel the journey holds all the reward,
and that it's you NOT the world who decides

No one's watching, or judging. Really no one keeps score
And if they do, man, quite frankly, who cares?

Take a rest stop, plan detours. Heck, plan a whole different trip!
And if you do, that's no business of theirs!

So don't sweat "where to next?" or even "when will I reach?"
(though it may feel like a race against time)

What should matter most really is that you live what you love
and experience your grand purpose sublime

The sign "Welcome to Life" passed you a long time ago
Don't hold your breath. You've got nothing to prove

The trick to this trip's just keep driving ahead
and don't forget….always breathe as you move!

Breathe as You Move
Walt's Life Rhyme #287

"I share what I know,
so that others may grow!"
www.LifeRhymes.com

Commentary for Walt's Life Rhyme #287

It's all too easy to get caught up in what you perceive as your "final destination" and lose sight of the fact that you're already living your life right now! This is it! The reality of your ideal life will always be just an extension of the here and now, so in effect, you've already "reached." You're simply on a leg of the journey defined by today's set of goals.

Now, don't get me wrong. All the efforts, struggles, setbacks, triumphs and milestones are necessary and noble parts of the pursuit of the goals that we seek. But, remember, there will ALWAYS be new goals, and as long as you're here, every day lived is an extension of the journey. Therefore, don't delay your enjoyment to some future date when you've "made it." Instead, make every effort to live in a "NOW" that includes the laughter, the enjoyment, the travel, the time spent with friends and family, and every ideal that you associate with your "destination."

The sign that you're looking for that says "Welcome to your Life" is one we all passed on day ONE! Don't put your breath, or any other aspect of living on hold waiting for it to come by again! Breathe.

Walt's Life Rhyme #286: ...the process becomes inspiration

What can I do now that's never been done?
What words do the work that will still feel like fun?
What can I say that the cards haven't captured
What can I say that will leave you enraptured?

Trying to express what's a matter of heart
Leaves me quite lost as to what to impart
For with sonnets and poems and songs that exist
I ask, "What can I add that the others have missed?"

Hmmmm. Well maybe today I should go with the flow
And offer the thoughts that we all love and know
With no twists of plot and no thoughts too profound
But just simple advice for both seeker and found

For whether romance, a home or a business affair
It just goes without saying that love should be there
For yourself, for another, for the wide world at large
it's the basis of love that should lead every charge

For you'll find that with love--and not fear--at the helm
that your journey will move to a whole different realm
Where the people, events, every thought, word and deed
will confirm what's been said that "love IS all you need"

So perhaps there's no mystery today I've revealed
Just a journey of thoughts that express what I feel
But today, what I share, I can say with elation
That like LOVE, friend, the process is its own inspiration!

For Valentine's Day

...the process becomes inspiration...
Walt's Life Rhyme #286

"I share what I know,
so that others may grow!"
www.LifeRhymes.com

Walt's Life Rhyme #285: Tell Me How to Picture You

Tell me how to picture you
Make it clear to me
What image best defines success
in visions that you see?

Tell me are you traveling
to lands great, far and wide?
Or, do you sit at home at peace
with time to look inside?

Tell me are you free now
from constraints that make you seethe?
No deadlines! No commitments!!
Time to.. >Aahhhhh<...relax and breathe

Tell me what's that thing you'll do
the passion that you love
The thing that fits you perfectly
as hand will fit to glove?

Speak it into realness, yes
and dream the dream aloud
You'll lift the veil of doubt
and pull away the mental shroud

This snapshot of success for you
developed in my mind
Gives both of us more options
to create results in kind

So tell me what to picture
For it's vital that you do
Your dreams develop faster
with more minds focused on you!

How Should I Picture You?
Walt's Life Rhyme #285

"I share what I know,
so that others may grow!"
www.LifeRhymes.com

Commentary for Walt's Life Rhyme #285

As students of metaphysics, philosophy and theology know, great power is activated and harnessed "when two or more are gathered" in the name of a particular purpose or goal. The resulting irresistible force of the collective intention, energy, thoughts, words and actions of many individuals focused towards a single outcome is what all great social movements, corporations, sports teams and marriages are all about.

As the Passion Profit Company goes through some rapid expansion, I have frequent opportunities to meet, network and form alliances with various companies and individuals. When forging a direct relationship with someone who's being considered for my "Passion Prophet Dream Team," one of the things I insist upon is that he or she tell me (or the team) what his or her goals, aspirations and personal vision of future success look like. My belief is that if all of us, for example, know that "Wendy's" dream is to own her own horse stable, then she's got a roomful of supporters, well-wishers, visionaries and "can do" people who will encourage her, send her any information they happen to come across, and, most importantly help her dream to come true by "picturing" her already there. It's what I call the "How Should I Picture You?" exercise.

Before we start the meeting, we take turns answering the question: "Tell us, Wendy, how should we picture you? What does your personal success look like? What's the one image we should all hold in our minds that epitomizes your success, and the creation of the lifestyle and feelings towards which you strive? Are you on a beach? Are you skiing in Aspen? Are you a millionaire now doing good by serving food in a soup kitchen for the homeless? Are you simply grinning from ear to ear knowing that you have enough money so that you don't have to worry about money?" This exercise provides a safe haven for our team members to express their "radical" images of success, and gives us, as well as them, a powerful mental tool with which to achieve it.

Those who know me know that one the little great pleasures of my own life is having the freedom to "go see movies in the middle of the day." My personal picture of freedom ALSO includes being out in some ecologically pristine, wide open, natural setting (the mountains, a desert, an ocean) with my Internet-equipped laptop, food for the journey, and the freedom to wonder and wander through the experience, soaking in the sunshine, all the while knowing that my company is running smoothly without me being physically present. As I gaze up at the beauty around me, I'm buoyed by the peace of mind that comes from knowing that operations are streamlined, that things are being "taken care of" to my satisfaction, and that my books, tapes and videos are providing guidance to others so that they can create the same outcome! That, my dear family and friends, is how you should picture ME! But enough about me, how should I picture YOU?

Walt's Life Rhyme #284: These Walls *(aka "The Very Thing I Seek")*

Not all who peer through prison bars
are equally confined
Some roam free in chains
while some are shackled by their minds

The fact he even asked it
is what took me by surprise
The question blocked the options
that were there before my eyes

(I'd called him to enlist his aid
to plan my great escape
His crazy scheme, quite frankly
well, it bent me out of shape!)

For here I was in dire need
and yearning to be free
What he advised seemed likely
to extend captivity

But, now on closer viewing
it's embarrassingly clear
I didn't see the options
what I saw instead was fear

Proposed, he did, a question
young and old should learn to speak:
"How can I bring to others' lives
the very thing I seek?"

Ironic, yes, but safe to say
and surer still to bet:
Sometimes your safety lies
where there appears the greatest threat

And options that on first glance
might seem drastically opposed
Might just provide the answer
if the question's rightly posed

What first I saw as prison
did in fact have me confined
But now I'll scale these walls
using the very chains that bind!

These Walls
Walt's Life Rhyme #284

"I share what I know,
so that others may grow!"
www.LifeRhymes.com

Commentary for Walt's Life Rhyme #284

A friend and mentor made a suggestion recently to which I immediately and uncharacteristically, responded, "Heck, No!" His suggestion seemed so far in opposition to my desired outcome, that I thought it was patently absurd! (How often do you get to use the phrase 'patently absurd' in a real-life situation?)

I'm good at web design. But while fun, it isn't the sort of service I would consider offering to others as it would be too time-consuming. And, freedom is the very thing I'm committed to creating for myself.

In helping me to solve my own financial challenges as a full-time entrepreneur, he asked if, as a means to an end, I would consider offering web design services to others. I answered no, because in my view, this would have immersed me in the very situations, and time-depleting challenges I'd been facing, but hoping to eliminate all these years.

What I hadn't immediately recognized was that that specific experience—needing web design services as a pressed-for-time passionpreneur—equipped me with an understanding of the frustrations, as well as a first-hand idea of what an ideal solution would look like. I now possessed insights, skills, and even valuable contacts, therefore, to be AN AGENT for that solution to other individuals equally burdened and frustrated. But, as long as I saw myself as being personally responsible for solving the challenge for others, I would miss the opportunity the situation presented. Ironically, in my Passion Profit workshops, I do this for others by connecting to people who are frustrated employees as I once was, but I didn't see the same option in my own situation.

Ask yourself, "How can I bring to others' lives, the very thing I seek? What is the thing I dream of in my own life? Can I be or make that dream come true for others? What is the thing I'm running away from? Can I provide escape for others as well?" That way of thinking has led many a frustrated individual to a great invention. For instance, think how many of the now popular and profitable dating services might have been started by people interested in meeting Mr. or Ms. Right themselves?

Walt's Life Rhyme #283: Enough

We're lost in the illusion
that we're all here to compete
The fear of insufficiency
lights fires at our feet

We've bought the grand deception
that in life there's not enough
We fight for love and money
and we view our lives as rough

But ask yourself this question
when abundance is in doubt:
If all of us are really one
who really goes without?

It's naught but misperception, friend
this instinct to "survive"
It's based on the belief
that in some real way we're deprived

The more we're separated
is the more we feel in need
Once wakened from this slumber, though
from struggle we are freed

The more we feel connected
is the less there is to fear
We're part of One. One's all there is.
Of this you should be clear!

Commentary:

Think about it. If we were all more attached to each other; if we felt and experienced a real connection with everyone else, then my joy and pain would be yours; your happiness and fears would be mine, and the experience of everyone would be felt by us collectively. In such a world there would not be the sense of, or need to grab, collect, and acquire in a state of competition, that which another has, for there would not be that sense of "another-ness" that so pervades our society. In fact, there are societies that operate closer to this ideal. Today, strive to feel connected and feel and experience the world and its wealth and abundance from a feeling of "ours" rather than "mine."

Today's Life Rhyme is inspired by Neale Donald *Walsch's Communion With God*, and the FOURTH of the Ten Illusions of Humans. These ten beliefs form the basis of the flawed perception of reality that causes all of mankind's woes. The ten illusions are

1. Need Exists (see Life Rhyme #278)
2. Failure Exists (see Life Rhyme #280)
3. Disunity Exists (see Life Rhyme #282)
4. Insufficiency Exists (today's Life Rhyme)
5. Requirements Exists
6. Judgment Exists
7. Condemnation Exists
8. Conditionality Exists
9. Superiority Exists
10. Ignorance Exists

Enough
Walt's Life Rhyme #283

"I share what I know,
so that others may grow!"
www.LifeRhymes.com

Walt's Life Rhyme #282: The Sum of Parts

I've finally learned who peers out
from behind each pair of eyes
It's always been no one but me!
--my maker in disguise!

"Because he's not like me or us"
or words to that effect
Is how we seek to justify
a world that seems a wreck

We think of all as distant
separate beings unconnected
And therefore see no cause
to all the chaos we've effected

But think of what the world has known
that to this day persists
That's based on the illusion
that DISUNITY exists

And think of all the things YOU do
and that TO you are done
By people who believe the lie
we're all not really one

Then think of how your day would be
if all you say and do
Was done with the belief that
everyone is really YOU!

From play, to work, to world affairs
to strangers on the street
How would you act if now you saw
yourself in all you meet?

And love and hate, and good and bad
and all that men allow
Might change if we were forced to think:
"Who's going to feel it now?"

The truth is, what I do to you
is done BY me TO me
I'm no more separate from the whole
than waves are from the sea

So now amongst each other
with our maker in our hearts
Let's see ourselves as whole
and more than just the sum of parts!

The Sum of Parts
Walt's Life Rhyme #282

"I share what I know,
so that others may grow!"
www.LifeRhymes.com

Commentary for Walt's Life Rhyme #282:

It's the age-old refrain of doing unto others as you would have them do unto you. But, indeed no greater wisdom was ever spoken, because, in truth and in fact, anything we do to another, we do to ourselves. Any judgment we make, any pain we inflict, as well as any support, praise and love we extend to another, is visited on us. This is true on an interpersonal level (in our relationships), on a global level (as members of the collective called earth), as well as on the ultimately spiritual level (as spiritual expressions of all that is).

There's really just one of us here, experiencing itself through trillions and trillions of expressions of itself. You are but one of these expressions. But the whole of which you are a part remains the same. You can't escape it, because you are it.

Therefore, extend the awareness of who and what you really are to every level of your interaction with everyone you meet today. In every face you see, stop long enough to ask: "How would I act towards this person if I believed I was interacting with another part of ME?

Today's Life Rhyme is inspired by Neale Donald *Walsch's Communion With God*, and the THIRD of the Ten Illusions of Humans. These ten beliefs form the basis of the flawed perception of reality that causes all of mankind's woes. The ten illusions are

1. Need Exists (see Life Rhyme #278)
2. Failure Exists (see Life Rhyme #280)
3. Disunity Exists (today's Life Rhyme)
4. Insufficiency Exists (see Life Rhyme #283)
5. Requirements Exists
6. Judgment Exists
7. Condemnation Exists
8. Conditionality Exists
9. Superiority Exists
10. Ignorance Exists

Walt's Life Rhyme #281: The Outward Path

Or your life may be a circle
growing outward from the core
Like an ever widening sphere
each passing day including more

Things inside this sphere of life
all represent your comfort zone
Things you've seen and know and do
while things outside remain unknown

So the trick to living fully
reaping all the good you sow
Is to clear the outward path
and give your sphere some room to grow

Therefore, clear away the clutter
tie and store away loose ends
Fix those nagging bits and pieces
speak forgiveness, make amends

Clear away all known obstructions
things not done you've known you should
For in some way, shape or form
these things are keeping back your good

And address all matters equally
unrelated though they seem
Oft the thing you've most avoided
is the key to your life's dream!

Once you deal with each obstruction
(to this truth I can attest)
More and more life will bestow on you
it's good, better... then best!

The Outward Path
Walt's Life Rhyme #281

"I share what I know,
so that others may grow!"
www.LifeRhymes.com

Commentary:

Some of the good things you aspire to in life will only happen when the path is clear. But the path isn't always in front of you. Sometimes the blockages to our forward motion (what I prefer to see as an outward expansion of a circle or, more accurately, a sphere) are not just in front of us (the things you need to do), but to the left, to the right (the things in related areas of our lives), the things above us (spiritual matters), and even behind us (the things in the past).

Our lives will improve, therefore, and expand to include more within its enclosed area, when the things that block the expansion are removed. Those blockages can be words that need to be spoken, feelings that need to be expressed or tasks from the past that need to be accomplished. Take the time to take care of all this "stuff" that in some way is blocking your sphere from expanding fully in the outward path!

Walt's Life Rhyme #280: No Such Thing

How can my thoughts betray me
if my thoughts and I are one?
My thoughts and words are simply tools
by which my will is done

Failure as an outcome
in my world does not exist
But let's explore this fully
so my point here isn't missed

The life that you've been living's
been the outcome of your will
No matter how you end this year
this fact stays that way still

When fate is seen as punishment
imposed on from without
Then fear of failure looms
and every outcome seems in doubt

But goals and resolutions
brought to failure or success
Reflect OUR daily choices
nothing more and nothing less

There's no such thing as failure
there's no way to lose a game
Where both player and opponent
made and maker are the same!

No Such Thing
Walt's Life Rhyme #280

"I share what I know,
so that others may grow!"
www.LifeRhymes.com

Commentary:

Today's Life Rhyme is inspired by Neale Donald *Walsch's Communion With God*, and the SECOND of the Ten Illusions of Humans. These ten beliefs form the basis of the flawed perception of reality that causes all of mankind's woes. The ten illusions are

1. Need Exists (see Life Rhyme #278)
2. Failure Exists (today's Life Rhyme)
3. Disunity Exists (see Life Rhyme #282)
4. Insufficiency Exists (see Life Rhyme #283)
5. Requirements Exists
6. Judgment Exists
7. Condemnation Exists
8. Conditionality Exists
9. Superiority Exists
10. Ignorance Exists

Walt's Life Rhyme #279: The Need to Be Right
A Moment's Resolution

All manners of assertions
criticisms and the like
Are mostly said so we can say
"You see there, I was right!"

So much of all our earthly ills
and heartaches that we face
Are caused by us replaying
tapes we really should replace

It blocks all human progress
makes us trade plowshares for guns
It keeps addicts in denial
and turns mothers against sons

And those whose views you trample
and who leave feeling "less than"
Leave not with warm intentions
but with vengeance as their plan

But ask yourself, "What outcomes
might my words produce instead
If rather than choose conflict
to myself I simply said:

"I'll let you keep your dignity
and self-esteem intact
We'll both be free to choose new ways
to be and interact

And though we won't agree
or see eye to eye on everything
I'm open to the change and growth
this new outlook will bring

It's just a pyrrhic victory
being "right" at your expense
A love that's based on right or wrong
is naught but false pretense

So from this moment onward
despite how it's always been
I know I won't always be right
but now we both will win!"

The Need to Be Right
Walt's Life Rhyme #279

"I share what I know,
so that others may grow!"
www.LifeRhymes.com

Commentary for Walt's Life Rhyme #279

Here are a few personal qualities and traits you need in order to sustain harmonious relationships: a desire to heal, a willingness to communicate, knowing the intentions behind another's statements, the ability to apologize, and giving up the need to be "right."

The need to be right takes many forms in our lives. We often hold views and opinions about people and situations (e.g. All engineers are geeks", or "it's too hard to start my own business") that serve us in some way. They keep us safe and feeling protected so we never have to venture out into the unknown and risk what we've come to think of as "failure."

The need to be right comes up in our interpersonal relationships. We hold on to images of others and ourselves, of past hurts, errors in judgments and mistakes, so that we can feel justified in our suffering. We can blame others for our present conditions and thus never have to face the responsibility for changing them.

The need to be right justifies our interactions with strangers. We can lash out at drivers who cut us off on the highway, shoppers who try to jump ahead in line, all because we're in the right, and they're wrong, so we won't give in. Think of all the energy you've wasted over the past year defending your delusions, asserting your dominance, justifying your judgments, while diminishing others' own self-esteem by your need to prove them wrong and prove yourself right.

You say: *I'm smart. I'm in control. You were wrong. I was right. He is bad. I am a victim. The world is evil. They don't understand. Things are difficult. I always lose at this game.* And, when the world turns out just as you believe it to be, you get to say, "See, I was right!"

SUGGESTION: For the new moment that approaches, instead of asking, "How can I be right today?" ask instead, *"What can I learn? Whom can I help? Knowing that the only way I can truly succeed and raise my own self-esteem is by raising the self-esteem of others, how can I support [name of person] in his/her journey without making him/her feel 'less than'? What new ways of understanding people, situations, and myself are being presented to me? What interpretations of these situations will aid my growth and development, rather than reinforce stereotypes, fears and animosity? Is this really important enough for me to fight for? Will the energy I expend in proving my point get me the willing support, admiration and warm wishes of my adversary, or is there another way?"*

You might be surprised at what new realities you can create when you give up your need to be right!

Walt's Life Rhyme #278: Nothing That You Need

Despite your protestations
over all you think you lack
You've got all that's required, friend
for nothing's been held back

Success, wealth and abundance
and to have and eat your cake
Exist first as decisions
and are choices that you make

In other words, your happiness
and how you feel today
Are not results dependent on
things going a certain way

And all you think you needed
that you think will hold life's key?
You're here, alive, without them
so how crucial could they be?

Life is its own complete reward
know this and you'll concede
For you and for your maker
that there's nothing that you need!

Commentary:

Today's Life Rhyme is inspired by Neale Donald *Walsch's Communion With God*, and the FIRST of the Ten Illusions of Humans. These ten beliefs form the basis of the flawed perception of reality that causes all of mankind's woes. The ten illusions are

1. Need Exists (today's Life Rhyme)
2. Failure Exists (see Life Rhyme #280)
3. Disunity Exists (see Life Rhyme #282)
4. Insufficiency Exists (see Life Rhyme #283)
5. Requirements Exists
6. Judgment Exists
7. Condemnation Exists
8. Conditionality Exists
9. Superiority Exists
10. Ignorance Exists

Nothing That You Need
Walt's Life Rhyme #278

*"I share what I know,
so that others may grow!"*
www.LifeRhymes.com

Walt's Life Rhyme #277: Nothing's Wasted
"Masterpiece in the Making"

PROLOGUE: Snapshot
For life's not a pose nor a picture, my friend
where one click shows "the life of my dream"
It's a river 'round hills, over stones and down falls
gathering strength for what's waiting downstream

Don't belabor the absence of this thing or that
nor stress over 'wrong' turns that you took
Don't despair that you're not where you thought you would be
with reminders everywhere that you look

No the years were not wasted though seemingly so
(I know progress feels slow and painstaking)
But each heartache and triumph and laughter and tear's
been your masterpiece life in the making

Nothing's wasted. It all led you here to this day
with experience and skills you can use
And when viewed as a path things may start to make sense
when life's seen in this way you CAN'T LOSE!

Nothing's Wasted (Masterpiece in the Making)
Walt's Life Rhyme #277

"I share what I know,
so that others may grow!"
www.LifeRhymes.com

Commentary for Walt's Life Rhyme #277

As they assess the "success" of their lives, many people feel that if things aren't presently as they wish them to be, that not only have they failed, but that everything they've done up to this point has been an exercise in futility--a wasted effort.

I suggest to you that no job you've ever had; no relationship you've ever been in; no business venture that didn't quite take off--has ever been a waste, unless you choose to see it that way. Although I spent 7 years in the corporate world in a job I didn't like, I recognize the benefits of the experiences, skills, friendships and serendipitous events that being there have brought me. I see the unifying theme that runs through my early life in Jamaica, my high school experiences, my college years, my radio station stint, my artist management debacle, my record label downfall, the unique network marketing experience, the leap into being a full-time entrepreneur, the resulting debt, the evictions, and all the ongoing ups and downs of this journey that I'm on. I see how it all worked in divine order to bring me here today.

I see clearly that in order for me to effectively help others to achieve their dreams of turning passion into profit, that I NEEDED to go through every single one of the setbacks and triumphs that I did. What kept me going is the simple belief that there's a masterpiece in the making, and that EVERYTHING is necessary. Remember: Once you know that you're in pursuit of your passion, you enjoy the journey regardless of the ups and downs and detours you experience. Nothing's Wasted!

Walt's Life Rhyme #276: Mastering Me

PROLOGUE:
Before, within your shadow
all I saw were cloudy skies
the forecast's not as gloomy
when I see with my own eyes

I'm getting through it daily
though indeed it's quite a course
Unlike before, my answers now
come from a different source

I've learned now how to separate
and choose a different train
The scenery here's much different
skies of blue instead of rain

I've learned now how to recognize
where I and you both end
What's yours is yours, what's mine is mine
this truth I now defend

I've learned how early thoughts of me
all made me feel "less than"
I've learned now to reframe the world
in ways that say "I can!"

I've learned a whole new set of rules
designed to help me grow
To former thoughts of smaller MEs
I've learned to just say no

So now when I am tested
by things I once just couldn't see
I pass with flying colors
For now I'm finally mastering me

Mastering Me
Walt's Life Rhyme #276

"I share what I know,
so that others may grow!"
www.LifeRhymes.com

Commentary for Walt's Life Rhyme #276

When your mind is young, people can have an inordinate influence and impact on you and your identity. If you're fortunate and determined, however, you can *unlearn* views of you that don't serve you, and develop mastery of whom you ought to know yourself to be. The steps are: Separation, Recognition, Reinterpretation, Growth and Mastery.

Separation
You first must be able to physically separate from the oppressive or negative environment. Even the proximity to such thoughts can keep you trapped.

Recognition
The next step is the recognition of your separateness. Not a real separateness, of course, because we are all connected. But separateness in that the issues that another individual deals with in his or her life on this plane are uniquely their own. Once you recognize this, you can seek definition of yourself from other sources.

Reinterpretation
You must now develop the skills of introspection and critical thinking that will allow you to create new truths for yourself.

Growth
Realize that life is indeed a journey, not a destination, and commit yourself to the journey of self-growth and discovery.

Mastery
Once you separate, recognize, re-interpret, and grow, then you'll find that the thoughts, words and actions of others that used to define you, now merely amuse you. Once you realize that you aren't being pulled in, you can rest assured that you've grown, for you've passed with flying colors!

Dedicated to those who are breaking free to discover themselves anew.

Walt's Life Rhyme #275: And Butterflies DO Fly
(Not If But How and When)

It may seem quite presumptuous
but still, just hear me out
The only thing that's stopping you
is that you're plagued with doubt

You need no one's approval
for the things you want to do
The most the world can tell you
is what THEY'VE seen to be true

But trust me when I tell you
less than you have tried and won
They simply chose to disregard
what men said can't be done

Accept someone's opinion
you accept their truths and fears
Don't be surprised if, therefore, you live
not YOUR life but theirs!

Again there's no one out there
who can know what you can do
The only expert on your life
You got it, friend: It's you

For butterflies DO fly quite well
despite what experts say
Without a doubt you too can fly
and have things go your way!

So, guidance? Yes. Approval? No.
Don't switch the two again
And from now on the question is
not "if", but "how" and "when!"

And Butterflies DO Fly
(aka "Not If But How and When")
Walt's Life Rhyme #275

"I share what I know,
so that others may grow!"
www.LifeRhymes.com

Commentary:

In listening to a client's story last week, it was evident that despite many of the great ideas and dreams she had over the years, she never pursued them to her own satisfaction. I further realized that, as a result of her own feelings about her potential, she was asking for input from others in a distinct way. It seemed she was awaiting the approval of others she assumed were further ahead in the journey, or whom she thought somehow had a handle on what was possible for her.

The suggestion I offered to her is that the determining factor in whether you succeed at a particular task is not what others think is possible, but simply the degree of personal conviction with which you pursue the result. Even "known" laws of physics are limited by human perception. According to a piece I once read, the butterfly's body design and wing structure violates all principles of aerodynamics. In other words, according to expert opinion, butterflies can't fly. But fly they do, don't they?

Walt's Life Rhyme #274: The Absence of Bad

"With the presence of good
the bad are no better.
With the absence of bad
the good are made better"

It is never enough to
lay claim to respect
citing all the good things that you do

It's essential, my friend
to win favor and fame
that you stop doing all the bad things too

For the presence of good
may endear you to some
but in truth is just half of success

It's the absence of bad
that secures you your name
and each goal towards which you progress!

The Absence of Bad
Walt's Life Rhyme #274

"I share what I know,
so that others may grow!"
www.LifeRhymes.com

Commentary:

Here's a question for you to ponder today: Are we "good" to the degree that we do the right things, or to the degree that we don't do the wrong things? In other words, are you a "good" person because you help senior citizens cross the street? Or are you good because you choose not to shoot them?

You'd likely agree that one can not be a good Samaritan on Sunday, and a killer on Monday and still lay claim to, or qualify for the distinction of good. Similarly, in your quest for health, you can't claim to be on the road to health simply because you eat fruit in the morning, while bingeing on processed, refined, high fat, high cholesterol food in the evening. In order to achieve health, you must add the "good", while removing the "bad" in order to fully qualify. In fact, it's the absence of "bad" that really determines how healthy you are.

Consequently, any pursuit of success, be it wealth, health, love or spiritual peace, must incorporate a two-pronged approach in order to be effective. For example, to achieve

FINANCIAL WEALTH: pursue income, while removing debt/bad money habits

PHYSICAL HEALTH: eat healthy foods, while eliminating unhealthy ones

LOVE: pursue relationships while removing barriers to intimacy

The same is true in many other aspects of personal and business life. Realize that a single blemish on your credit history, a transgression in your past, or a single irate customer (all instances of the "bad") can do more damage to your reputation than the combined instances of the "good" can do to maintain it.

Walt's Life Rhyme #273: I Simply Listen

I start by asking questions
and the answers that I seek
Give focus to your dreams
and help your inner heart to speak

I listen for commitment
in the promises men make
A man will get results
when it's his happiness at stake

I listen for the hunger
in the dreams women pursue
For that predicts the measure
of the things that they will do

I listen for the anger
and the ire that men vent
For many worlds of wealth
have grown from seeds of discontent

I listen for the value
people place on what they love
You'll find that's what they'll likely choose
when push comes down to shove

And sometimes what I hear
are things you wish but never voice
And all I do is offer thoughts
that show you have a choice!

Commentary:

This Life Rhyme is in response to the young lady who, at a recent Passion Profit™ workshop, asked my secret to helping people find their inner passions the way I do.

I Simply Listen
Walt's Life Rhyme #273

"I share what I know,
so that others may grow!"
www.LifeRhymes.com

Walt's Life Rhyme #272: A Cup of Sugar & a Little More Thyme

Just a little bit of sugar
might have sweetened the pot
with the result that all might have been fed
But your choice of ingredients has soured the meal
and now one will go hungry to bed

Just a little bit of thyme
might have bettered the taste
but older recipes instead were defended
Just a little bit of patience
would keep all in good cheer
But instead, the whole banquet has ended

A Cup of Sugar, & Little More Thyme!
Walt's Life Rhyme #272

*"I share what I know,
so that others may grow!"*
www.LifeRhymes.com

Commentary:

A business supplier I've had for the past 5 years was recently bought out by a larger company. The new management recently took over and consequently, I no longer have direct personal contact with the Billing Manager. I also quickly learned, that I no longer enjoyed the flexibility of the payment plan I once enjoyed with the previous owners. The new billing manager threatened to cut off my supply in 1 week unless all previous balances were paid in full. While it's certainly within every business' right to do what he did, I, on principle, decided to take my business elsewhere.

I always have a plan "B," because I believe that any plan for success that is based exclusively on the good will of a single individual or entity is inherently flawed. So, I spent the next several days preparing to use a new supplier. I made the transition smoothly just a day before the deadline.

So what have I learned from this? Well, from my point of view, it's a blessing (as are all events in my life). I've found a new supplier whose prices are less than 10% of what I was paying before, and which will, therefore, save me thousands each year! When I think about my previous supplier, I think of all the thousands of dollars of income which he might have received but for the price of a little leniency and patience. Don't let YOUR business, relationship, or success suffer for want of a cup of sugar, and a little more thyme!

OUTTAKE:
*Just that one cup of honey
might have filled every cup
and in time brought you all you deserved
But without it the flavor has turned bitter instead
with the result that now no one is served!*

Walt's Life Rhyme #271: Sometimes a Banana

My friend says I analyze things way WAY too much
and take everything out to the extreme
She says that some things are to be felt and not known
and that some things are just what they seem

She says if I lived life just as much as I thought it
that I'd be happier with how things unfold
And if I act first from heart and not logical mind
I'd live a life that's much brighter and bold

For she says people will do just what people will do
without regard to any research or stat
And that sometimes a banana is just a banana
Hmmm. I wonder what she meant by that?

Sometimes a Banana
Walt's Life Rhyme #271

*"I share what I know,
so that others may grow!"*
www.LifeRhymes.com

Walt's Life Rhyme #270: How Likely?

We're powerless, she said
That's how the world seemed through her eyes
And I, not one to judge, said
fair enough, let's analyze

The way you've framed your outlook
I can see why you're not striving
It's like your life is moving
in a car that you're not driving

But ask yourself this question
and perhaps you'll think anew
If others rise from depths of woe
I ask then, why not you?

The urge to grow and prosper
and the feeling that there's more
Are clues we have a purpose here
of this I'm very sure

What works best is a view
that gets you where you want to go
Not one in which you're victimized
and jostled to and fro

To me, all things are possible
what's hard is just believing
To think you've got no say
is just an act of self-deceiving

It makes no sense
we're born with dreams our inner eye can see
And not the means to reach them?
Hmmm. How likely could that be?

How Likely?
Walt's Life Rhyme #270

"I share what I know,
so that others may grow!"
www.LifeRhymes.com

Commentary:

Early on in my journey of personal growth, I encountered a concept in Brian Tracy's *Psychology of Achievement* which had a tremendous effect on me. He stated: "Nature is not capricious. We wouldn't be given the faculties to dream of, and aspire to goals without also being equipped with the equally necessary means to achieve them." It made sense and formed the basis of my belief system from that moment onward. The way I look at it is, you've got nothing to lose by believing this idea. If you're right, then you can achieve anything you set your mind to. If you're wrong, and we have no control, then at least you've lived a life with a feeling of empowerment as opposed to one of futility and dejection! So it's a win-win either way!

Walt's Life Rhyme #269: Switchboard
(The Enemy Within)

I marshal all my forces
and I launch my best attack
With plans to smash and conquer
loot and pillage, sweep and sack

And just when all is ready
for that one deciding blow
The tables turn, and now
I have become my own worst foe

And now my new dilemma
seems ironic, almost fated:
I find myself reacting to
a battle I've created

With plans revised I strike again
intent this time to win
This close to calling "checkmate"
and the board gets switched again!

To win at such a conflict
where the enemy's not clear,
My strategy must change:
I must become the one I fear

Yes, think like my arch nemesis
whose thoughts will hold the key
But, wait. Oh, no! I see it now.....
.....the enemy is me!!

I'll never win this battle
out to crush, kill and destroy
I'll win when all "his" troops
are also mine too to deploy

Offensive and defensive
must be one mind and the same
When both serve the same outcome
that's the way I'll win the game!

Switchboard (The Enemy Within)
Walt's Life Rhyme #269

"I share what I know,
so that others may grow!"
www.LifeRhymes.com

Commentary for Walt's Life Rhyme #269

Armand Dimele, host of *The Positive Mind*, a favorite radio program on Pacifica Radio, describes an interesting technique he used to teach people how to play chess. According to Armand, the game would start as usual, with each player making their moves based on their own strategy. Ten minutes into the game, however, he would turn the board around, and force each player to continue playing from the "other side," i.e. with his or her opponent's pieces and strategy.

This creates an interesting dynamic. If you're the weaker player, it allows you the advantage of proceeding now from a position of strength with a "better" board. If you're the stronger player, you now find yourself in a weaker position, defending against a superior attack, the very attack you created! In either case, you are now experiencing the game from your opponent's viewpoint.

What a great metaphor for the game of life! Metaphysically, you can be sure that whatever plans of attack you lay out for another will eventually return to you, for the simple reason that there's no one else out there but you. So, after the "board of life" is switched enough times for you to notice, you'll hopefully revise your strategy and realize that soon you may be playing with your opponent's pieces, so the strategy that will work best is one where both of you have the opportunity to win. For the victory you create may be your own!

Perhaps the best strategy in any aspect of your life, therefore, is communication, not conflict. Perhaps, when there is conflict, you can create a dialogue between the two parts of you that are in conflict (the "fat" you & the "skinny" you; the "rich" you & the "poor" you; the "happy" you & the "sad" you; the "old" you & the "young" you), and allow each equal time to meet, greet and work together towards a mutual understanding, acceptance and harmony where both will win.

Walt's Life Rhyme #268: Nowhere To Hide

I come in search of answers
and you make me look inside
You dispel my delusions
and I've no place left to hide

I bring to you my issues
when my time I choose to bide
You challenge me with clarity
and force me to decide

A mentor and a teacher
seems you've always been a guide
Directions are suggested
(so as not to hurt my pride)

You're loyal to the truth
so you won't always take my side
Myself I'll fool, but never you
with you there's no free ride

Attempts to skirt and sugar coat
those come to naught. I've tried
It either is or not, you say
what is won't be denied

You help me find reality
when dreams and life collide
You help me find the truth of me
when to myself I've lied

I hope you have a friend like mine
with whom you are allied
A voice of reason ever clear
in whom you can confide

For robbed of your excuses
and with no place left to hide
The place where you're left standing
is the place where truth resides!

Nowhere to Hide
Walt's Life Rhyme #268

"I share what I know,
so that others may grow!"
www.LifeRhymes.com

Commentary for Walt's Life Rhyme #268

In this journey called life, it's vitally important to have someone to talk with. It's important to have someone who has your best interests at heart who will keep you grounded in truth and reality as you address the challenges you face. A true friendship is one which helps you quickly get to the truth of an issue rather than support you in the delusions and lies that you are likely to engage in as you attempt to escape.

When choosing your friends, don't look simply for blind loyalty. Look for someone loyal to a code of ethics. A friend without a moral compass can only keep you company as you both slide down into decadence. They can't help you on the journey towards the light.

Don't look merely for shared interests. You need an openness to growth. A friend without the propensity for personal growth can play your game quite well, but will never teach you any new ones.

Don't look just for intelligence, but seek introspection. Sometimes the answers to the great "out there" are to be found in the "great within." You need someone who knows where to look.

Seek that friend. Be that friend. And enjoy the ride!

Walt's Life Rhyme #267: Great Intentions

What makes this moment different from
all those that came before?
Good question. One to think about.
I'm honestly not sure

But trust me when I tell you, though
that this my friend is IT!
And if it's not, well that's cool too
'cause trust me, I won't quit

Unphased by past experience
I'm up for one more try
I can't envision giving up
success ever draws nigh!

I came. I tried. I stumbled
but I won't rehash the past
I view each new day's options
as more thrilling than the last!

I always get excited,
'cause the hope is always there
that this next "IT" will be the "IT"
that takes me over there!

So why is THIS time different?
Well, I can't say that I know
But possible or not, friend
great intentions make IT so!

Great Intentions
Walt's Life Rhyme #267
© Walt F.J. Goodridge
"I share what I know,
so that others may grow!"
www.LifeRhymes.com

Commentary:

As we prepare to launch a new venture, an associate mentioned how having the right intention and the appropriate script in one's mind brings players, possibilities and purpose to the forefront to make things happen. He commented on how contagious the joy and excitement I was expressing towards the new venture was for all involved. He remarked how seamlessly the components fell into place to build and launch our project within about 96 hours of conceptualization.

I thought about that for a moment, and recalled a similar conversation about how entrepreneurs always believe that their "pot of gold" is always waiting at the end of the next rainbow they see. In many areas of life, be it a new romance or a new business, I believe the ability to get excited about the future, and what it can and will be is critical to success, no matter what the present or the past may appear to be.

So today's Life Rhyme is just some pure unadulterated excitement, enthusiasm, joy and encouragement from me to you to help you get through whatever you may be facing. Trust me, it too shall pass, and you'll be that much stronger and ready for the next pot of gold that surely will be there as long as you keep moving towards it!

Set your goals, state your intention and don't rest until you see it in your reality!

Walt's Life Rhyme #266: From Root to Fruit

If life were seen to be a tree
desire would be the root
And choices become branches
and then outcomes fall like fruit

From Root to Fruit
Walt's Life Rhyme #266

"I share what I know,
so that others may grow!"
www.LifeRhymes.com

Commentary:

During a recent workshop in New York, a participant stood to answer the two questions I always pose at the beginning of each workshop:

1. What is your passion?
2. What is the challenge you face to bring it to reality?

A.R. spoke of his desire to retire early, to be able to spend time with his family, and to really enjoy his life. He said that at the root of his quest was his passion for freedom, and proceeded to elaborate on the tree analogy for the benefit of all in the room. I was impressed with his choice of metaphor, and offer to you this short paraphrase of A.R.'s words.

Walt's Life Rhyme #265: The Easier Game

Anyone can coach you
when you play the easier game
Despite the years of joyless scores
the game plan's still the same

Everyone's an expert
in this game we know quite well
First school. Then college. Then a job.
Don't question. Don't rebel.

In time once you discover
that in this game no one wins
You'll run to play the harder game
and then the fun begins

You'll find no lack of coaches
saying "do this thing or that"
Be wary though of sideline stars
who've never held a bat

You'll choke, strike out and fumble
ill-prepared you won't know why
Take heart, it's just a different game
the old rules don't apply

New rules. New game plan. New rewards
New way of keeping score
In time you'll see: with greater risk
the payoff's often more

But some, disheartened, give up hope
and blame it on fatigue
Returning to familiar fields
back in the minor leagues

So choose it if you wish but
heed these words from one who knows
That just because you're scoring high
don't mean you're in the pros!

The Easier Game
Walt's Life Rhyme #265

"I share what I know,
so that others may grow!"
www.LifeRhymes.com

Commentary for Walt's Life Rhyme #265

In a recent coaching session, a client and I discussed the "expensive" outcomes of some of the business risks she's taken. I comforted her (only partly, I'm sure) by reminding her that years ago she chose to play a different game than the average individual, and whatever outcomes she experienced, (whether "good" or "bad") were going to be different than those of the average person, who chooses to play an easier game.

Society encourages us to play the easier game. The easier game is called "Employee for Life." If you opt for the security of a regular job, you can pay the bills that will keep the utilities on, keep the roof over your head, pay the car note, maintain your credit and keep everything working great! And, by the criteria of the easier game, you're high in the rankings if you manage to keep things in relative equilibrium.

However, the game of "Succeed on my Own Terms" is naturally a harder game for the simple reasons that 1) fewer people play it, 2) the strategies and rules aren't as well known, 3) the rewards, and thus the risks are greater. Few utility companies, landlords, banks and creditors will be supportive while you work out the kinks in your strategy for playing the "harder game." So, if you choose to play it, you've got to be prepared for greater tests of your commitment, patience, resolve and stamina. It's just the nature of the game.

So, for you passion seekers who've opted for the harder game, don't be misled by the apparent high scores (car, clean credit, working telephone) of your friends. You chose a different game, so you'll have to learn to rank yourself based on other criteria (freedom, purpose, fulfillment, creative expression) while you work out the details of your strategy! But rest assured, the rewards will make it all worthwhile.

Walt's Life Rhyme #264: Ways and Means

To put your dreams
on hold and mourn
all in the name of lack's
like coming to conclusions
way before you've got the facts

You never know
what good may come
along the road ahead
but first you've got to
take the trip
in spite of what you dread

I've heard it said
our feelings will,
in ways not understood,
attract the folks and circumstance
that bring to us our good

So focus less
on ways and means
and more on how you'd feel
And walk with the conviction
that the path will be revealed!

Ways and Means
Walt's Life Rhyme #264

"I share what I know,
so that others may grow!"
www.LifeRhymes.com

Commentary:

Hi Walt,
I have been a little sad because I was trying to do the right thing by going to school and I'm finding out that it is so expensive. Even though I was honored with some grant money, I would be in so much debt, and that's really not in my financial plans right now. XYZ University is one of my 1st choices, but since that one is so expensive I did not take the placement test and send off my paper work. Do you have any suggestions?
-My Academic Reality Yearnings

Hi M.A.R.Y.

Do the paperwork and send it off! Expect that if it's meant to be, that the money will come. I didn't get my scholarship to Columbia until AFTER I was already accepted and already in my first semester. A counselor at the school submitted my name and I got the scholarship. Education is a great thing! And if it's always been your goal, then go for it!

At the same time, if your reason for pursuing the education is to make more money, there might be other ways for you to increase your value in the marketplace. You're already exceptionally qualified to earn millions if you're willing to take some risks and put yourself out there in ways other than being an employee.

In either case, remember to live from the feeling of the wish fulfilled. In other words, the key to achieving your goals is to pretend that the dream is already a reality and to live, think, breathe, walk, talk and be just as you would be if your goal were realized. That process of feeling the desired outcome sets up almost mysterious vibrations, that, like a tuning fork, harmonizes with other similarly tuned people and circumstances, and attracts the necessary ways and means into your life! So, don't worry about HOW! As a friend of mine is fond of saying, "HOW is none of your business!"

Walt's Life Rhyme #263: The Primary Illusion

What's real cannot be threatened
What's unreal can't exist
So says the Course in Miracles
and what it means is this:

The world you see about you
is really but a dream
A world of your perceptions
as real as it may seem

You first see what's inside you
and this you then project
Untrue beliefs in separateness
you're choosing to protect

This primary illusion
has caused a world of fear
If life looks grim, I say to you
you're seeing what's not there

What's real is "we're connected"
What's real is "nothing dies"
What's real is "what we see
depends on where we cast our eyes"

So seek first perfect vision
without it, here's the deal:
You'll find yourself defending
what in truth, friend, isn't real

Yes, focus on reality
despite what "simon says"
All else is mere distraction
for really, love is all there is

The Primary Illusion
Walt's Life Rhyme #263

*"I share what I know,
so that others may grow!"*
www.LifeRhymes.com

Commentary:

An excerpt from A Course In Miracles:

"We look inside first, decide the kind of world we want to see and then project that world outside, making it the truth as we see it. We make it true by our interpretations of what it is we are seeing. If we are using perception to justify our own mistakes -- our anger, our impulses to attack, our lack of love in whatever form it may take -- we will see a world of evil, destruction, malice, envy and despair. All this we must learn to forgive, not because we are being "good" and "charitable," but because what we are seeing is not true. We have distorted the world by our twisted defenses, and are therefore seeing what is not there. As we learn to recognize our perceptual errors, we also learn to look past them or "forgive." At the same time we are forgiving ourselves, looking past our distorted self-concepts to the Self That was created in us and as us."

Walt's Life Rhyme #262: Work?
A Labor Day Life Rhyme

It's really not work if you love it
this I've said to you time and again
As I spend my days doing the thing that I love
well, I guess I'll just say it again

It's really not work if you love it
that special thing that you cannot NOT do
For no matter how far and how wide that you hide
that ol' thing seems to always find YOU

It's really not work if you enjoy it
this special calling that you ever must heed
And as much of a gift as it is to the world
within you, too, it fills a real need

It's really not work if you crave it
and can't imagine if it didn't exist
And know somehow, somewhere you'll be under its spell
for its pleasure you're not strong to resist

It's really not work if it's in you
and is the you that all others are seeing
No, don't call it work for it's much more than that
for it's really your reason for being!

Work?
Walt's Life Rhyme #262

"I share what I know,
so that others may grow!"
www.LifeRhymes.com

Commentary:

To my new friend in Chicago who realizes that no matter what else she has ever done in life, and no matter how she tries to avoid it, she knows beyond the shadow of a doubt that her love of things bridal (her passion is a unique style of wedding dress) is her true calling. She promised that she wouldn't rest until she gave that gift to the world! The world awaits YOUR special gift. Don't keep us waiting too long!

Walt's Life Rhyme #261: Conditions of Necessity

Conditions of necessity
both natural and contrived
Just make me more resolved to say
this too have I survived

Challenge and adversity
while stumbling blocks to some
Just give me all the strength I need
to face and overcome

I seem more motivated
when all others give up hope
My fighting skills get better
when I'm up against the ropes

I seem to run my fastest
when the clock is running out
I act more boldly often
when the outcome is in doubt

A week left for a six-day job
and that's when I'll begin
I get much more productive
when a deadline's closing in

I'm using voids and vacuums
to create some sort of lack
I'm ready to move forward
when the wall's against my back

So often when I have a goal
I'm yearning to complete
Conditions of necessity
are the fire at my feet!

Commentary:

So, here's what I've learned about myself: I'm a "pressure addict." I work better with deadlines. Whenever I have a project, say a book, or other goal to accomplish, I find or create some sort of external pressure which I use to motivate myself towards completion. For example, when I write a new book, I'll often pre-sell it (even before I've started writing it), and promise to deliver it to my customers by a specific date. The pressure of all those customers waiting for their merchandise is what I use to drive me ever forward. I do the same thing with other goals. I create a condition of necessity, of "having to," that spurs me on to do the thing that needs to be done. Perhaps not the healthiest method, but quite effective.

Conditions of Necessity
Walt's Life Rhyme #261

"I share what I know,
so that others may grow!"
www.LifeRhymes.com

Walt's Life Rhyme #260: The Incomplete Begun

a million irons in the fire
a million things half-done
the list gets longer every day
the incomplete begun

so many new things to explore
that tug this way and that
not long enough to see them through
the incomplete begun

it always starts off with a bang most times
but then excitement wanes
you're off again to seek new thrills
the incomplete begun

I know the feeling well, my friend
I've traveled that road too
but here's the trick I used to end
my incomplete begun

first I--

The Incomplete Begun
Walt's Life Rhyme #260

"I share what I know,
so that others may grow!"
www.LifeRhymes.com

Commentary:

Oops, look at the time! I have to start packing for an event. So, hopefully I'll continue this later. I really wish I could have finished this one, especially because I know many people battle with just this challenge. But anyway, I know you guys won't mind, right?

But, meanwhile, PLEASE reply to me and let me know what you think of it so far, and maybe you could help me complete it, by adding the last few lines. Personally, I think this may be my best one so far! What do you think? Really, I'd like to know. Even if you've never emailed me before, please just take the time to respond. It would really mean a lot. Wow! The time is just slipping by! My flight is in an hour, and I haven't started packing yet! *Inspired by Shawne*

Walt's Life Rhyme #259: The Incomplete Begun Part 2

Life Rhyme #260 was a wake-up call for those who tend to begin but not finish what they start. It was also a bit of a challenge to those inclined to add their own verses to aid its completion. Here are some of the best responses from members of our mailing list all with valuable tips and laments on their own incomplete begun!

***Evie Writes**:

first I prioritized my 'to do' lists
to find what was really big
giving each task a long hard look
the incomplete begun

I consolidated all the tasks
and deleted what no longer mattered
a new list is what I needed
the incomplete begun

And once I had my new list ready
I stopped procrastinating
I stopped thinking
"but what if this....or what if that..."
I stopped creating (or imagining) any blockade
to achieving the goal I am striving for
It's time to get to work

so my incomplete begun
and soon I will be reporting back to you
how much of my incomplete is done!
(finally found a rhyme at the end) :)
thanks for the 'homework'

***Edwin In New York Writes**

I write three columns labled A, B, C,
then list my things to do in priority.
Let my conscience guide my choice,
while listening to my inner voice.

I handle tasks like a performing plate spinner,
concentrate on each project equally a winner.
Keeping all things in perspective.
helps me achieve my set objective.

Walt, great topic.

Walt's Life Rhyme #259: The Incomplete Begun Part 3

***Patricia Writes:**

Hi Walt;

I enjoy your newsletter very much. I have never written to you before but I could not resist your invite. My advice/solution to overcoming incomplete beginnings is:

To enjoy the true beauty is in the journey. It is continual, with no set starting points. We step aboard wherever we are and we can change directions as needed. Life is an ever-changing adventure. Age, race and gender does not matter, everybody travels their own way, at their own pace and time. We each have our own methods. Some race through life while others take things slower. There is no right or wrong, only whether it works or not. No one can define the process, which works for us. When we arrive at the crossroads of our own truth, we become more aware of where we have been and where we desire to go. Until we get to that point, why not enjoy the ride anyway? (taken from article printed in Premyeir.com)

Written By Author/ Contributor
Patricia Alli-Hines, CEO
Exclusive Services Consulting
About Exclusive Services

***Ricky Writes:**

Dear Walt,

I hope you like my response. I finished your poem for you. You'll find it below. This is definitely one for the record books. I and so many others close to me struggle with this dilemma. I think I'm going to follow my own advice and find out what has worked for me in the past (before I got bored and moved on) and begin doing it again & STICK to it. This was a very clever inspiration. Hats off to you for all the good work you are doing. Sometimes all I have is your inspirations to keep me going. See you in NY in November! Keep up the GREAT work & may God bless you.

Sincerely,

Ricky

first I--Take the time to think about all my accomplishments
and remember what I started in the past before my incomplete begun

Then I make a plan of action to begin again where my incomplete begun

Walt's Life Rhyme #259: The Incomplete Begun Part 4

Carlos Writes:

Walt:
As I read your "Incomplete Begun" I started to chuckle. I just couldn't help it. Once again you picked me out of the crowd. You see, I'm a software engineer and on my spare time I write software for my own use and knowledge; you know to keep the blades sharp. Most of the time, when I write some code, I almost never get back to finishing it before I come up with a new idea or deciding that I have something new to learn. My wake up came when you [virtually] walked away at the end. Here's my attempt at finishing your thought:

first I sit back and think
at the end of the day
was it all a waste of time
was it really thrown away
    or
first I think is this one too for naught
then a new idea comes to mind
and once again my latest thought
an incomplete begun

Enjoy, and thanks for all that you do!

WALT ADDS:
And with that, my friends,
we've done what seemed a monumental feat
with words of help from all
what was begun is now complete!

The Incomplete Begun Parts
Walt's Life Rhyme #259

"I share what I know,
so that others may grow!"
www.LifeRhymes.com

Walt's Life Rhyme #258: So, What Do You Do?
By any other name

"What's my definition now?"
she asked eager to know
All my life I've had a role
But now I want to grow!

I want to share my story
and help others to succeed
I want to show a clearer path
where others may mislead

I want to travel 'round the world
and charge to give a speech
I want to make a ton of cash
while sitting on the beach

I want to do so many things
heck, even write a book!
But, give up all this education?
man, how will it look?

And better yet, please tell me this
and help me think this through
In Heaven's name what will I say
when asked, "what do you do?"

See, everything I've ever done
fit in such nice neat frames
What title will this new me have?
What role shall I proclaim?

(I see you wrote a book,
So, Mr. Passion Profit Man
It seems you've got some answers
so, please help me if you can)

Tell them first you have no job
that concept's just a myth
Tell them that you play a game
they're not familiar with

Tell them that you're just a light
your goal here's just to shine
Tell them what you do on earth
no earthly words confine

Tell them that your mission
is to be all you can be
Tell them, "Ask tomorrow
for today I'm being me!"

So, tell them anything you like
it matters not the name
What matters is to do the thing
that sparks your inner flame!

By any other name you'll find
what stays the same is you
as Willie* says to thine own self
is whom you should be true!

*(*Willie Shakespeare, of course!)*

So, What Do You Do? By any other name
Walt's Life Rhyme #259

www.LifeRhymes.com

Inspired by and dedicated to S.Stafford

Walt's Life Rhyme #257: What Have I Learned?

Am I where I wish to be?
What titles have I earned?
What truths do I now know to be?
What lessons have I learned?

Have I learned compassion
yea just like the prophets teach?
Or have I yet to walk the talk
and practice what I preach?

Have I learned forgiveness
at those times I feel attacked?
Have I learned to walk away
or must I still fight back?

Have I learned that fairness
means "it's not always about me"?
Or do I only take from life
and give back grudgingly?

Have I learned that justice
and that vengeance aren't the same?
Or do I think that victims' hearts
are soothed when they can blame?

Have I learned to share my gifts
and know that there'll be more?
Or do I think what's mine is mine
and vilify the poor?

Have I learned that ethics
matter most when I'm alone?
Or do I seek the limelight
and make all my good deeds known?

Have I learned in life
that things will sometimes go awry?
Or confronted with life's stresses
do I throw a fit and cry?

So, am I who I say I am?
There's just one way to know:
Put me to the test and
see what colors start to show!

Commentary:

Why might all those experiences be coming your way? What possible good can come of the bad attitudes, selfishness, and tests of your "last nerve" that people seem to be good at giving you these days?

Well, they might simply be opportunities for you to know if you are who you know yourself to be. You only know you can swim when you are submerged in water. You only know you're a master, when there are students around.

Inspired by and dedicated to Zahrah
and the Zen Experience

What Have I Learned?
Walt's Life Rhyme #257

"I share what I know,
so that others may grow!"
www.LifeRhymes.com

Walt's Life Rhyme #256: Conventional Wisdom

Believe what prophets tell you
and you might jump ship and flee
And live your life in terror
fearing what you cannot see

Put your stock in forecasts
and you mayn't survive the crash
And all that worthless paper
will be good for naught but trash

Believe what pundits tell you
and the world is only hate
You're apt to see all things
as based on how they speculate

I've seen it time and time again
how life reflects the mind
And others' worlds are nothing but
THEIR thoughts returned in kind

So be not lemmings
blindly chasing those ahead who lead
But choose advisors wisely
question those whom you would heed!

Commentary:

Whether the "wisdom" is the state of the world, political views, or another's idea of what you should do with your life, realize that the only advice another can give you is one drawn from the world in which they've personally inhabited. Before accepting their conventional wisdom, therefore, ask yourself, "Is this person living the sort of life I wish to live?"

Conventional Wisdom
Walt's Life Rhyme #256

"I share what I know,
so that others may grow!"
www.LifeRhymes.com

Walt's Life Rhyme #255: Never Me. Never Mine. Never Mind

"Please don't take it personally"
you've heard it said before
It's true more often than you think
here's how you can be sure

Most people choose their roles in life
based on their inner fear
And act on how they view the world
no matter who's out there

A prior hurt, a troubled past
a life of sticks and stones
All this in them you may evoke
through no fault of your own

It's not the you they'd likely love
that they're responding to
But every thought of what life's been
or what THEY'RE going through

So on those days you find yourself
the target of their fears
It's never you they're seeing, friend
with that in mind, who cares?!

THE MORAL:
You're not what others think you are
you're not the things they say
You're not the things they do to you
and neither too are they

Commentary:

Having said that, dear reader, your mission is to identify less and less with the you of others' thoughts and expectations, the you of your job or what you do, and the you of the outer facade. Once you really feel that you are truly a unique being defined by something other than what is seen, then you'll realize that what others typically respond to is NEVER YOU at all!

From now on, when faced with what you previously thought was rejection, or the feeling of being misunderstood, or unappreciated, remind yourself silently

"You act from what you see. Never me.
Your fears control your life. Never mine.
Your eyes, therefore, are blind. Never mind."

Never Me. Never Mine. Never Mind.
Walt's Life Rhyme #255

"I share what I know,
so that others may grow!"
www.LifeRhymes.com

Walt's Life Rhyme #254: Ask the Inspirer
The Lesser Stress (aka Boathouse Blues)

Walt,
I have a dilemma. It's very expensive here - so I will probably have to be sharing - yet need space and privacy for my project. Also, since I hate my job, I keep thinking that I should move somewhere cheaper, so can work at something that I like more - but make less money. But - where is that? I go into a tailspin as I ponder all this. So, my focus right now is to find something fairly temporary - that is less than what I now pay - and work less hours so that I can get my passion project on the road!

P.S. I have found a beautiful boat that I could live on - in the Sausalito harbor. However, it is about $300 or so more than I now pay - but living on a boat and around boats is a dream of mine. So, do I go for this dream at hand - and have to continue at a job I hate - and give up freedom - or focus on the project now, live in a traditional boring apartment - and keep envisioning life down the road?--J

Hi J
I know the sound of crashing waves
would soothe your furrowed brow
But longer days and higher rent
makes no sense, does it now?

It seems to me the goal right now
to live life at its best:
Make clear and sound decisions
while you seek the lesser stress

Resist the urge right now
to bite off more than can be chewed
(We handle life less gracefully
when pressure rules our mood)

As ships and planes in peril
will first jettison dead weight
So too in life you'll float and fly
with less stuff on your plate

And have no fear this detour's
but a temporary measure
That keeps you free to see and reach
your true and wished for pleasure!

MORAL:
The options life presents us
as towards our goals we strive
are lost in the distractions
as we complicate our lives!

Ask The Inspirer:
The Lesser Stress (aka "Boathouse Blues")
Walt's Life Rhyme #254

"I share what I know
so that others may grow!"
www.LifeRhymes.com

Walt's Life Rhyme #253: The Me I Get To Be

The me I choose to show you
or the me you think you know
May not be me at all but just
the right one for the show

The you you felt you had to be
to win the world's attention?
A product of true genius
and may be your best invention!

But think how freeing it would be
to find and know ourselves
And give the world what's real
instead of offering what sells

No judgments, no agendas
no posture and no pose
Just free and clear acceptance
of the self that no one knows

I love who I can be now
as within your gaze I bask
A flawed yet perfect treasure
with no need to don a mask

The ultimate excitement
that our journey holds for me
Is coming face to face now
with the me I get to be!

Commentary:

According to talk show host Armand Dimele, what is ultimately most attractive about a new love is not what the other person brings to you, but what you become in their presence.

You are attracted most to how you get to view yourself when you're around this person. This may indeed be triggered by them fitting a certain image, or having certain traits that you find desirable, but ultimately, the heightened self-appreciation is the most addictive component of the love experience.

The Me I Get to Be
Walt's Life Rhyme #253

"I share what I know,
so that others may grow!"
www.LifeRhymes.com

Walt's Life Rhyme #252: The Silent Fall of Fences and Walls

They said my escape could be easy as pie
Truth be told I just didn't believe
I'd gotten so used to the fences and walls
that I'd limited what I could achieve

They hinted that freedom might already be mine
I replied, "Oh, but surely you jest."
That new worlds might appear in the blink of an eye?
No, such promises seemed empty at best

But one day something happened! A shift DID occur!
When and where? Hmmmm, I just can't recall
But now left, right and center things fall into place
and it seems I do nothing at all!

I feel all at once I've been living a lie
How much further I'd be if I'd known
That these fences and walls I had built as a child
all this time I had long since outgrown

But when did they crumble? No trumpet was blown
no fanfare, no crash to discern
In the quiet of thought did my jail disappear
from this fact here's the truth that I've learned:

The breakthrough will always be silent, my friend
it's an elusive sound you won't hear
For no noise marks the fall of your fences and walls
because the truth is they're really not there

The Silent Fall of Fences and Walls
Walt's Life Rhyme #252

*"I share what I know,
so that others may grow!"*
www.LifeRhymes.com

Commentary:

It could happen at any minute. Who knows what may set it off. Who knows who or what may be the catalyst. The walls may fall while you sleep and you might wake up tomorrow morning with the rubble at your feet. Unpredictable, yes. But you might be able to speed the process along by creating more quiet moments in your life to listen for the silent fall.

Walt's Life Rhyme #251: The Best of All Goodbyes

She came. She grew. She graduated.
Not much more to say
Her words were clear and to the point
and now she's on her way

Exactly what she said was:
"I don't need you anymore"
You served a purpose in my life
new realms I must explore

What struck me most about it
was there was no room for tears
I smiled in silence and rejoiced
She's overcome her fears!

Yes, some have been here from day one
some left and then returned
And millions more are yet to know
what insights might be learned

I must admit that words like this
make what I do great fun
Completion, growth and gratitude
ah, yes, my work is done

And if I'd ever doubted
well, at least this truth I know
I've shared a bit of what I know
and others really grow!

The Best of All Goodbyes
Walt's Life Rhyme #251
© Walt F.J. Goodridge
"I share what I know,
so that others may grow!"
www.LifeRhymes.com

Commentary:

I received the following email from "L" last week, and honestly this ranks among the top 5 BEST that I've ever received in relation to the weekly inspirations!

FROM: "L"
Dear Walt,
Please unsubscribe me.
I don't need you anymore.
But, 2 years ago, when I first started reading your material -- I was fascinated. I was intrigued. I was really touched.
So much had to eerily do with what I found myself suddenly dealing with.

So I just can't say 'unsubscribe'.
I just have to say thanks for taking the time to have a web presence. You're insights are extraordinary.
(I especially like the elephant under the rug #164)*
There were critical times that I forwarded these to a friend. I've found myself deleting you the last 3 or 4 months. And, I'm rather pleased. I feel much more confident, and strong. I see your email, and I say, "I don't need to read this anymore." And that's that.

I sure hope other people are getting out of it what I did. In fact, there was one really, really meaningful one I added a beautiful ocean picture to when I forwarded it to my friend. Looked like a poster. Still have the printout. It was around June 2nd 2000.
[If Only For A Moment #145]*
That's it for me. Best of luck with all your work! --L

Walt's Life Rhyme #250: Turning Stones

For sure you'll think I'm crazy
or at best a tad insane
But wait, I think I've learned the trick
to winning at this game:

Seek out stones in numbers
seek them everywhere they lie
Small ones, big ones, boulders too
just do it, and here's why

Stones that block and trip you
even stones that cause you pain
Are really life's great teachers
though you may think them your bane

Once a stone is found and lifted
then hurled out the way
Excuses that lay hidden
are exposed to light of day

Even stones that others throw
revealing inner wrath
Come with some life lessons
you can use well on your path

Make sure none are left unturned
for once each stone is gone
What's left to see are just the steps
of paths you should be on

Yes, each stone hides an answer
that removes a bit of doubt
And seeking stones and turning them's
what winning's all about!

Commentary:

So what are stones? Stones are life's hardships, the hardened beliefs, and the obstacles that block your path. They are also the hard opinions and judgments that others pelt you with that cause you pain.

But understand, each stone hides a step in your path. If stones are blocking your path, then for each stone that you leave unturned, you hide a step that you should be taking in order to move forward on your journey. A step not taken is called an excuse. And, as you know, failure follows excuses.

Once each stone is experienced, felt and dealt with, then the doubts of
"Perhaps I didn't try hard enough"
"Perhaps I should have given more"
"Perhaps I don't have enough experience"
"Perhaps, perhaps, perhaps"
all disappear. The only thing left will be "the way."

The reason some people take longer to succeed than others, is that they stroll passively through life avoiding stones. They merely talk about the steps they imagine lie hidden beneath them.

But you, my friend, will do things differently. Seek out the obstacles. Follow the fear. Meet the challenges. Stretch the boundaries. Give more. Post a "Help Wanted" sign for unemployed obstacles to come to you for work. Remember, the quickest way "out" is "through."

Turning Stones
Walt's Life Rhyme #250

*"I share what I know,
so that others may grow!"*
www.LifeRhymes.com

Walt's Life Rhyme #249: A Conversation of Choice

SHE SAID:
"I had it planned so perfectly
It was to be my day
The 'best laid plans of mice and men'
just didn't go my way"

"Perhaps a change of scenery
will lift me from this mood.
I'm hoping this vacation ends
my tendency to brood"

I SAID:
A good idea, I offered
At least it couldn't hurt
Might I suggest the thoughts I use
to start to 'mood convert'

A thing once done, as Shakespeare wrote,
cannot be then undone
Accept what's done then let it pass
like day at setting sun

Then waste no time on mulling
and let your thoughts not stew
Unless there is a cure to cook
or remedy to brew

You know well my philosophy:
Why choose what makes you sadder?
"All for the best" and "silver linings"
yadda, yadda, yadda

First choice, then change, is how it's done
so rather than be vexed
Your mood and manner's yours to choose
so ask yourself, "What's next?"

A Conversation of Choice
Walt's Life Rhyme #249

"I share what I know,
so that others may grow!"
www.LifeRhymes.com

Walt's Life Rhyme #248: Cost of Living

"I'll do it if you pay me"
my friend was known to say
And had no qualms in mind or heart
with viewing life this way

His view of life's transactions
revolved around the cash
And traded time and energy
for C-notes in a flash

"There is another option,
my friend, might I suggest
Life offers more than ways
to feed the fiscally obsessed."

For when you work for money
your dreams take second place
And winner though you'll be
you might be running the wrong race

Consider rating options
based not on what you earn
But seize the opportunities
that offer ways to learn

Desire, wisdom, knowledge
are the currency of dreams
Time spent on less depletes your stash
though lucrative it seems

Time is the cost of living
you give to life your days
No job can ever buy more time
no matter what it pays!

Cost of Living
Walt's Life Rhyme #248

*"I share what I know,
so that others may grow!"*
www.LifeRhymes.com

Commentary for Walt's Life Rhyme #248

I assume that you have goals. While some of those goals can be measured directly in terms of accumulated cash (buying a home, paying for kids tuition, savings, etc.), there is a vision of yourself and what you've been sent here to do, to which you cannot attach a dollar value. If that's so, then please recognize that living that vision is just as important as paying the bills.

In business, and in every aspect of life, we are presented with requests for our time and talents. Some appear to be worthwhile, and others do not. Too often, however, we use only one type of yardstick to measure the options before us. There may be much more being offered than we may recognize, because opportunity is often a master of disguise. The chance for us to live our dreams may not immediately appear alongside a huge paycheck.

A business acquaintance (I'll call him Joe) and I were both approached by a client to help with a project. Joe asked, "What do you need done? And, how much are you willing to pay?" When he discovered that there was no money allocated to the project, Joe saw a client with big dreams, but no budget and turned the offer down.

I asked, "What do you need done? And then I asked myself, "Can being a part of this help me to achieve my grand vision?" "Or maybe," I thought to myself, "this is simply a chance to rack up 'universal karma points' by doing a good deed. I mulled it over for a while from several different angles, and, based on the client's willingness to share in some tangible and intangible assets he also possessed, I created an opportunity to help myself move forward on a path I was already on. So, I accepted the project.

Now there's no right or wrong to this story. I'm sure Joe had some immediate cash needs and time constraints that made taking on the project a drain on his resources. And not every opportunity is right for everyone at every time. And I, too, am running a business, with cash needs and time constraints. But, I've learned that the way I spend my time is what's really important to me. I'm no longer willing to spend the days SIMPLY accumulating cash. So when presented with requests for my time, I ask myself, "If I do this, will I spend my days doing something that is fulfilling and/or that helps me paint the bigger picture of my vision of myself and my life? If so, I'm there!

Walt's Life Rhyme #247: Precisely Then

A shelter's not a shelter
if it crumbles in a storm
It must withstand bad weather too
not only when it's warm

A friendship's not a friendship
that dissolves when times are bad
You'll know then for a fact
if it was real or just a fad

Commitment's not commitment
until things come to a head
For only then you'll know
if what you'll do is what you've said

Security's just posture
'til it's tested by some threat
What good is an umbrella
that allows you to get wet?

Your faith is just lip service
if it's lost when brought to bear
It really only matters
when you choose it over fear

A bridge is rendered useless
if it buckles under stress
And weak resolve won't serve you
on your journey to success!

Precisely Then
Walt's Life Rhyme #247

*"I share what I know,
so that others may grow!"*
www.LifeRhymes.com

Commentary:

I believe that the words you use don't just *describe* your reality, but actually *create* it. Therefore, in my workshops, and before coaching my clients, I always set a few ground rules around the use of words.

Recently, I mentioned to a particular client that, in order for him to achieve his goals, that we needed to work on his language. He agreed that from then on, he would not use words like "problem", "try", or "can't" in favor of words like "challenge", "intention" and "choice."

So one day as I listened to him handling a heated, stressful situation I heard the word "problem" continually popping up in his conversation. I interjected and reminded him of our agreement. With a look of exasperation, and a dismissive wave of his hand, he replied, "Not now, Walt, I'm really stressed out!" So, I had to remind him then and there that it was precisely at those moments of greatest stress, that the commitment to his agreement with himself really mattered. Otherwise it was just lip service to a cute concept.

So, I ask you:

Are you living up to your decisions precisely when things don't go your way?

Are you sticking to your diet precisely when it's *inconvenient*, and even when you're tempted?

Are you in love with your partner precisely when they DON'T do what you want them to?

Are you pleasant to your customers and clients precisely when you're having a bad day?

EPILOGUE: In his defense, my client realized that he had to take his commitment to another level and today is much more conscious of those special moments when it really matters!

Walt's Life Rhyme #246: Before You Can Smile

Before you accept
all the things that go wrong
You first must believe
that you're where you belong

Before you can watch
without getting involved
You first must believe
that all problems get solved

Before you can let
others be who they will
First choose not to judge
(yes, that might take some skill)

Before you can deal with
life's sorrows with grace
You've got to draw strength
from a spiritual space

Before you can smile
at the things people say
You can't hold out hope
that we'll all think your way

Before you'll take chances
that might just risk all
You've got to believe
you'll survive any fall

The day you're not phased
by the things people do
Is the day that you're free
of perceptions of you

And before you'll let go
and just go with the flow
You must trust that paths
lie beyond those you know!

Before You Can Smile
Walt's Life Rhyme #246

"I share what I know,
so that others may grow!"
www.LifeRhymes.com

Commentary:

So I'm cruising around the city the other day, and I notice a few incidents of people reacting to each other's "driving styles." I hear a string of expletives, and I think to myself, "You know, it's just as easy to choose to smile instead of curse." But, of course, making that choice presupposes you believe in a few things about who you are, who others are, and the way the universe works. Here are a few core beliefs that make it easier to handle life's little challenges. It's easier to smile if you believe that

-I walk protected.
-Everything happens for the good
-Everything happens in due time
-No one can harm the real me
-There's always a solution that works for the good of all
-I can choose my responses to everything

Walt's Life Rhyme #245: Five By Ten (and Shrinking!)

My world fit in a five by ten
and still had room to spare
So how much more to go
until I live without a care?

Intent I was to free myself
and cut away these strings
I searched to find a storage space
for all my earthly things

For reasons of frugality
I chose the smallest size
And packed and wrapped up all I owned
and said all my goodbyes

Concerned I was that what I had
would fill and overflow
Imagine my surprise to find
that lo, it was not so

My world fit in a little cube
but what can I deduce?
Perhaps I'm bound until
that storage size I can reduce

This metaphor for freedom
told in terms of length and width
Shows freedom's not in having more
in truth that's just a myth

True freedom comes when all I own
are thoughts in mind and then
I'll walk free of encumbrance
and won't need a "five by ten!"

Five by Ten
Walt's Life Rhyme #245
© Walt F.J. Goodridge

Commentary for Life Rhyme #245

I'm a minimalist. That means I strive to have less and less in my life. Less attachments. Less complexity. Less things. If you're among the close friends who've visited my place, you'll know what I mean. But then, my minimalism extends to my social interactions too, and social minimalism means I also have, well, less close friends. (Hmmm. Maybe I need to rethink this.)

Anyway, I've also realized I am an extremist. Which means I'm an "all or nothing" person who goes to extremes for what I believe in. For example, I'm not just a vegetarian, I'm a vegan--a "fanatic vegetarian", as my friends prefer to call it!

I also believe in freedom. I left the corporate world to pursue my passion because I wanted freedom. Minimalism lends itself to creating true freedom because the less things I have, the freer I can be to pick up and go.

So, as a freedom-obsessed, extremist minimalist, I've recently putt my possessions (the heavy ones which are a burden to keep moving) into storage. So, now with just a laptop, a phone, and an order fulfillment company at my disposal, I'm free to indulge my nomadic lifestyle. (Make that a freedom-obsessed, extremist, minimalist, vegan *nomad*, thank you very much!)

Now, what's that you ask? Why does a minimalist need to put his belongings in storage? Why not just throw them out? Well, some things I just can't seem to part with yet-- my records and books. The records have sentimental value and are a connection to my past as a radio deejay, and they provide hours of nostalgic enjoyment and keep me in "the zone" when I write. And the books, well, they're mostly the inventory of my own self-published books.

So, anyway, back to the storage story. It occurred to me, as I pulled the metal gate shut on storage space No.575 on the 3rd floor, that everything I owned had just fit in a 5' x 10' space, and that I was free of the weight. But then I realized, too, that real freedom will come when I can throw away the key and simply walk away!

Walt's Life Rhyme #244: Walk With Giants

Play with pros
and soon you'll raise the level of your game
Fly with stars
and soon you'll raise the status of your name

Work with happy people
soon you too will start to smile
Run with winners
cross the finish line in just a while

Dine with kings
and soon life's every feast will grace your plate
Talk with prophets
in due time you too create your fate

Stand on mountains
just like that much more comes into view
Walk with giants
sure enough your world gets bigger too!

Commentary:

One of the most consistent keys that 90% of millionaire passionpreneurs have cited that helped them grow past the elusive million-dollar income milestone and into the big leagues has been having a mentor guiding them in the business of business. The next most important thing has been the cultivation of relationships with a network of similar-minded individuals. I call such mentors and associates "giants."

Giants are not the small (minded) people who can lift you no higher than they themselves have reached in their thoughts. They are not those of minor vision who can see for you nothing higher than they themselves can see. Giants are those unique individuals who, by virtue of their stature, step wider, see more and reach farther, and encourage you to do the same. So, who do *you* walk with?

Walk With Giants
Walt's Life Rhyme #244

"I share what I know,
so that others may grow!"
www.LifeRhymes.com

Walt's Life Rhyme #243: Societal Expectations
Excerpt from the Tao of Wow

There are 9 factors which must be taken into account if you are to wage wow successfully.

(1) Societal Expectations
(2) Assets and Means
(3) Challenges
(4) The Bar of Present Output
(5) The Wow Master Ideal
(6) Method and Discipline
(7) Mood of the Masses
(8) Reactions
(9) Energy and Inspiration

1. SOCIETAL EXPECTATIONS

What men are known to do as men
will men expect of you
So leap beyond that fence for men
and men will bow to you

All Wow is based on exceeding expectations. The Wow Master must therefore be aware that the greatest opponents to the recognition of Wow are the expectations of the average of men.

The world is prone to see their expectations of you rather than the truth of you. Therefore, every effort must be made to see yourself first as you wish others to see you.

The world is wowed when it is evident that their preconceived expectations have no power in the creation of the reality of who you know yourself to be.

Societal Expectations [Excerpt from Tao of Wow]
Walt's Life Rhyme #243

"I share what I know,
so that others may grow!"
www.LifeRhymes.com

Tao (pronounced dow, as in Dow Jones) is a Chinese word which, loosely translated, means "way." The Tao of Wow, contains wisdom which, applied appropriately, results in success in any facet of life! (www.TaoofWow.com)

Walt's Life Rhyme #242: The 45 Ways of Men
Excerpt from the Tao of Wow

STUDENT: Master, why do men do the things they do?
WOW MASTER: Men do what they do because:

1-2
Some men have come here to cause things to be
and ACTIVATE others to move
Some men have come with a SPIRITUAL goal
the existence of God they must prove

3-4
Some men have come here to fight for a CAUSE
through their deeds many others are fed
Some men have come to LEAD masses of men
and by them many masses are led

5-6
Some men have come to be makers of ARTS
to add beauty through word and through sound
Some men have come to wreak havoc in life
their goal to IRRITATE and confound

7-8
Some men have come here though simply to feel
their EMOTIONS are always their guide
Some men have come here as LONERS in fact
and seek always to withdraw and to hide

9-10
Some men have come here as JESTERS in court
content just to make others smile
Some men have come here as VICTIMS of sorts
and are here only for a short while

15-16
Some men have come here to take away pain
HEALING ailments of ordinary men
Some men have come here avenging all wrongs
and seek JUSTICE by sword or by pen

The Wow Master knows that men have come to be. That is, that men have come so that they may be that which they have chosen to be. Men are here to learn what it is like to walk the path they choose. The Wow Master recognizes this choice as purpose. The Wow Master also recognizes that choice can be chain and that purpose can be punishment. And that the masses of men are in a constant state of battle because their choices may be both wing or weight. The Wow Master sees the 45 ways of men as the necessary expression of the Eternal Wow in a state of manifestation and therefore, is neither shocked nor shamed by the things men will do.

The 45 Ways of Men [Excerpt from Tao of Wow]
Walt's Life Rhyme #242

"I share what I know,
so that others may grow!"
www.LifeRhymes.com

Walt's Life Rhyme #241: How Can I Help?

Perhaps it's still a virtue
or maybe it's a curse
I'm often found dispensing aid
as if I was a nurse

You weary? Let me help you
You lost? Then take this road
Confused? Think on this option
You weak? Give me your load

It happens without pretense
No interest in applause
Just feels like it's the thing to do
no reason, just because

But why are some more giving
while some seem not to care?
What motive lies behind the actions
Selfishness or fear?

Perhaps it's for approval
Perhaps to gain control
Perhaps because the act of giving
fills the giver's soul

But people do their best
to get through life while they're here
You'll notice different ways they cope
Just know their heart's still there

But keep YOUR heart wide open
and know when you're in doubt:
The time spent helping others
is what life is all about!

How Can I Help?
Walt's Life Rhyme #241

"I share what I know,
so that others may grow!"
www.LifeRhymes.com

Commentary:

At a recent poetry gathering, I had a chance to discuss some interesting topics with several of the guests. During the course of a chat with one individual in particular, I noticed two separate instances in which he showed himself to be particularly skillful at noticing the needs of others in the immediate area, and offering his help to make things easier for them. (And he wasn't the host!) That got us into a discussion of the prevalence and/or absence of that unique trait of helpfulness among the general population.

Why are some people more helpful than others? Why will some hold the door for you while some will not? There are undoubtedly a million different reasons. Perhaps it's a coping strategy developed early in life by a child seeking approval and a parent's love for being Mommy or Daddy's little helper. Perhaps those who aren't as helpful are avoiding the pain of being hurt or taken for granted.

Of course, a discussion like that could last forever, so it was left unresolved with the simple suggestion that because there are in fact so many factors that govern an individual's behavior, we shouldn't expect everyone to be on the same page at all times. And don't get upset at others for not being as giving and as helpful as you'd like, but don't let THEIR way of being jade YOU to the virtues and benefits of giving.

Walt's Life Rhyme #240: Not For Gold Or Silver

Not for gold or silver
no, those days have long since gone
You think I'll dance for dollars?
Then you've got me figured wrong

Not prestige nor position
makes me do the things I do
I chase a bigger vision now
that you're not privy to

No prize, award or statue
ever holds me in its spell
You can't afford the core of me
what's more, I'll never sell

Perhaps for love and laughter, though
you'll see me jump through rings
But tempt me not with paper
for I seek not earthly things

Perhaps to make a difference
just because I passed this way
But not for fiscal benefit
I'd do this without pay

For legacies that linger
that help others to succeed
But not because you promise
me some title or some deed

Integrity for income? No
that's not a trade I'll make
So find another carrot, friend
I've got too much at stake!

P.S.
So keep your gifts and bribes
and take this worthless ransom letter
And thanks for calling, try again
....once you know me better!

Not For Gold Or Silver
Walt's Life Rhyme #240

"I share what I know,
so that others may grow!"
www.LifeRhymes.com

Commentary for Walt's Life Rhyme #240

Got an interesting call yesterday from a customer who owes me money for an item he purchased a few days earlier at an appearance. I had let him have the book if he promised to send payment at a later date. He was now calling to make good on his promise, but additionally wanted to use that fact to get me to meet with him (he preferred to pay me in cash) so he could also pitch a business idea.

When I instead told him to send the payment to my Post Office box and to forward the business proposal to my office for my review, he was taken aback by the fact that I wasn't willing to alter my way of doing business to get his money.

At one point in our conversation, he suggested that since he was only willing to pay in cash, that I take *his* number and call *him*, when I was prepared to meet him to get my money!

The truth is, I know I can't force him to do what he doesn't intend to do. I'm not a collection agency. So, if he *really* wants to complete our original transaction and pay for the book he received, he'll do it with a check or money order because it's the honorable thing to do. And, if he wants me to consider his proposal, he'll send it according to the process I've outlined.

Now don't get me wrong. In the game called "business," cash flow is a key component of that game. And perhaps with other people, or at a different time in my own life, he might have been able to use the carrot of cash as leverage to get his way. Unfortunately for him, however, I won't place my standards on hold, or allow myself to be manipulated for a few dollars. Those days are long gone!

Walt's Life Rhyme #239: Master of Separation

PROLOGUE:

What else was I supposed to do?
How else was I to cope?
The safety of a separate me
is all that gave me hope

THE CHALLENGE:
We fear the world will change too fast
and life will be too hard
We fear the world will harm us
so we always walk on guard

We fear the world will fail us
so we put our trust in none
We fear the world will leave us
so we're always first to run

We fear the world won't hear us
so for love we never ask
We fear the world won't love us
so we hide behind a mask

THE RESPONSE:
Life's pain has made you bitter
so you did what most would do:
You found a way to keep the world
from ever hurting you

You made a separate image
of a you that others see
You've mastered separation
and now strive for PhD

But what you use to keep you safe
(or so at least it seems)
That self-same thing will keep you from
accomplishing your dreams

THE MORAL
The perch from which you view the world
from which you feel protected
Keeps people at a distance
and life's not what you expected

EPILOGUE
To find the you you were
before the pain that has you scarred
Become again the child you were
before your heart got hard.

Master of Separation
Walt's Life Rhyme #239

"I share what I know,
so that others may grow!"
www.LifeRhymes.com

Commentary for Walt's Life Rhyme #239

There was a time when you thought the world was safe. But something happened that shattered your beliefs and forced you to adapt accordingly. To keep yourself safe, you learned how to separate yourself from who you were and to become who you thought you needed to be in order to spare yourself any more pain. So by the time you reached adulthood, you'd become an expert, a Master of Separation working on still higher degrees.

But now you're realizing that you're stuck. You're in limbo somewhere between your memories of childhood bliss and an imagined future you can't seem to get to. So, what's the answer? What's the solution? How do you get from here to there? You've got to unlearn all the "education." Unlearn all the skills that you mastered, and take a remedial class on how to be that child again. For in the naiveté, bravery, trust confidence, love, honesty and self-acceptance of childhood lies the only hope of becoming a true adult.

Walt's Life Rhyme #238:Within The Context Of Commitment

Within the context of creation
every challenge is a tool
Every obstacle will aid your growth
and failure is your fuel

Within the context of advancement
all distractions fall away
All the suffering is justified
and even work can seem like play

Within the context of achievement
every risk may lead to gain
And the unknown's an adventure
with rewards beyond the pain

Within the context of improvement
facing fear becomes the norm
And your mission is your shield
that helps you weather every storm

Within the context of your purpose
all your fearfulness is cured
Former habits lose their grip
and life's pain can be endured

Within the context of commitment
the world becomes a different place
For what you once saw as a hindrance
spurs you on to win the race!

Within The Context of Commitment
Walt's Life Rhyme #238

"I share what I know,
so that others may grow!"
www.LifeRhymes.com

Commentary:

Just yesterday, a friend and I were reminiscing about our involvement in a business venture which required us to stretch ourselves and to do things outside of our comfort zones. Essentially we had to become salesmen in order to achieve the success we envisioned for ourselves. We had to conquer our fears of approaching people, our fears of rejection, and the tendency to settle for mediocrity. We had to subordinate our habits and tendencies in the interest of achieving a particular goal. Today, we can say we're better individuals for having put ourselves through the ordeal. But, we asked ourselves, how and why we were able to do it?

The truth is, we never considered the tasks themselves fun, but we saw them as necessary in the attainment of our goals. We also had the benefit of working with people and in an environment that made the experience otherwise quite enjoyable.

But the ultimate reason for our success was that we were committed to creating something. We were all about creating something for ourselves and for those whom we loved that didn't exist. We were on a mission
to make our worlds better places. And within the context of that bigger dream of what we were creating, all the late nights, the fear, the weariness, the rejection, and the pain were all secondary, all minor, and all doable.

Today, much of what I do : writing books, doing workshops, and consulting, are all done within the context of my mission to "share what I know, so that others may grow." People say I work too hard. But, I've always thought that it's not "work" unless you don't like what you're doing.

I encourage you to find the greater context for your own life that makes the challenges you face all worthwhile! What shall you create today?

Walt's Life Rhyme #237:Straight to My Heart/The Five Fears

Straight to My Heart

I'm not what's in my head
How liberating this could be!
It's true my thoughts create my world
but never define ME

I'm not what's in my head
though errant thoughts may be in charge
I'll take the power from my fears
before they grow too large

I'm not what's in my head
but like a world that's yet to be
The real me is inside my heart
just yearning to be free

Straight To My Heart & The Five Fears
Walt's Life Rhyme #237

"I share what I know,
so that others may grow!"
www.LifeRhymes.com

The Five Fears

CONTROL says "Do it my way."
For I'm safe when I'm in charge."
But freedom says, "I'll set you free
to do what floats your barge!"

UNKNOWN says, "Don't take
chances!"
I am safe with what I know."
But freedom welcomes newness
and will treat life like a show

FAILURE says, "I'm not enough
not brain nor beauty's mine."
But freedom says, "I'm worthy
to have much more by right divine."

DEPENDENCY says, "Trust you?"
Heavens no! I've been betrayed."
But freedom says detachment's key
lest life's misfortunes jade

ALONE says, "How will I survive
with none to help me through?"
But freedom says, "I'll make it
frankly with or without you."

So take the time to face the fear
and change how you respond
And know that on the other side
true freedom lies beyond!

Commentary for Walt's Life Rhyme #237

Last night, on the local PBS channel, I was watching Dr. Wayne Dyer, a self-help author, speaking on his new book, *There's a Spiritual Solution to Every Problem*. In a quite illuminating exercise, he asked the audience to participate in a simple task. He asked everyone in the room to point to themselves. (So, before you go on, I'd like you to do the same. Right now, free a hand and use it to point to yourself.) He then asked everyone in the room to look around and notice everyone else doing the same thing. Now if you're like EVERYONE in the room that evening, you too are now probably aiming your finger directly at your heart. Notice that you're not pointing to your head, your foot or your shoulder. It's evident, therefore, that you know the real you is nowhere inside your head. This gives you another tool to eliminate the fears that are holding you back. According to Armand Dimele of the radio show *The Positive Mind*, we all struggle with one or more of five basic fears:

1. the fear of losing control,
2. fear of the unknown
3. fear of failure,
4. fear of dependency,
5. fear of being alone.

So with the real you in your heart and not in your head, you'll know that these fears are not real, but just mind-dwelling ideas that you've devised to create a false sense of security. You are one step closer to freedom, because through your heart, you are connected to and part of a greater something with which you are never out of control, never on unfamiliar terrain, never inadequate, never betrayed and never alone!

Walt's Life Rhyme #236: Lend Me Your Eyes

Baseless concerns
goal-less actions
Unwarranted fears
and overreactions

Humorless outlook
blurred perception
Low self-esteem
misguided direction

Do you happen to see
the same thing I do?
Does the world that I see
appear likewise to you?

Or have I been tricked
by a past that's been hard?
Been fighting so long
that I'm always on guard

This house that I've built
seems about to collapse
So lend me your eyes
for a moment perhaps

Then maybe I'll see
something new that I've missed
And then maybe I'll know
what new options exist!

Lend Me Your Eyes
Walt's Life Rhyme #236

"I share what I know,
so that others may grow!"
www.LifeRhymes.com

Commentary:

Do you know someone whose past has made them a bit negative? Do you know someone whose self-image has been shaped to such a degree that they don't see the good in others or themselves?

Sometimes the best help you can provide that person is simply to lend them your eyes. You may be fortunate enough to have eyes that have not seen depression, defeat, destruction and dismay. Or, you may have eyes that have seen pain, but have also seen hope. Share your eyes. Tell that person how you see the world. Tell them how you see THEM in the world. Sometimes the most powerful form of therapy is simply to let someone borrow your eyes. Try it right now!

Walt's Life Rhyme #235: Give it Yourself

When no one has called you to come out and play
and folks you depend on are causing dismay
When phones aren't ringing with dates to hang out
and you once had big dreams but you're starting to doubt

When you've used all your options and emptied your cup
and no one will offer a sip or a sup
Or you've come to a fork in life's oft lonely walk
And those who could help you are nothing but talk

When you've come to a standstill and don't understand
why in a world full of people no one gives you a hand
Or it just seems unfair that as great as you are
that your best goes unnoticed and none see your star

I'll suggest to you this, you can take it or not
That it's not that you're trapped in a conspiracy plot
But when things that you want seem withheld on a shelf
That perhaps that's the gift you should be giving yourself!

Give it Yourself
Walt's Life Rhyme #235

*"I share what I know,
so that others may grow!"*
www.LifeRhymes.com

Commentary:

At last week's music industry workshop, two of the participants, a NY based Hip Hop group, addressed the topic of how to overcome the apparent obstacles to their rise to stardom. After detailing all the closed doors, shady dealings, and "fame blockers" that they encountered, and with the help of myself and the other participants, they arrived at a significant paradigm shift.

They decided that instead of waiting for promoters and producers to recognize their talent and hire them for performances, that they would take matters into their own hands and put on their own performances to create the reality they envisioned for themselves.

It immediately clicked and made sense. They realized they already had the experience and know-how of doing just what they needed to have happen in their careers, and that ironically, it was they themselves who had not been recognizing their own talent!

So if no one is inviting you to parties, throw one yourself! If no one is calling you for acting roles, put on your own performance! No one inviting you out? Treat yourself to a night out!

More often than not you'll find you have the talent and ability to do the very thing you're expecting others to do for you. And *that's* precisely why it seems that you've hit a wall and can't seem to find anyone *out there* to help you. Why? Because you're looking in the wrong place!

Walt's Life Rhyme #234: Ask the Inspirer
A Nicer Place

The world's a nicer place today
with one less angry word
There's one less victim crying foul
afraid she won't be heard

The world's a peaceful place today
with one less war to fight
There's one less person trying hard
to prove he's always right

The world's a hopeful place today
for one less dream was killed
There's one less person blocking you
from seeing yours fulfilled

The world's a cheerful place today
there's one more laugh you'll hear
There's one less person frowning
'cause she lives her life in fear

I know beyond a doubt
the world's a better place to be
Because that peaceful, hopeful
cheerful, fearless person's ME!!

Commentary:

Hi Walt,

After work yesterday, I decided to take the bus just a few blocks to Penn Station to head home. As I'm sitting on the bus, I noticed two people interacting heatedly a few seats away. Seems one woman sitting on the aisle seat had an empty window seat next to her. Another elderly women asked if the seated woman would
be kind enough to let her pass so she could sit there.

I couldn't believe what happened! The woman sitting did not want to move to let the other woman sit next to her. Can you believe that? She did not want to be inconvenienced!!! On public transportation!!!
Is this ridiculous or what?? What kind of world are we living in???

So, anyway, after all was said and done, I did what I could to add a bit of niceness to it all and, and as the second woman was leaving, I said with a smile, "Please try to have a nice evening!!" I just know that she needed those encouraging words. And she smiled back at me as she left!

I REPLIED:

Hey Mary,

The way I look at it is that at the end of the day, you can confidently and happily say that there was
one less fight in the world, because you didn't start one. One less bitter person in the world, because you chose not to be one. One more smile in the world, because you decided to give one. One more nice person on that bus, because you decided to be one!

A Nicer Place
Walt's Life Rhyme #234

*"I share what I know,
so that others may grow!"*
www.LifeRhymes.com

Walt's Life Rhyme #233: Short and Sweet

Do all you can and please enjoy
life, time and those you meet
And live your days so you can say
life may be short but sweet!

Short And Sweet
Walt's Life Rhyme #233

"I share what I know,
so that others may grow!"
www.LifeRhymes.com

Commentary:

Act now, for once the chance is gone
there may be no repeat
Throw caution to the wind
and then jump in with both your feet!

Walt's Life Rhyme #232: What Kind of Life?

Every stranger is a suspect
Every glance may pose a threat
Every movement's competition
Acts of kindness create debt

Every question is a challenge
Every gesture is a slight
Every misstep is an act of war
that makes you want to fight

Every handshake hides a motive
or intention to deceive
Even smiles will make you question
what lies lurking up the sleeve

Every gift comes with a string
And every offer has a catch
Who draws near evokes suspicion
of possessions they might snatch

Every whisper makes you wonder
who is planning an attack
Everyone is out to get you
so you never turn your back

What a burden you must carry
walls and weapons right and left
Watching warily for danger
poised in waiting for some theft

But there's naught the world can rob
and no real treasures they can steal
When you're safe, secure through knowing
all you own is how you feel

Feel the world is mostly evil
evil's what you'll mostly find
Feel that world is full of goodness
goodness is returned in kind

In your fear-based self-assertions
the thing of value you might lose
Is not position or possession
but the priceless right to choose!

Make new choices in your living
and your life could turn about
Choose to see the good in people
and guess who benefits from the doubt?

What Kind of Life?
Walt's Life Rhyme #232

"I share what I know,
so that others may grow!"
www.LifeRhymes.com

Commentary for Walt's Life Rhyme #232

I see it in the way some people interact with the world. I see it in the way some people drive—never giving an inch to merging traffic, as if their entire trip and their very lives hinged upon preventing one specific car from getting into the flow of traffic. I see it in how people wait on line at the post office—assigning themselves as "Queue Police", ever-vigilant (often to the point of paranoia) for anyone trying to cut ahead. There's an underlying fear that somehow every interaction provides the world a way to take advantage of them in some way. A fear that somehow they lose something by being kind to others. Do you know some people who live that way? Ahem. Maybe it's you.

Now don't get me wrong. I know people may be selfish. I know that there are users and abusers out there. But I decided a long time ago that it was much more liberating to choose my responses to those types of people than to allow them to choose it for me. For example, I used to think it was the greatest affront in the world if someone stepped on my foot (without an apology) on the subway. I would expect and seek out an acknowledgement and apology. In time, however, I got tired of feeling so suspicious, so vigilant, and consequently so tense every time I rode a train.

Somewhere in my self-help readings, I discovered the idea that instead of an automatic response of anger and vengeance, that I could choose unique responses and choose instead, for instance, to smile! Once I discovered this amazing truth, it was the beginning of freedom! So I developed some new habits.

These days, I choose to smile when someone is selfish. I choose to let the other driver merge into traffic with the hope that they'll get safely to their destination. I choose to be calm when someone picks a fight. And strangely enough, I still get through my days. I still get to where I'm going just as quickly. And, I'm not as stressed always expecting the worst. And, you know what? I like the kind of life I'm living!

So what kind of life are YOU living?

Walt's Life Rhyme #231: The Key To Happiness

To know just where you fit in
To know where you belong
To know your choice of actions
teach you lessons right or wrong

To see the best in others
To see life's other side
To see if what you're doing's
based on principle not pride

To own all you require
To require less and less
To break the need to show
you live a life filled with excess

To feel your life's progressing
To feel you're on your way
To feel that things improve
however slightly day to day

To share your wealth with others
To share it through the lack
To share the hope that what is lost
in time will come right back

To find your life's great purpose
and the means to make it real
To find the key to happiness
is a joy no one can steal!

Is this all that's required then
despite what we've been taught?
As simple as a change of mind?
Perhaps. It's just a thought.

Commentary:

Hmmmm. Perhaps it IS just a thought.

The Key To Happiness
Walt's Life Rhyme #231

"I share what I know,
so that others may grow!"
www.LifeRhymes.com

Walt's Life Rhyme #230: Letting Brian Speak

Today, I'll be inspired along with everyone else, simply by LETTING BRIAN SPEAK

Dear Walt,

You don't know me, but I've been a faithful reader of your Friday Inspirations for about three years now; and they've inspired me. Here's a little info about me. I've suffered depression for most of the past 19 years; and a year and a half ago I made a serious suicide attempt, actually I was trying to decapitate myself. Came real damn close too.

But as you know, life is strange; and as a result of that attempt, I've found a true home at the oldest mental health therapeutic community in the nation. I've been here 10 months now, and it's been a blessing.

Through it all, the good and mostly bad, the Friday Inspirations and the two books I've bought from you, *Lessons in Success* and *Turn your Passion into Profit*, kept alive a thread of hope for the possibility of making my passion dream come true.

Now back to my depression. I've long known that my depression was mostly habitual and not medical; although I believe they affect each other. Yet I could not, or did not, change my habits. That is, not until recently.

Several months ago, the nurse here led a relaxation session, and at the end of it she suggested that each night we write down "3 things I can feel POSITIVE about Doing Today." At the time I didn't give it a real effort. Then several weeks later my sister-in-law said to my brother and I, "Your problem is you have a negative outlook on everything." While I had known that for a years, hearing it at that time from someone else really hit home with me. It reminded me of the parts in Chapter 2 in *Turn your Passion into Profit* concerning thinking differently and thoughts creating reality and the order of things being Be, Do, Have. In my gut, and in my heart, I knew my sister-in-law was right, and that I had to change how I thought.

I went back to what my nurse had suggested, and every night I wrote down "3 things I can feel POSITIVE about Doing Today." It snowballed. I started to see myself forming new, and positive, habits. I had heard from a previous counselor of mine, and also read somewhere, that it takes 21 days to form a habit, or break an old one. So I defined a new habit as one that occurred 21 times in a row.

So far I've formed 9 new daily habits that I did not have before. They are:

1. Taking a Multi-Vitamin everyday,
2. Changing clothes everyday,
3. Shaving everyday,
4. Eating a fruit everyday,
5. Becoming a vegetarian!
6. Brushing my teeth every night before going to bed,
7. Flossing my teeth every night before going to bed,
8. Not taking my prescribed-as-needed sleep medication, and sleeping just fine, and the most important of all,
9. Writing down 3 things I can feel POSITIVE about Doing Today!!!

Walt's Life Rhyme #230: Letting Brian Speak (continued)

I'm now on Day 88 of writing down "3 things I can feel POSITIVE about Doing Today" and I've continued to maintain all these habits. I am working on creating more new personal habits concerning eating healthier, exercising regularly, and turning my living environment, a small room, into a more orderly, warmer, and inviting place to live.

While all these habits concern just me, the truth is that each day the majority of the things on the "3 things I can feel POSITIVE about Doing Today" list are ways I've helped or interacted with others. That's because, as is your practice, when I say 3, I always make sure it's 4; and I actually write down everything POSITIVE I can think of that day, sometimes as many as 15 things.

I'm a long way from Turning my Passion into Profit, but I'm finally headed in the right direction. Turning my Passion into Profit would be great. Turning my Passion into Reality without making a profit would be great still. But just getting through the first two chapters of *Turn Your Passion into Profit* and taking them to heart is priceless. This is so even if this means my current Passion doesn't become Reality. Being turned around 180 degrees in thought and headed in the right direction and trusting that path is the beginning of a new wonderful journey that is beyond having a price tag put upon it.

What you do for free with your Friday Inspirations and for a very small price with your books, given their invaluable guidance, is a noble and honorable gift. You improve many lives, and in ways you don't know.

Thank you Walt!

P.S. While this email is too lengthy to share in its entirety, I was hoping, especially for people experiencing depression and other mental illnesses, that you might mention the "3 things I can feel POSITIVE about Doing Today" list and the 21 days to form a new habit concept in a future Friday Inspiration.

Walt's Life Rhyme #230: Letting Brian Speak

Walt, I have also written a poem:

Looking Back

When the future looks bleak
And you're feeling weak
And it takes all your might
Just to put up a fight

And negativity abounds
All around
And the view holds no promise
Just a jungle amidst a forest

And all you want to do is shout
"What's it all about?!"
Then it's time to change the direction you view
And look at what you do with a different hue

For each night a choice is yours
Look at tomorrow with dread
Or today and all the good you did
The decision is key

For you see
The key
To having a positive outlook
Is having a positive look back

-Brian,

Thank you Walt!

P. S. Walt, your Life Rhyme #220, "Here to Hide?" was particularly inspiring for me as I began
turning my life around. Thank you!

If you would like to communicate with Brian, email him with subject: "To Brian" at brian@liferhymes.com

Letting Brian Speak
Walt's Life Rhyme #230
© Walt F.J. Goodridge
"I share what I know,
so that others may grow!"
www.LifeRhymes.com

Walt's Life Rhyme #229: The Magical Moment

As if some memo's circulating
As if by order or decree
It seems the world has taken notice
and turned their eyes squarely on me

As if I'm now a fad trendsetter
and all now harken to my cry
Don't get me wrong I'm not complaining
I'm just real eager to know why

Just yesterday the sky was empty
and not a rain cloud could be found
But now from rain it's gone to pouring
and things are starting to rebound

What magic magnet is now active?
what mystic force do I exude?
Is it through wish, or will or whimsy
or just the Universe's mood?

Some say such fortune starts in heaven
with plans for us we'll never know
Some say a little drop of water
compels entire crops to grow

Alas, perhaps through all my seeking
I'll find no reason and no rhyme
Or just perhaps, through all my thinking
I simply thought that it was time

The Magical Magnet
Walt's Life Rhyme #229

"I share what I know,
so that others may grow!"
www.LifeRhymes.com

Commentary:

Have you ever found yourself sitting at home, minding your own business without a single telephone call coming in for a long stretch of time? And then, as if by magic, one, then two, then three people all call at the same time? Or, maybe you've been looking for a job, with no success, and then, as if by magic, one, two, then three job offers all roll in at the same time? It happens all the time in matters of money, relationships, and sometimes even rain! First none, and then, as if by magic, it rains and then pours. It's almost as if some universal memo got sent out that everyone and everything now feels compelled to respond to! Strange, isn't it?

Well, what if that memo was sent out on the wings of your own thoughts about what you were ready to accept in your life? What if the moment or the night before, somewhere in the recesses of your own mind, you could simply say "I'm ready," and the next second or the next day it was so? Wouldn't that be exciting?

Well, don't wonder any more. Let's just assume that that's the way it is, and the degree to which it works is in direct proportion to your actual degree of readiness and faith that accompanies your thoughts. I call the bull market of good fortune that ensues after such a thought, the "magical magnet" in action. It can start with a little drop of water from above, or from within, and then your own thoughts about what is possible creates a magical magnetic force that attract more and more of the same stuff into your life.

So, tell me, what are you really ready for?

Walt's Life Rhyme #228: Just a Little Bit of Water

She said, "I'd be delighted!"
and the world just turned my way
It's funny how a few nice words
can brighten up a day

He said, "Why not be open?"
and it proved some good advice
And the next time that it happened
she said yes, and didn't think twice

Esteem is resurrected
then takes flight on new found wings
All from having someone take the time
to say all the right things

For a life at times may wither
like a rose that's dry with gloom
But just a little bit of water
is all it takes for it to bloom!

Just A Little Bit of Water
Walt's Life Rhyme #228

"I share what I know,
so that others may grow!"
www.LifeRhymes.com

Commentary:

Maybe it's a simple suggestion from a good friend to do things a little differently. Maybe it's a compliment at a moment of low self-esteem. Maybe it's a yes to an invitation to hang out that turns into Something Really Cool. Never underestimate the power of a little attention, a well-placed word, or a bit of encouragement. It just might be the drop of water that saves a dying rose. Share the blessing and the difference your words can make in another person's life.

Walt's Life Rhyme #227: Arbitrary Lines

What if they said that every day
would start at half-past three?
We'd all reset our clocks
and change our lives now wouldn't we?

What if they said the best friends
in the world you've ever had
Were not the ones you liked
but just the ones who made you sad?

What if they said the time of life
that offers most to learn
Are two years AFTER college
and the rest? of no concern

How random do those lines all seem?
Well here's some breaking news
They're really no more random
than the ones that we now use

Imagine for a moment, though
that life is just a stream
Of magical "now" moments
that just flow from scene to scene

And people come and go
with either joy or pain in store
No judgments in your mind
that make you rate them good or poor

And every moment matters
with no more or less at stake
For each holds equal promise
of a new life you could make

For time knows no beginning
and it surely knows no end
So let's erase the lines
on which we all too oft depend

And choose to spend our time
free from this view that undermines
And live our lives unruled
by all these arbitrary lines!

Commentary:

What if you didn't divide time into years, or derive your motivation to make changes in your life by the approach of an arbitrary day on a ancient calendar? What if you simply lived your life the best that you could from day to day? What if you didn't divide your life into periods defined by your education? What if you didn't rate your friendships, and your relationships and your marriages as good or bad, but simply saw them as the comings and goings of people you've met who each had something to share with you before they moved on? What would life be like then?

Arbitrary Lines
Walt's Life Rhyme #227

"I share what I know,
so that others may grow!"
www.LifeRhymes.com

Walt's Life Rhyme #226: Patterns

Look for order in the chaos
common threads and ties that bind
Recurring themes in every story
matching thoughts in every mind

Listen and you'll hear the echoes
same refrain but different song
Find what's true in every version
Find what's right when men are wrong

There's one thing that all are seeking
a single goal to every game
Faces change and bodies differ
See what always stays the same

Find the patterns all around you
the lessons in the cards life deals
Make connections in your choices
and find the answers life reveals!

Patterns
Walt's Life Rhyme #226

*"I share what I know,
so that others may grow!"*
www.LifeRhymes.com

Commentary:

When I was growing up, my mother and I used to play a card game called "Concentration." To play the game, we'd first lay out all 52 cards across her bed. Then, taking turns, we'd proceed to pick up a card, call it out aloud, and then replace it back in the same place in the arrangement. The object of the game is to use one's memory to find matching cards. If, for example, I picked up an ace, I might recall exactly where in the arrangement I had seen another ace earlier in the game. If I reach for where I think that card is, and I'm correct, I win that round. I keep those matching cards, and pick again. When all the cards are matched, the winner is the person who makes the most connections.

The ability to detect such patterns plays an important part in success in all areas of life. There's an underlying order to all things in the universe, in everything from people's behavior, the stock market, the weather, and even the choices you and I make. Therefore, the quicker we can spot those patterns and make the connections, the better able we are accept, change, control or master the results and consequences of those patterns. And just like in Concentration, life's winners are the peoples who make the most connections.

Walt's Life Rhyme #225: Room For Rent

Make some room in your mind
for a new set of thoughts
and evict those
that currently reside

Make some room in your heart
for another to dwell
and from you
love will no longer hide

Make some room in your days
for some new things to do
and enjoy
more that life has in store

Make some space in your life
for those other than you
and you'll soon
hear a knock on the door

Fill the void in your life
by creating some space
or what you seek
may not ever come in

So clear out the cobwebs
and hang out a sign
so that all know
to apply now within!

Commentary:

If you were expecting a house guest, chances are you'd make some sort of preparation for his or her arrival, so that he or she would feel welcomed and accommodated. Why not do the same for anything you wish to come into your life? Make physical as well as emotional room for your "tenants" and "house guests." Friends, love, money and happiness all need a place in your life to stay when they come to visit. And, if you make it really comfortable for them, who knows, perhaps they'll even move in!

Room For Rent
Walt's Life Rhyme #225

"I share what I know,
so that others may grow!"
www.LifeRhymes.com

Walt's Life Rhyme #224: Pathway to the Core

The feelings are the symptoms
but your history is root cause
Beliefs are now the scars of wounds
To heal you've got to pause

First probe through to emotions
for they'll lead you to the cure
But treating them alone, my friend
still leaves more to endure

It starts with something deeper
Things aren't always what they seem
Keep asking why, and who, and when
and what does this thing mean?

Deny it all you like
The treatment's easy to resist
But rest assured I tell you
that no other cures exist

For only at the center
does it all make any sense
You do the things you do
most likely as your heart's defense

Now ask yourself, "What new thoughts
do I choose to have instead?"
For on the pathway to the core
is how you move your life ahead!

Commentary:

Any time you are unhappy, it's because you are suffering from an erroneous perception which leads to an unmet expectation. There's a "fatal flaw" with how you perceive yourself, people or the world. Don't waste time dealing with the beliefs, or simply finding ways to justify them. At the core of who you are is the answer that needs to be uprooted. Once you make the connection, the strangle-hold starts to weaken. Address the core issue, not the symptoms, because nothing else matters.

Here's some homework for you to do to address that area of your life that's causing you the most grief. Write out and list thoroughly the answers to these questions:

1. What/how am I feeling?
2. What do I believe about myself, others and the world that is causing these feelings?
3. In other words, what expectations did I have that weren't met?
4. What experiences have led to these beliefs?
6. Are these beliefs getting me what I want?
7. If not, what new beliefs would help me achieve what I desire?

Inspired by Asher

Pathway To The Core
Walt's Life Rhyme #224

"I share what I know,
so that others may grow!"
www.LifeRhymes.com

Walt's Life Rhyme #223: Make it Right

Sometimes your head will lead you
but your heart will want its way
Still, either one will serve you
if you first make it OK

Sometimes you'll need departure
from your normal way of being
Just know that you're still you
with just a different way of seeing

Sometimes you'll make new choices
and the hardest thing you'll do
Is learning how to live and love
the ever-changing you

Sometimes you'll know what must be do[ne]
but fight it tooth and nail
To make sure that your view of you
will triumph and prevail

No action's ever taken
'til we run it through this test:
"Is this the me I want to be,
or will I now be less?"

Most times the question's easy
but the battle that we fight's
Not finding the right answer, no
but how to make it right!

Commentary:

Psychologists say that humans are incapable of doing something they know to be wrong unless they can somehow first justify it in their minds and make it "right." Similarly, we often need to justify any new course of action as being "right" for us before we can take it.

Think about a challenge you're facing right now. Think about the possible ways you could address it in order to have things the way you wish.

Chances are you already know what the BEST course of action is, but something is preventing you from taking it. Perhaps you fear the consequences. Perhaps you doubt your abilities. Perhaps you fear being vulnerable. Perhaps you worry what it says about you and how others will see and think about you if you do it. Perhaps you're clinging to old tapes of who you know yourself to be even when it has ceased being effective.

All of these reasons are simply meanings that YOU'VE attached to these actions. And, therefore it's within your power to change what's right. The struggle is often not "What route shall I take?", but "Am I still me if I take it?"

Before you can take any new course of action, you have to be OK with being that new person you believe you'll become. You'll need to change your judgment of the type of person you believe it will make you.

Don't worry, you'll still be you....just a bit more.

Make It Right
Walt's Life Rhyme #223

"I share what I know,
so that others may grow!"
www.LifeRhymes.com

Walt's Life Rhyme #222: Busy Looking Left

In the chain of
sought and seeker
no one's looking to the right
For all are looking left
at that which
grabs and holds their sight

In the quest for
troves of treasure
some will mine for wealth afar
And miss acres of diamonds
that exist
right where they are

In due time when
you stop running
and slow down enough to see it
You might find the thing you're chasing
has been there
right at your feet!

Commentary:

The irony of the dating game is that each person is often "looking to the left," to the object of their desire, and therefore fails to notice the interest of the person standing to their right, who in turn is missing the gaze of the person to THEIR right, in an unending chain of unrequited love.

So it is, too, in other games of search and seek that we miss the thing most sought because it is too close to be seen. But, the wise always look both ways before they get cross!:-)

Inspired by the witticisms of C. D.

Busy Looking Left
Walt's Life Rhyme #222

"I share what I know,
so that others may grow!"
www.LifeRhymes.com

Walt's Life Rhyme #221: The Appropriate Level of Self-Advocacy

And who will fight my battles
making sure I get what's mine?
And clear my path of swindlers
who might call a six a nine?*

And who will sing my praises
making sure the world will know?
And champion the cause called me
and lift me when I'm low?

And who will plead my case
when others' goal is to condemn?
And hold me in esteem
and love me more in spite of them

I know you know the answer
for even I myself can see
Who else can I depend on
if I can't rely on me?

The Appropriate Level of Self-Advocacy
Walt's Life Rhyme #221

*"I share what I know,
so that others may grow!"*
www.LifeRhymes.com

Commentary:

I can always rely on my good friend Chris to give me food for thought, and the occasional catchy phrase for a Life Rhyme. While discussing the details of a contract between two parties, she commented that people often act against their own best interests, and that often because of low self-esteem, we can't always rely on ourselves to exercise "the appropriate level of self advocacy."

So true, for while it's great to have people in your corner cheering you on, ultimately it'll be you who has the responsibility, as Bob Marley says, to "Get up, stand up! Stand up for your rights!"

**"A SIX FOR A NINE??" In Jamaica, when someone says "him want give you a six for a nine" it means someone's trying to trick you (for example, offering something of lesser value for something of greater value)--hoping you won't notice the deception because of the similarity in the digits. (a "6" being an inverted "9")*

Walt's Life Rhyme #220: Here to Hide?

I have a friend who lives concealed
who keeps herself inside
I feel she's got so much to live
At times I've almost cried

A fugitive from fun, it seems
"But why so shy?" I pried
"Is there not more to life than this?"
and here's how she replied:

"My precious time is wasted
doing things I've never tried
I like the things I like," she said
I'd rather stay inside."

It seems instead of facing life
your time you've come to bide
Say yes to life for once, I urged
it's time to turn the tide

And do some things you've never done
For time's short, I implied
And show the world the gifts you've brought
Don't let them be denied

And share with some the things you've learned
you might be someone's guide
Whoever said you walk alone
believe me, friend, they lied

And take the time to see the world
and travel far and wide
There's much to see, and well, who knows
you might enjoy the ride

So to my friend who fears the fun
once and for all decide
Are you here on earth to show and tell
or are you here to hide?

Here To Hide?
Walt's Life Rhyme #220

"I share what I know,
so that others may grow!"
www.LifeRhymes.com

Commentary for Walt's Life Rhyme #220

To paraphrase a great quote I heard today on the *Gary Null Show*, it's not the time you spend on your strengths that creates your legacy, but the time spent on your weaknesses. We all have both strengths and weaknesses, but it is the work we do to keep our weaknesses from undermining our strengths that makes us rise to the greatest levels of accomplishment.

My good friend who inspired today's Life Rhyme has tremendous assets to offer the world. But the fact that she allows her fear of venturing out to keep those strengths from getting the greatest possible exposure, is what may ultimately limit her service to and enjoyment of the world, and what causes me the most sadness.

I'd like to be able to sprinkle some magic dust over her and have her wake up more open to new ideas and ways of being, and live beyond her weaknesses. But, alas, I know that decision is hers alone to make.

In any event, I can relate to her situation. I, too, tend to remain in those environments in which I feel most successful. Every time I immerse myself in my next book, website, or business venture (those areas of my strengths), I neglect to carve out the appropriate time to work on the areas where I need the most work. (i.e. my social life, romance, etc.)

Perhaps my greatest legacy will not be the books, websites and ventures, at all, but the simple act of letting someone else inside to share it all with. I, too, have to remind myself I'm not here to hide.

Walt's Life Rhyme #219: Load Test

Seems each day more weight is added
you take more hits than you can bear
But before you call it madness
listen close to what I'll share

You can smile through disappointment
you can laugh despite the pain
When you really know what's going on
there's much that you will gain

Every object (man's or nature's)
must be put under some stress
It's the only way to know
if it's been built to pass the test

Every structure gets load tested
if it gives under the strain
That just means it's time to go
back to the drawing board again!

Think of buildings in your city
floor on floor up to the skies
Just the strongest of foundations
add more stories to their rise

Even seeds don't have it easy
damp and packed there in the mud
They too face all types of stress
to overcome before they bud

So don't break under the pressure
simply smile now that you know:
Every thing must be load tested
for under pressure's how we grow!

Load Test
Walt's Life Rhyme #219

*"I share what I know,
so that others may grow!"*
www.LifeRhymes.com

Commentary:

As a former civil engineer, and now as the owner of several websites, I'd like to introduce you to a concept call "load testing." In construction, a structure like a bridge, or a building is subjected to weight to determine if it can and will support the loads (cars, people etc.) for which it's being designed. A similar process happens in website design. Before a website "goes live" (i.e. is launched), it is subjected to a test that simulates thousands of simultaneous visitors to see if it can handle (without crashing) the million "hits" (visits) per day that a successful advertising campaign might generate.

Well, wouldn't you know it, something similar happens in life, too. The minute you decide YOU want to "go live", or take yourself to another level, the universe sends a load test your way. You'll know when you're being load-tested because you'll feel the pressure of everyday life increasing, or you'll find that everything you attempt seems to go wrong, or you might meet upon a hundred roadblocks that test your patience, commitment, strength and will power. You'll feel like you too are receiving a thousand hits a day, or a thousand pounds per square inch of pressure! The question is, Are you ready to "go live?" Can your structure support the load and the pressure? Once it's determined that you've got what it takes, then like a building, another story will be added to your rise. (Get it? Story?) Or, you'll be ready to go "live!" So, the next time you're going through an obvious load test, you can smile, because NOW you know what's really going on!

*Think of buildings in your city
floor on floor up to the skies
And the stronger the foundation is
the higher it can rise*

Walt's Life Rhyme #218: Fearless

There are those who think me fearless
that my blood must run quite cold
I'm just at peace with life's outcomes
so my actions seem quite bold

For I, too, face those decisions
to go where none have gone before
I always choose the path less traveled
to see what life may have in store

They see my choices and they tremble
asking "What kind of man is this?
Who walks where others fear to tread
and welcomes every risk?"

Well, I'll share with you my secret
faced with challenges each day
I conjure up my worst scenario
and then this is what I say:

Whatever be the outcome
of this next choice I shall make
I'm prepared to face the consequence
and results that's in its wake"

For no fall is everlasting
there's no wall that never ends
All I need is strength and time
to overcome and start again

For in this life there's just two choices
either live it or you don't
One choice leads to where you're wishing
the other, well, quite simply won't

So, am I fearless? No, I face demons
towards the goals for which I strive
I've just learned to see beyond them
and have faith I will survive!

Commentary:

There is no risk. There are simply choices with consequences. One choice holds the chance of getting me where I want to go. The other does not. Since I'm committed to getting to my goal, there really is no other choice that I can make. For me, the greater risk is inactivity.

As long as you can deal with the outcomes, what others see as a risk is nothing but the opportunity to succeed. Eventually, what others will consider your fearless approach to life, you'll know simply as a commitment to your own success, and the only choice you could make.

Fearless?
Walt's Life Rhyme #218

"I share what I know,
so that others may grow!"
www.LifeRhymes.com

Walt's Life Rhyme #217: The Big Secret

If it ever made the headlines
there are those who'd lose their minds
But if they stopped and looked around
they would surely see the signs

If the masses ever knew this
man, what mayhem would ensue
It would re-write all their history
and they'd know not what to do

If by chance it ever got out
yes, the faint of heart would flee
Just imagine how unsafe they'd feel
with knowledge running free

If the news were ever leaked out
all advantage would be lost
"There must be no disclosure
keep it hidden at all cost"

If the truth was common knowledge
there'd be riots in the streets
Those of high regard and status
might be toppled from their seats

If the secret was discovered
we'd have no place we could hide
We'd have to face the world
with just what comes from deep inside

So, what's this secret that lies looming
most will learn when it's too late?
That even through the chaos
We Are Makers Of Our Fate!

The Big Secret
Walt's Life Rhyme #217

*"I share what I know,
so that others may grow!"*
www.LifeRhymes.com

Commentary

Destiny is not about where we end up. It's about where we are. Question the assumptions.

Walt's Life Rhyme #216: Like Others Before You

Some have tripped and fallen
but arose to walk the path
Some have faced the gauntlet
and survived the pelters' wrath

Some have reeled from punches
but bounced back to win the fight
Some have walked through darkness
and emerged bathed in the light

Some have lived in exile
with their faith their only friend
Some have faced destruction
but have triumphed in the end

Some have withstood trials
that most average men would fail
Some have beaten hopeless odds
o'er which none should prevail

Some have conquered illness
with naught but their inner will
Some have kept their winner's smile
despite life's bitter pill

So when you find you're grieving
over life's unbalanced scale
Think of those who've been through worse
and lived to tell the tale!

Commentary:

Feeling sorry for yourself
for all you're going through?
This too and more have I endured
and so, my friend, can you!

It is the human will to survive and prosper that has helped others before you meet their trials and overcome them. Know too that you possess that same potential to overcome anything that befalls you.

Like Others Before You
Walt's Life Rhyme #216

"I share what I know,
so that others may grow!"
www.LifeRhymes.com

Walt's Life Rhyme #215: An Alien Soul Observes *Human Conflict*

It's making much more sense now why there's always war & strife
The basis of it all is fear of losing one's identity
For each asserts himself and so desires eternal life
And still thinks conquering others brings the hope of immortality

And others hang on tight to modes and manners of religion
Believing in their smugness they alone have found the path
That others not converted somehow threaten their existence
They battle for beliefs and in their gods' name wreak their wrath

They all define themselves in terms of being, doing, having
Not being, doing, having then is just like death you see
They fear the way they self-relate will be stripped from them
And tolerance of others means they somehow cease to be

So call it what you will it's all the "fear of not" in essence
Man simply fears the death of what he knows himself to be
Through scarcity of reason feels that all is competition
And never once suspects that all might coexist quite free

Yes, those who live in conflict rest assured will boldly tell you
What I believe is sacred but your world and you are doomed
They miss the fact ironic that in their struggle for survival
That lo within their very fears are they themselves entombed

An Alien Soul Observes Human Conflict
Walt's Life Rhyme #215

"I share what I know,
so that others may grow!"
www.LifeRhymes.com

Walt's Life Rhyme #214: There's Still Road Ahead
In the Aftermath of Sept 11

The journey has not ended
although some have gone away
The road ahead still calls us
one foot forward every day

The mountain is still looming
although some have stopped their climb
More peaks for us to conquer
goals to reach one at a time

The marathon's not over
though there're some who won't be back
Find a partner you can run with
bit by bit take up the slack

There's a void of dreams and visions
left by those who've taken flight
So whatever task befalls you
take the time to do it right

Just as birds fly in formation
all involved must do their part
Gain your strength from those around you
flap your wings, and don't lose heart

There's Still Road Ahead
In the aftermath of Sept 11
Walt's Life Rhyme #214

"I share what I know,
so that others may grow!"
www.LifeRhymes.com

Commentary:

Ever notice birds flying in V formation? Researchers discovered that in such a formation, each beating of a bird's wing provides a boost of air that gives an extra lift for another in the group and helps them all fly up to 70% farther than if each traveled alone. Each one has a vital part to play in the success of all.

There is still a job to do. No task is too small. No task is too insignificant. Every part of the puzzle contributes to the whole. Children still need to be taught. Floors still need to be swept. Do not be deterred in achieving the vision of who you wish to be. It is still a part of the progress of the whole. The collective advances one individual at a time. Do not be afraid to laugh. Do not be afraid to sing. Do not be afraid to dream. Do not be afraid to soar. There must and will be an "after" to this "now." But what lies beyond exists first as an idea in the mind of he or she who is brave enough to conceive it, believe it, and achieve it.

Originally published Sept 28, 2001

Walt's Life Rhyme #213: The Meaning of the Moments

She said,
"If I knew back then what I know right now--"
But stop, for that's not fair
For hindsight scatters clouds
and makes your vision crystal clear

So therefore, I submit to you
a different point of view
Instead of rating best or worse
let's focus now on you

They come, they go and life goes on
but what have you become?
Is there some gift you did extract
or really was there none?

For every interaction holds
a truth for one and all
A blessing and a benefit
despite what you recall

I'd like to think that each and every
person whom I've met
Has helped me see a part of me
I'd not encountered yet

Through good or bad their role was such
that had you only known
You might have seen a teacher
in some way you might have grown

To love, to laugh, to learn, to live
cannot be done alone
In relation to another's how
these vital skills we hone

The meaning of the moments
spent with people whom we know
Exists in what we learn about ourselves
and how we grow!

The Meaning of the Moments
Walt's Life Rhyme #213

"I share what I know,
so that others may grow!"
www.LifeRhymes.com

Commentary:

I was having a conversation with a friend who rates all her relationships as either 'good' or 'bad'. She first considers how long they lasted, then by assessing how much of that time was pleasurable, determines whether the relationship overall was a good one or bad one.

Well, my view is a little different. I believe it's not the nature of the interaction that makes the relationship good or bad, but whether you use the opportunity that the circumstances provide to help you define and develop who YOU are and wish to become.

Stop beating yourself up for your past choices. You can't make any better choices than those that you see as available to you at the time. And the truth about life is that you see with different eyes every new day of your life. So you ALWAYS make the best and only choices that you CAN make given who you are at any moment.

Walt's Life Rhyme #212: Commandment

Thou shalt not just stand idly by
while others might be saved
Or take freedom for granted still
while others are enslaved

Thou shalt not forsake others
who through sickness are in need
Or overlook the famine
and the many we could feed

Thou shalt not through indifference
miss the chance to simply pause
And choose to lend a helping hand
no matter what the cause

Commandment
Walt's Life Rhyme #212

"I share what I know,
so that others may grow!"
www.LifeRhymes.com

Commentary:

Yesterday, I came across the story of Elie Wiesel, a World War II concentration camp survivor who has dedicated his life to helping others. In the article, Elie was asked about people's indifference and arrogance. He replied that, on the contrary, he meets so many *sensitive* people from all walks of life that he couldn't generalize.

He added: "A doctor in New York read a quote of mine that sparked her involvement. Somebody had asked me, '[Mr Wiesel], what is the most important commandment in the Bible?' and I said, 'Thou shalt not stand idly by.' So she packed up her office and went to Macedonia."

Walt's Life Rhyme #211: The Law of Obligation

The Law of Obligation
say's There Ain't None, that's a fact
So don't go thinking somehow
you'll dictate how people act

If all would do their 'duty'
and would simply do what's 'right'
Sure, things would go much smoother
there'd be one less war to fight

It would be nice I'll grant you
and yeah, that's all well and good, but
No binding code of conduct
makes the world do what they 'should'

No one will do a thing now
just because you want them to
For everyone's got issues
and a different point of view

You can't control the masses
so here's what I suggest to you
Just live your life with honor
still despite what others do

And though you can't determine
what reward your action brings
There is a thing called justice
in the grander scheme of things

Commentary:

Ah, yes! This may be a tough lesson to learn, but people really aren't obligated by YOUR sense of right and wrong, to do what YOU want them to. We all live in a society in which we hope the accepted standards of conduct will be adhered to by everyone. We hope people will say 'please' and 'thank you.' We hope others will take our concerns seriously, hold up their end of a bargain, return our calls on time, pay back what they owe, allow us to merge into traffic, hold the door open for us, treat us as we treat them and so on. In our daily interactions with others, we hope people will play along with our game plan. The truth is, however, these are just expectations of what others should do.

And remember, unhappiness is nothing but an unmet expectation.

Can you accept that others will do as they please? Can you still keep smiling when you don't get your way? Can you give up the victim game and stop waiting for someone to treat you in a specific way? If you can, you might find the road a little less bumpy and less aggravating. Now that doesn't mean you'll accept abuse. Neither will you allow yourself to be taken advantage of. And you'll remove yourself from destructive people and situations as soon as possible. And for heaven's sake, don't lower your expectations of people. Simply detach yourself from any specific outcome. You might be surprised how liberating it might be!

Keep doing what you know to be right, and know that all will be balanced—if not from 'him' or 'her', but through another, and the universe at large.

The Law of Obligation
Walt's Life Rhyme #211

"I share what I know,
so that others may grow!"
www.LifeRhymes.com

Walt's Life Rhyme #210: If You Only Knew & Something to Look Forward To

If you only knew your power
it might go straight to your head
Your days would be quite different
and you'd never go to bed

If you only knew the power
that you have to change the world
You'd spend your days doing more than
simply watching things unfurl

If you only knew the power
that's inside for you to wield
What wrongs would you be righting?
and what hurts could you then heal?

Imagine what you'd be like
if you woke one day to find
Your thoughts had crossed the border
to another state of mind

Imagine you're no longer bound
to earthly points of view
And people's thoughts
will not define for you what you can do

If you knew the world awaits your say
to make real all your plans
You'd feel like you could almost fly
and bend steel in your hands

Imagine too it's not just you
but people everywhere
Who've conquered limitations
and have vanquished all their fear

But sadly, though, it's just a dream
for most will never know:
The only thing that stops them
is the will to make it so

I woke up a different person
yeah, I know it must sound trite
But trust me when I tell you
for the first time things feel right

For almost overnight
some things are happening like I've wanted
The little and the big dreams
that for years have had me haunted

My eyes see much more clearly
and the pressure? It just stopped!
My good now overfloweth
like champagne that's just been popped!

An angel's visitation?
man, who knows, I couldn't say
But let's just say I'm grateful
and I hope it stays this way

Was just about to settle
but I'm glad that I held out
Imagine where I'd be now
if I'd given in to doubt

But if you try to reach me
to explain what's going on
I'm out living the good life!
but I'll leave my voicemail on!

If You Only Knew &
Something To Look Forward To
Walt's Life Rhyme #210
Walt F.J. Goodridge
"I share what I know,
so that others may grow
www.LifeRhymes.com

Walt's Life Rhyme #209: When Do I Quit My Job?

There's no such thing as future time
'cause time does not exist
To think there's more than "now", my friend's
a trap you must resist

It's tempting to construct your life
in terms of "if" and "when"
But "if" and "when" don't always come
and if they don't, what then?

Your question begs an answer
but assumes one lie is true
That somehow cause for what you'll do
exists outside of you

The critical decision
is not based on time or tide
Whoever claims a formula
quite frankly, friend, they lied

You'll need to choose your view of you
despite what terms are met
And asking "when" might simply mean
you haven't chosen yet

Identity decides
the why and when of what we do
Decide first who you are
and then you'll know what you should do

(For fish will do what fish will do
and that's the reason why
No pension, perk or paycheck
ever gets a fish to fly!)

Don't complicate the matter, then
with all this extra "stuff"
But simply choose by asking
"Do I want it bad enough?"

When Do I Quit My Job?
Walt's Life Rhyme #209

I share what I know,
so that others may grow!"
www.LifeRhymes.com

Commentary:

During a recent group teleclass coaching session, someone asked, "So, when do I quit my job?"

I replied, "You quit your job when you want to be successful." Other answers include, "You quit your job when you don't want to work there anymore!" Or "When you want the alternative bad enough."

My feeling is that most people would like to have a formula to use to determine when, at some time in the future, all the pieces of the puzzle are in perfect alignment and they can cheerfully and confidently wave goodbye to their boss! The truth is, the answer to the question has nothing to do with any facts or figures and everything to do with your identity. When you become a passionpreneur in the deepest concept of yourself, you'll know the answer to "When do I quit my job?"

Walt's Life Rhyme #208: Back in The Game

You can hide out if you want to
take time out if that's what's best
But remember wings are strengthened
when you fly after you rest

You can heal your wounds from battle
skill and strength strive to regain
Those who fight and flee the fracas
in due time must fight again

Make thee well your plan of action
find some allies in this fight
For with friends to help it's safe to say
this time you'll get it right

In a new young state of mind
now marching to a different song
King of the hill and now triumphant
you'll be back where you belong!

Ah, the game in all its glory!
feels so right, you will confess
Soon you'll taste the spoils of victor
smell the sweet smell of success!

Back In The Game
Walt's Life Rhyme #208
© Walt F.J. Goodridge
"I share what I know,
so that others may grow!"
www.LifeRhymes.com

Commentary:

Some are returning to businesses. Some are returning to relationships. Some are returning to ways of thought that helped them well. Some are returning to people and places of past experience. Not all returns are about the past, however. Some are about the future. Make sure your return helps you face forward.

Walt's Life Rhyme #207: In Regard to Limitations

The funny thing 'bout life is this
I know it won't seem kind
The view of you held most by you
is often what you'll find

The world is like a mirror, see?
it matters not the face
You'll only see reflected
what's already there in place

But what if in this case instead
you took the winner's lead
And argued for yourself
as if you're likely to succeed?

The evidence is often there
all you need to do is look
Examples of your winning ways
could often fill a book

Pretend that you're defending
all opposing points of view
And launch a case of what could be
and argue against you

So try this trick right now, my friend
it's worked for me because
Defending your potential
shows the world you have just cause

If you argue limitations, friend
your limitations stay
Present your case against them
and you'll chase them all away!

Commentary:

Whenever I do my Passion Profit Workshops, I often start by encouraging participants to resist the temptation to argue on behalf of their limitations. Many people are so accustomed to seeing the glass as half-empty that in the course of their conversations, they seem bent on defending their right to failure.

They'll quote chapter and verse, forwards and in reverse in support of why their great idea WON'T work, or why they're destined to fail because of the odds. Consequently, I find myself arguing on behalf of THEIR potential and possibilities while THEY defend their limitations. How would their words and attitudes be different if they chose instead to work WITH me and argue FOR their potential?

In Regard To Limitations
Walt's Life Rhyme #207

"I share what I know,
so that others may grow!"
www.LifeRhymes.com

Walt's Life Rhyme #206: A Process of Recovery

The sun is always shining
though you may not see the light
You always know the answer
though you may not get it right

A process of recovery
is what learning's all about
Though knowledge is in easy reach
you may not pull it out

The genius, sage and gifted
bless them all but know this too
The same fountain of knowledge
is available to you

No more or less, no good or bad
no smarter they than you
How much you choose to reconnect
is all you'll ever do

No different in reality
oh so different in perception
Acceptance of your failings
are degrees of self-deception

The choice is yours to be much more
despite what you are seeing
To lift the cloud of conscious
limitations on your being

No nothing is beyond you
but believing makes it so
All growth is just remembering
things your soul already knows!

A Process of Recovery
Walt's Life Rhyme #206

"I share what I know,
so that others may grow!"
www.LifeRhymes.com

Commentary:

It's my contention that some intelligence is nothing more than the ability to connect to information that is "floating" in the ether awaiting anyone to "tune" in to the right frequency. There is no truth that cannot be readily grasped by any mind that is tuned correctly. And there is no truth that is not already intuitively known by every soul. My tutoring and consulting sessions start with that basic premise-- that everyone can understand any concept given the right explanation and sequence of steps to get from where they are in their understanding to where they need to be.

Anyone who doesn't exhibit the traditional signs of great mental skill or intelligence is simply operating without all the information. Remember that, and be patient with yourself or with that certain someone you know as you guide you or them through the process of recovering the forgotten pieces.

Walt's Life Rhyme #205: Out of Order

If everything in life
happens according to plan
then nothing can ever be late

Contemplate this
as you reach for your dreams
and it'll help pass the time while you wait

For if a leads to b
and then b leads to c
then by design does your daily life move

It might not seem to fit
any schedule or plan
but there's order and this I shall prove

Like each note in a song
played too soon and it's wrong
out of time and the tune goes astray

It's not due to ill will
but a sequence to fill
that's at cause when things don't go your way

Would a playwright begin
without pencil or pen?
would a bird dare to perch in mid flight?

It seems the trick then to get
any goal that you set
is know the steps and then order them right!

Out Of Order
Walt's Life Rhyme #205

"I share what I know,
so that others may grow!"
www.LifeRhymes.com

Commentary: *(this rhymes too)*

I met a naysayer, a dream stealer, last week, who tried his best to rain on my parade.
My feelings were hurt, my resolve called to bear all from a single biting comment he made.

The sentiment he expressed really threw me for a loop, and I was tempted to respond and cut ties.
But I took time to think, and finding no evil intent, I concluded he was simply unwise.

Who are you to think that, all my dreams will fall flat? That was so out of order, I did muse.
But if his concept of things were out of order it seems, then so too would be all of his views.

Anyone who insists that a thing can't be done suffers not just from merely poor sight.
But convinced that no path leads to where they would dwell, are then doomed to fail, try as they might.

The naysayers are unwise to the order of things, be on guard lest you too be misled
Every point does connect to one point just before all you need is to know where to tread

All goals are reachable if you tread wisely and in the right sequence!

Walt's Life Rhyme #204: BE On Your Way

To have the world respond at once
and answer when you call
Step up from thought to being
for being takes no time at all

Don't think about it too much now
much precious time you'll lose
Go straight to BE and don't pass go
to live the life you choose

What is, just is right now, that's all
that's where you should begin
For chances are with too much thought
you'll never just jump in

For being is the quickest route
to get to BE from A
You'll always BE more than you think
So just BE....on your way

BE On Your Way
Walt's Life Rhyme #204

"I share what I know,
so that others may grow!"
www.LifeRhymes.com

Commentary:

Now that you know that your thoughts create your reality, what's the next step? Well, remember that the cycle of success is 1)BE, 2) DO, 3)HAVE. Many people have it reversed and think they must first "HAVE" in order to "DO", and as a result will "BE." For example, "If I HAD a lot of money, I could DO the things I want to do and then I would BE happy." However, those of us on this journey of self-discovery know that first we must BE, then DO, and the HAVING will take care of itself! Being comes first, even before thought. In fact, thinking is a form of "doing" and therefore must be preceded by a "being." What you are *being* causes the thoughts you need to create your reality. So start with Be! And BE on your way to having!

Inspired by Friendship with God *by Neale Donald Walsch*

Walt's Life Rhyme #203: Spinning Wheels

I want to do things differently
but just can't figure how
I want to be a better person
not next week but now

I want to make a bigger list
of all that I should do
And one by one address them all
like I've been wanting to

I want to live a life of faith
and trust my fellow man
To know despite appearances
things unfold as I plan

I want to tap the mother lode
of all my inner wealth
And live life to its fullest state
in happiness and health

I want to move things quickly
I've been stagnant for too long
Dance boldly to a different beat
and sing a different song

But darn, my wheels are spinning
as if they just don't touch the ground
I feel like I'm in limbo
'til I learn something profound

And then a voice reminds me
of something I already know
"To hold the thing you most desire
you first must let it go"

"On levels way below our sight
is where we make our fate
And sadness comes because
we rarely want what we create"

"Don't waste your tears on outcomes
that surely is your safest bet
Seek not to get to make you pleased
be pleased with what you get!"

Spinning Wheels
Walt's Life Rhyme #203

"I share what I know,
so that others may grow!"
www.LifeRhymes.com

Commentary:

In creating results in your life, remember this: Until you reach a level of effective creative mastery, what you intend is not always what you end up creating. You may simply be unaware of a more powerful creative process that is taking place on a subconscious level (i.e. "on levels way below our sight"). Therefore, you should be open to the seemingly unanticipated occurrences that come your way. For example, if you plan and work towards A but end up getting B, do not be alarmed and distressed, but simply accept it. Unhappiness is caused by unmet expectations held too firmly. The more attached you are to a particular outcome, the unhappier you'll be if you do not achieve it at first. Seek your outcomes, yes, but don't be too attached.

In addition, "be pleased with what you get" does not mean to be *satisfied* with what you get. It means simply to accept it as your own creation, grow from that awareness, then continue to create from an ever-evolving state of mind. Remember this when it seems your wheels are spinning and things aren't happening.

Walt's Life Rhyme #202: Trust Me

For every parent who's wanted the best for a child; For every leader who's wanted the best for her people; For every teacher who's held a student's future in his hands; And for every coach who's team has looked to her for guidance.

Trust me when I tell you
you'll get nothing but my best
I've been there many times before
I've taken that same test

Trust me when I tell you
if it was all left up to me
I'd make the journey worry-free
and joy is all you'd see

Trust me when I tell you
if you walked long in my shoes
I'd pave the way a winner
so you'd never have to lose

Trust me when I tell you though
I'm not quite there as yet
I'll share with you each secret learned
the closer that I get

But if you put your trust in me
No doubt I'll show and prove
There're limits on what I can do
the rest? well, that's your move!

Trust Me
Walt's Life Rhyme #202

"I share what I know,
so that others may grow!"
www.LifeRhymes.com

Walt's Life Rhyme #201: Self Growth 101

You'll first need to accept the fact
that things you're prone to do
Reveal more about who you are
than you believe they do

Accept that everything on earth
is ruled by natural laws
And everything has meaning then
and all effects have cause

Accept that you're accountable
for each new situation
Acknowledge that in some weird way
you've helped in their creation

Accept your role as writer
not just actor in this play
If things are not as you might wish
then edit them away

And then proceed to ask yourself
what might my actions mean?
If ultimately I'm root cause
what message can I glean?

What image of my world and me
am I perpetuating?
(It's usually our low self-worth
we aid in validating)

Though circumstances in your past
affect who you've become
It's what you do right now
that will affect your next outcome

So just in case you didn't know
the truth is now you know
It's where you look for answers
that determines how you grow

So never stop your seeking
for the answers to these questions
For discovering the answers
will make future days the best ones!

SelfGrowth 101
Walt's Life Rhyme #201

"I share what I know,
so that others may grow!"
www.LifeRhymes.com

Commentary:

The journey towards the life of your dreams begins when you make a commitment to personal growth.

Walt's Life Rhyme #200: My Secret Wish

What words can I now share today
that haven't since been said?
What food for thought is mine to give
on which you have not fed?

For if I had to choose one gift
to leave you with today
I'd wish my weekly words had strength
to help you in some way

I'd wish there was some magic dust
some spell that I could cast
To bring to life a death-bed hope
undo a pain-filled past

I'd wish that those who live in fear
would find their own brave heart
I'd wish that those who loved and lost
could just forget that part

I'd wish that those who yearn to climb
who stumble, fall and cry
When faced with mountains from now on
won't even ask how high

I'd wish that those who've lost the strength
to fight that inner fight
Would find the will somewhere inside
to simply set things right

I'd wish that those whose pleas for help
seem oft to go unheeded
Would find the ones whose need to give's
what makes them feel most needed

I'd wish that everyone could know
the pleasure of the day
That starts with a reminder
that you've made life your own way

Perhaps next week I'll find the words
to make my wish come true
Perhaps you'll find your inspiration
lives right where you do

So if by chance next week, my friend
you fail to hear my voice
I hope the echo urges you
to live life by your choice!

My Secret Wish
Walt's Life Rhyme #200

"I share what I know,
so that others may grow!"
www.LifeRhymes.com

Walt's Life Rhyme #199: What I Learned From Al

Today while listening to performers in Farragut Park in downtown D.C., I shared a bench with an elderly gentleman named Al. We chatted about life and music and acting and passions, and about his sons. What was most curious was that while they (his sons) had both achieved some impressive milestones in their individual pursuits, they still hadn't reached the point where they were 100% financially self-sufficient through their creative endeavors. I wondered what the missing ingredient was. Eventually, he told me!

Today I met a man named Al
whose sons were on his mind
For both pursued their passions
but still both were in a bind

For neither one had made their mark
to claim the title "great"
Despite their own best efforts
it was Al who filled their plate

"Work hard", he said, "and I'll support"
you only have to call
Yes, Al was there to catch them both
if ever they should fall

They hadn't ever worked a job
(a blessing in disguise)
For freedom seems a grander goal
when seen through captive eyes

I told him what they need
is something Al could not provide
And truth be told his "help" 'til now
had crippled them inside

Unless they stumble, stall or sink
they'll never find their best
For even eagles fear to fly
'til pushed beyond the nest

They say a man who's taught to fish
goes through a mental shift
The pride of "I can do for self"
might be life's greatest gift!

What I Learned From Al
Walt's Life Rhyme #199

"I share what I know,
so that others may grow!"
www.LifeRhymes.com

Walt's Life Rhyme #198: The Harder The Battle

The games that we remember most
are those against the best
The matched opponent makes us work
and therein lies our test

The victories we savor most
are those for which we fought
Through sweat of brow and tests of will
hard lessons we are taught

The triumphs that we yearn to share
of which we are most proud
Are those over arch nemeses
to whom we never bowed

So revel in the game
and view the obstacles as par
A conquest without struggle
never gets you very far

The measure of our mettle
lies in what we must defeat
A victory too easy?
well, it's never quite as sweet!

Dedicated to Danielle,
and to the Philadelphia 76ers! :-)

Commentary:

You've heard the phrase, "The harder the battle, the sweeter the victory?" Well, recently, I had the chance to help a friend's 13-year old daughter with an online math-based mystery/sleuth challenge. We were up until midnight struggling to decipher the clues and compute different values needed to access the various parts of the puzzle in order to find the prize!

When all was clicked and done, I felt a tremendous sense of accomplishment and pride for her, knowing that she was able to solve the assignment and present it in class the next day. I'm sure that her confidence has been boosted by the experience and that a valuable life lesson regarding the rewards of commitment and perseverance has been indelibly etched in her mind.

Along the same line of thought, I was recently reminded by a mentor that every game is defined by three things, 1. an objective, 2. freedoms, and 3. barriers. Anything of any value that we desire in life, love and the pursuit of happiness has all these elements. Without any individual component, the "game" doesn't quite work. A basketball game, for example, without an objective, or without the freedom to advance on the court, or without an opposing team providing barriers to our advancement, isn't quite a game at all. Our mission in life is to accept that all three elements are necessary for us to really benefit from the challenge. So revel in the freedoms, accept the obstacles, and never, never, never give up on reaching your objective!

The Harder The Battle
Walt's Life Rhyme #198

"I share what I know,
so that others may grow!"
www.LifeRhymes.com

Walt's Life Rhyme #197: Points For Trying

You DO get points for trying
just not enough to say you've won
The game goes not to those who try
but those who get more done

You'll get an "A" for Effort, yes
but that won't mean you'll pass
For Effort's just a minor course
Results, now THAT'S the class

You'll win the hearts of some
but fame alone won't swing the vote
Until you risk and sink or swim
you're trapped in the same boat

For doers aren't remembered
for the things they TRIED to do
They're known for their results
and yes, the same applies to you!

Points For Trying
Walt's Life Rhyme #197

"I share what I know,
so that others may grow!"
www.LifeRhymes.com

Commentary:

"At least I tried" may be good for some, but no bridges were ever made, no laws were ever changed, no battles ever won by those who were content simply to try. The only purpose a try serves is to increase the chances of actually doing a thing. Results are what matter.

OUTTAKE (opening stanza):
You DO get points for trying
just not enough to change the score
The game's not won by those who tried
but those who just do more

Walt's Life Rhyme #196: This Time Tomorrow

To get beyond the ups and downs
just look ahead with glee
Anticipate the moments
when of worries you'll be free

I know it might feel hopeless now
it seems the world has ended
There'll come a day you'll look back from
by then things will have mended

You'll be with friends, you're woes will end
a brand new sun will shine
Just know this moment cannot last
you'll see, things will be fine

So have no fear it'll be alright
time triumphs over sorrow
Just know that this thing too shall pass
by this time tomorrow!

This Time Tomorrow
Walt's Life Rhyme #196

"I share what I know,
so that others may grow!"
www.LifeRhymes.com

Commentary:

As a child growing up, a favorite aunt would often create a sense of excitement for us—her nieces and nephews—by placing our thoughts in the anticipated future of a coming event. Whether it was an overseas trip, a graduation, or some family gathering, she would say with a smile, "This time tomorrow, you'll be doing such and such..." Now, at 8 years old, a day can seem like forever. So even though her words didn't quell the impatience of a 24-hour wait, it gave us practice in focusing our attention on a desirable future.

These days, I often use that technique to focus on the future when beset with broken promises, delayed dreams, setbacks and challenges. Yesterday, I was talking to a friend who was going through her own such challenges. She had already gleaned the lessons she felt the experience was teaching her, so there was not much in the way of advice I could give her. So, I offered what little consolation I could in the form of that trick I learned from my aunt. "Cheer up," I said. "By this tomorrow..."

Walt's Life Rhyme #195: Firewood

In light of life's unfairness
there are those who think they're cursed
They're just so blind to how it works
they've got things all reversed

They're opting not to work too hard
'til boss man pays them more
Refusing to commit to love
until they can be sure

They simply won't invest in life
for fear that they might lose
Unsure of just which path is best
they often never choose

But holding back from giving
when the outcome is in doubt's
Like choosing not to race
until you know how it turns out

In life you must give first
before expecting your return
You'll never get the heat
without some firewood to burn!

Firewood
Walt's Life Rhyme #195

*"I share what I know,
so that others may grow!"*
www.LifeRhymes.com

Commentary:

There's a popular cartoon depicting a man standing in front of a wood-burning stove yelling in anger, "Give me some heat FIRST, and THEN I'll give you the wood!" As silly as it seems, many of us do the same thing by expecting the rewards for our efforts before we invest adequately. The truth is: in your job, the raise comes AS A RESULT OF the effort you invest. In relationships, the love is maintained AS A RESULT OF the commitment you bring to it. The answers to what steps to take come AS A RESULT OF the choice of path you make. In other words, you've got to put the firewood in first, before you can expect the warmth in return.

Walt's Life Rhyme #194: Blue Light Special

Just one or two aisles over
there's a special going on
If you miss the next announcement
you'll arrive and find it's gone

There's a giveaway next weekend
you can have what you can hold
But alas your arms are empty
for it seems you were not told

High's the price you pay for wisdom
in life's inconvenience store
Friends' advice are like free coupons
for they've paid full price before

Closed I was to friends' suggestions
of another way to be
I was stuck paying full retail
for what I could have gotten free

I was stubborn for a while
no love nor logic could convince
Then I took their words to heart
and life's been special ever since!

Offer friends your blue light specials
share your wisdom and advice
Some will thank you for the discount
some will choose to pay full price

Commentary:

"Blue Light Specials" are words of advice that you offer to your friends and family to help them get a sale in life's store of lessons. They are also the words of guidance offered to YOU from those who've been there. But heed these words of advice about advice: Make sure you only give directions to places you've been, and only take directions from those who've been there.

**[For readers unfamiliar with the reference:] The term "blue light special" originates from a department store popular in certain parts of the US, which routinely announces special sales with a flashing blue light and an announcement directing customers to the appropriate aisle with the sale item.*

Blue Light Special
Walt's Life Rhyme #194

"I share what I know,
so that others may grow!"
www.LifeRhymes.com

Walt's Life Rhyme #193: Ask the Inspirer
A Doctor's Prescription for Success

Dear Walt,

I am challenged by a fear of failure. Most of my college life has been consumed with a relationship that aided in me neglecting school work and getting horrible grades in my classes. I graduated high-school with a 4.0 GPA [Grade Point Average], and now in college, I barely have a 2.0. Now, I've gotten rid of the relationship, but my GPA is still very low, and I'm afraid that after college, there won't be any opportunities for me because of my GPA. I know there's no way I can go to medical school as I've dreamed of since I was 5yrs old. Always helping others has been my best attribute, now I'm afraid that no one will give me a chance to exert my wonderful personality and humanity by becoming a doctor. Now, I'm not sure that I can even make good grades in school. I graduate next spring. Any advice would be greatly valued

Worried MD

Hey Worried MD,

I have a good friend who's an MD and therefore more qualified to give advice as it relates to your medical career. So I'll let her take it from here, then I'll wrap it up!

Hey Walt,

I would tell Worried MD that there is more to being a doctor than earning exemplary grades. Of course, med schools always give those students with excellent marks a first look. However, they also appreciate students who have a wealth of life experience, i.e.: work in the peace corps, extensive world travel, community service, overcoming of hardship, etc. These experiences offer a different kind of education that can only be learned through living them, rather than memorizing them from a book. They also help a future doctor connect with their patients on a human level. If someone is truly dedicated to becoming a doctor, but has poor grades, I would suggest that they take a couple of years off after college and do something meaningful to show that the have matured and gained life experience. They might also want to take a few post grad courses to show that they are capable of obtaining the marks. It also helps to seek out a mentor, preferably one who sits on an admissions board or has some influence or connection with a medical school. Also, there are always foreign medical schools, and osteopathic schools as an alternative. The most important ingredient is believing that you can do it. I didn't have a 4.0 GPA in high school or college, but I did have determination, focus, and a commitment to my dream. Even when I was on the verge of failing physics, I never once believed that I would not get into medical school, graduate, and become a doctor. It's amazing the things you can achieve when you adjust your mind to fit your agenda.--

Hope that helps, Worried. Now here's my life rhyme wrap up!

Walt's Life Rhyme #193: Ask the Inspirer
A Doctor's Prescription for Success (Continued)

The best grades that you'll ever earn
come not from class or book
The lessons learned throughout your life
depend on where you look

Look to the texts for lesson one
and there find fact and figure
Look to the world for lesson two
and find something much bigger

With basic human skills
I've come this far and learned one thing
No lessons learned in school compares
to those that life can bring

Our goals in life may often shrink
to fit our shriveled mind
Expand the mind to fit the goal
and here's what you might find:

The you in you is more than grades
believe and have no fear
For men care not how much you know
until they know you care

With thoughts like these ingrained in mind
quite soon you will be soaring
So heed these words two times a day
and call me in the morning!

A Doctor's Prescription for Success
Walt's Life Rhyme #193

"I share what I know,
so that others may grow!"
www.LifeRhymes.com

Walt's Life Rhyme #192: Ode to "You've Got Mail!"
(Confessions of an email addict Version 2.0)

I hear it in the bedroom
when I'm dozing off at night
It might mean someone likes me
'cause they took the time to write

I hear it in the shower
lathered up and soaking wet
And yes, I rush out dripping
(how addicted can you get?)

I even hear it sometimes
in the silence before dawn
And that's some scary stuff
because the thing ain't even on!

I wasn't this obsessed at first
quite normal I would say
But now it's at the point
I sometimes sit and wait all day

They say that I'm addicted
like some junkie hooked on crack
Well that would mean I couldn't stop
you hear that? ...Be Right Back

Oh that? Oh it was nothing
just some silly old chain letter
Said send to everyone you know
so Susie will get better

And others say get help
as if I'm strung out on cheap wine
But, I do this only socially
I'll stop at any time

It's not as if I'm gullible
or fall for each new hoax
I forward things of value
OK? And just a few good jokes

I never know what to expect
the fortune that it brings
I treat it like a phone call
that gets answered when it rings

So tell me, is this crazy
or a normal human quirk?
I sometimes send things to myself
to make sure it still works

At other times when dressed
and almost halfway out the door
I'll swear I hear it, run back in
and check it just once more!

How thrilling now to hear that sound
its pull I can't resist
It's constant validation
someone knows that I exist!

It's something that I yearn for
day and night now without fail
No other feeling quite compares
to hearing "YOU'VE GOT MAIL!"

Confessions of An Email Addict
Walt's Life Rhyme #192

"I share what I know,
so that others may grow!"
www.LifeRhymes.com

Commentary for Walt's Life Rhyme #192

NOTE: Users may substitute the appropriate chime, bell, flasher or other appropriate indicator of incoming email.

Like many home-based entrepreneurs, I maintain what psychiatric professionals might consider an unhealthy relationship with my internet connection. You see, my computer is on for almost the entire day because it's the lifeline between me and my websites. For me, email is not simply the harbinger of the latest joke, hoax, or chain letter. It's not just the newest means to facilitate banal chats with people in the next room or cubicle. No, for me email is a matter of survival. Incoming email indicates that someone may be clicking around on my website, filling out forms and placing orders! In my home-office, email carries with it the urgency of a ringing phone that demands to be answered right away for fear of losing that big order or opportunity.

But even without the promise of potential income, email has become the latest substance of choice for a world in search of its latest fix. It's the drug du jour for people of all ages. I have friends who just six months ago had trouble with the technical aspects of opening the box a computer might arrive in, who now find themselves rushing home in the evenings to see what adventure their inbox has in store for them. Countless others are finding themselves late for work, neglecting the kids, and rather than develop meaningful social interaction, find themselves curling up on a Friday night with a warm glowing computer screen. It is in this spirit of depraved dependence that I offer the world this Life Rhyme!

Walt's Life Rhyme #191: Suspended Animation

Just as soon as I get things together in life
then I'll do all those things I want to
I'm just waiting for things to get better in life
so I can make all my wishes come true

But the days come and go much too quickly in life
I progress but I'm never quite there
I remain in a state of stark fear towards life
all my days seem suspended in air

Seems I spend the time waiting and miss out on this life
delaying all my "now" moments 'til "then"
I forsake precious days and then curse at this life
Asking "Why not now?" "If not now, when?"

But it can't stay this way now forever in life
this I said and I thought it was true
But it will 'til I learn that the secret of life
is that dreams come to life when I do!

P.S.
So get up off your "buts"
and meet head on with life
from time's passage no one can long hide
No you can't stop the clock by delaying your life
for it's true time will not be denied

Suspended Animation
Walt's Life Rhyme #191

"I share what I know,
so that others may grow!"
www.LifeRhymes.com

Commentary:

DON'T LET THIS HAPPEN TO YOU! As I was writing today's Life Rhyme, I came across this excerpt from a book entitled *The Seven Stories of Love: And How To Choose Your Happy Ending by Marcia Millman*. It provided another perspective on the very concept I was writing about.

"Many avoiders of love were hurt before and don't want to risk being hurt again; postponers unconsciously equate making a commitment with aging and death; cynics focus only on their partners' flaws instead of looking within themselves and seeing that they are projecting their own self-hatred. People who postpone and avoid love commitments are often living in a state of suspended animation--they are not moving forward but are often frozen in a time of their past. They believe by delaying a commitment, they have stopped the clock. But while they put things on hold, time passes them by. Instead of preserving life, they lose it.

For people like this to change and open themselves to love, they must have a powerful shock that makes them see that it's really now or never. As long as people are comfortable living with the defenses they've constructed, they don't have any motivation to change and they'll live as if they have forever. Only those who find the courage to risk love, with all its dangers, truly gain life and a kind of immortality."

Walt's Life Rhyme #190: Don't Miss The Sun Rise

If the farmer missed the clues
that showed the crop was on the rise
Then he'd know not where to water
and the plant, neglected, dies

If the runner missed the signs
that showed the finish line was near
Then she might give up the race
and run instead towards her fear

If the sailor missed the stars
that showed him where the land should be
Then he might turn 'round too soon
and be forever lost at sea

If the seeker in her seeking
knew not where to cast her eyes
Then she might live on in darkness
for she'd miss the day's sunrise

Miss the clues you should be using
while instead lamenting strife
Miss the moment that your efforts
take on form and come to life!

Don't Miss The Sun Rise
Walt's Life Rhyme #190

"I share what I know,
so that others may grow!"
www.LifeRhymes.com

Commentary:

Of course, the trick is to understand how things work on the planet called success. In this strange new world, plants can grow in places where it seems you haven't planted seeds. So be vigilant. Finish lines appear when it seems the race has just been lost. So always be on your mark. Land appears when it seems you're adrift in deep waters. So keep scanning the horizon. And the sun may rise today from where it has always set. So look both ways for the coming of the sun.

Walt's Life Rhyme #189: Given That It Is

Given that things right now in fact
are how they seem to be
How then should you respond
instead of saying woe is me?

Given that things around you
didn't work out as you planned
How best to turn these cards you're dealt
into a winning hand?

It's all in the response
so, you can focus on the flaws
Or simply use events
to help you find your life's great cause

No answers come by saying
"My life's worse than hers or his..."
You find them when you start by saying
"Given that it is..."

Commentary:

Perhaps that was not who you were meant to be
Perhaps that was not what you were sent to do
Perhaps you are moving towards a goal you can't yet see
Perhaps you are creating a new edition of you

Given That It Is
Walt's Life Rhyme #189

"I share what I know,
so that others may grow!"
www.LifeRhymes.com

Walt's Life Rhyme #188: Make The World Go Wow

It doesn't take a lot
to set yourself above the rest
For most settle for second
when there are empty seats at best

Just do the thing not often done
and say what most won't say
A reputation thusly built
will grow from day to day

They'll beat a path straight to your door
and hang on all you do
The world will know you by your works
your works reflect on you

Impress your way to riches?
yes you can and here is how
Your dreams will come much quicker
when you make the world go wow!

Make The World Go Wow
Walt's Life Rhyme #188

"I share what I know,
so that others may grow!"
www.LifeRhymes.com

Walt's Life Rhyme #187: The Double Agent

Your confidante and friend
the one you trust beyond all doubt
Might one day turn and be
the very one who sells you out

The one who always comes to mind
when others call your name
May end up on a rival team
intent to thwart your game

So what on earth are you to do
when spies are all around
And each attempt to rise above
is prone to be shot down?

Just keep a watchful eye
but know through secrecy and stealth
The double agent in your life
might just be you yourself

The very thing that makes you *you*
may also hold you back
The you that makes the world go wow
may keep you steeped in lack

The tools you use for planting seeds
won't work for reaping fruit
And traits that help you run away
might fail you in pursuit

So strive always for balance
but let just one you take the lead
Assign the task to you who's
best equipped to do the deed!

Commentary:

It's often true that the thing that makes you a good business person, makes you rate poorly in relationships. The thing that makes you a great artist, hinders you from being able to take care of business. Our greatest talent is often our greatest stumbling block to success in another key area. Your relationship-oriented side has taken the lead in your private life, for example, and made you liked by all. But, in your business and professional life, it allows others to take advantage of you. It won't be easy, but there's an untrained, undeveloped side of you that needs to be given a different assignment.

Assign business tasks to the you who's better equipped for business success. Similarly, assign the gregarious you to meeting the social obligations that your personal life requires. Unless you delegate appropriately, you'll end up sabotaging the very dreams you seek.

The Double Agent
Walt's Life Rhyme #187

"I share what I know,
so that others may grow!"
www.LifeRhymes.com

Walt's Life Rhyme #186: Easier Than I Thought

You don't suppose? No way...you think?
How could I've been so wrong?
To let myself be duped and tricked
and fooled for quite so long?

Oh no, what if for all this time
it's been within my power
To choose not just the who and where
but month, week, day AND hour?

Oh, man, then that would mean, in fact
I've wasted precious time
Perhaps it's best if I believe
the choices were not mine

Each day more pieces fall in place
each day things follow plan
Just goes to show what you can do
when you just think you can

Yes, day by day the folly's clear
of all that I've been taught
I realize the truth....
and things are easier than I thought!

Commentary:

What a waste it would be if you lived your whole life and never even attempted to find out. I don't know about you, but I just couldn't live with the daily haunting of NOT knowing!

Easier Than I Thought
Walt's Life Rhyme #186

"I share what I know,
so that others may grow!"
www.LifeRhymes.com

Walt's Life Rhyme #185: Out And About

No they won't be comin' to get you
wish and wish as hard as you might
The only way you'll meet that perfect someone
is to be there in their line of sight

It won't come knocking at your door
that dream job that just sweeps you away
Seek help from above when you pray at night
but then shuffle your feet by day

It won't just be dropped there at your feet
the millions in cash that you desperately need
Just like fruit, the reward for all the good you do
comes down after you first plant the seed

No it won't just up and fix itself
this thing in your life that needs repair
Faith with works as they say is the way it goes
that's how it is however unfair

So don't waste your time in pine or whine
you can scream, holler, cry or shout
But the only way the world will find out what you're about
....is for you to get out and about!

Out and About
Walt's Life Rhyme #185

"I share what I know,
so that others may grow!"
www.LifeRhymes.com

Walt's Life Rhyme #184: Same Key. Different Twist

Crack the code and find the answer
no puzzle's made that can't be solved
Perhaps where heavy hands have failed
a feather touch should be involved

Look to the lock you turn with ease
and see what tactic works the best
Perhaps not force but faith
will turn the lock and end the stress

Self pity leaves no query answered
no riddle solved no lock undone
Combine persistence with the hope
the next attempt might be the one

Each door in life that we have opened
provides us with a key that fits
Sometimes new doors are ours to open
with same key, but just a different twist!

Same Key, Different Twist
Walt's Life Rhyme #184

"I share what I know,
so that others may grow!"
www.LifeRhymes.com

Commentary:

Have you ever struggled in vain to open a lock, only to have someone else (or perhaps you yourself) succeed a few moments later using the very same key you just tried? Have you ever worked yourself into a frenzy trying to solve a puzzle, then given up, only to return a few hours later and solve it easily? Why is that?

Well, the truth is, your potential to succeed it was always there. All that was needed was a different touch, or a slightly different perspective. Is there some "puzzle" in your life right now that's causing you to worry or wallow in self-pity? I believe that you already hold the key. Look to other areas of your life where you've been successful and ask yourself, "How can I use what I've learned in area "A" of my life, to solve this riddle in area "B"? Remember, there are no accidents. Everything you've ever done in your life has been in preparation for this moment. The key of understanding is there, just waiting for a slightly different twist.

Walt's Life Rhyme #183: One Step Inside

To pour, and pour and pour
and find you never fill the cup
To chase the thing most dear
and find you never quite catch up

Or worse to seize the thing you chase
and end up asking "Why?"
Or drinking from a cup now filled
and find it leaves you dry

The basis of pursuit is just
to get what you don't own
The objects change with each new catch
like dog after new bone

So, save yourself the million steps
of searching far and wide
The hunt for what completes you
starts and ends one step inside!

One Step Inside
Walt's Life Rhyme #183

"I share what I know,
so that others may grow!"
www.LifeRhymes.com

Walt's Life Rhyme #182: Ask The Inspirer How To Handle The Doubts

Dear Walt:
My question to you is how do you maintain your motivation and excitement when you encounter frustrating obstacles? How do you remove the doubt about whether this is the right direction on those mornings when you wake up and the first thought that jumps into your mind is "Am I crazy?" You know what I mean? There are several of us that are out on their own...and we all struggle with that issue.
Doubtful in Savannah

WALT'S REPLY:

The truth, dear Doubtful, is that there are no real doubts that I encounter, just frustrations and tests of my patience. You see, I believe that every challenge has a solution, every journey has a destination, and that the only way to find it is to keep looking. I believe that my destiny is not in the hands of anyone but me and my creator, so I never doubt that I can accomplish my goals. Once I made the decision to pursue my passion, the question became not "is this the right direction?", but "what do I need to make this happen?" In other words, I only ask "when?" not "if?"

The commitment was already made way at the beginning. The ups and downs are just part of the journey. I can't tell you why I believe this, or what series of events in my life conspired to give me this perspective, but I know that it is what keeps me going forward even through the setbacks, the evictions, the credit challenges, etc., (see *Turn Your Passion Into Profit* for my full story) that I went through during my journey.

But, as a result of your question, I started asking myself, "What is it that makes me this way?"

Maybe it's because I got encouragement at an early age for my accomplishments and therefore don't believe that there's any test that I can't master if I try hard enough.

Maybe it's because I'm prepared to fall without shame (I gave up the ego a long time ago. In fact, it's the first thing that needs to go if you're serious about becoming wealthy.)

Maybe it's because I'm a control freak who is fanatically driven to be in control of my life, and will settle for nothing less.

Maybe it's because I get physically sick if I have to work in a corporate environment, and decided long ago that I wouldn't remained trapped in the corporate world.

Maybe it's because I have a fear of mediocrity that won't allow me to settle for being an "also ran."

Maybe it's all these things, or none of them. I may never know the answer. What I DO know is that going back was never an option. Giving up my ultimate goal of freedom is not an option. Neither is giving up the desire to help others do the same.

I wonder how many people will really believe that it's within their power to change the outcomes they've been creating, and give themselves something different? Doubtful, I hope that *you* do!

Walt's Life Rhyme #182: How To Handle The Doubts (Continued)

No doubt there'll be doubts
as you build your dreams, but
Avoid second guessing
just measure and cut

Commit to the journey
do it once in advance
Then always keep striving
leave nothing to chance

For roadblocks don't mean
that the journey has ended
And spirit that's broken
can always be mended

When obstacles come
don't lose faith in your goal
When the ride becomes bumpy
simply tighten your hold

Commitment to outcome
precedes all success
And once convinced of your goals
daily doubts become less!

How To Handle The Doubts
Walt's Life Rhyme #182

"I share what I know,
so that others may grow!"
www.LifeRhymes.com

Walt's Life Rhyme #181: Are You Willing To See Things Differently?

I've got something to teach you
but let me ask before we start
Are you willing to see things differently?
If not, then let's just part

I know you feel quite justified
to hold tight to your view
So why on earth would I think that
you'd let it slip from you?

You've come equipped with tools and such
to shore your house of thought
Intent to get a full return
on viewpoints that you've bought

But if for once, you'd let them go
you might see what I see
If not it might be best to just
agree to disagree

For so intent we are sometimes
to paint the world our way
We often never take the time
to hear what others say

Are You Willing To See Things Differently?
Walt's Life Rhyme #181
© Walt F.J. Goodridge
"I share what I know,
so that others may grow!"
www.LifeRhymes.com

Commentary

It's been said "a man convinced against his will is of the same opinion still." No new thoughts can be introduced to a closed mind. Consequently, I sometimes find myself engaged in battles with individuals who are so wedded to their views of one reality, that they refuse to cooperate with my efforts to show them another. So, these days, before dispensing any advice, I first ask, "Are you willing to see things differently?"

Walt's Life Rhyme #180: Yet Another Test

When the weather is sunny and clouds are away
that's when all come to watch the parade
It's when rain sleet and snow start to threaten the day
that you see the committed who stayed

Any building can stand if the tremors are weak
any ship will fare well in the port
It's when trials and hardships reach an all time high peak
that you see who and who will abort

Even turkeys can fly if the tailwind is right
even underdogs win by default
But when threatened by forces that put up a real fight
then all pretenses come to a halt

Make your courage such that it will harden with heat
gain your strength and resolve from each test
Let life's challenges force you to stand on your feet
let adversity bring out your best!

Yet Another Test
Walt's Life Rhyme #180

"I share what I know,
so that others may grow!"
www.LifeRhymes.com

Commentary:

Don't think that the tests will ever stop. They just get more appropriate for your "grade level!"

Walt's Life Rhyme #179: The Price of Admission

If success said "Members Only,
show your pass, or move along!"
What proof could you present, my friend
to show that you belong?

If getting rich meant first
you had to answer "Tell me why!"
What story could you tell
to make it clear you qualify?

If joy said, "State your case
before the jury has its say!"
What closing statements could you make
to sway the vote your way?

And if you ask with each new day
"I'm waiting, why not me?"
The currency of time or talent
is how life takes its fee

Admission to your dreams
is not through luck or rolling dice
The door will open wide
when you decide to pay the price!

The Price Of Admission
Walt's Life Rhyme #179

"I share what I know,
so that others may grow!"
www.LifeRhymes.com

Commentary:

If things aren't moving forward the way you wish, it might be because you don't have the right ticket for the journey. But how do you get that ticket? What's the price, and whom do you pay? The answer is you pay with your time and/or your talent. Could it be that you need to invest more of your time in a project or to a cause? Maybe it's your talent you need to develop and offer to the world. With that outlook foremost in mind, you'll always be adding value to the world, you'll keep busy as you move toward the thing you desire, and no one will be able to deny you the right to gain admission!

Walt's Life Rhyme #178: Bigger Days

Bigger days are coming soon
don't ask me how I know
I feel it deep down in my gut
no way to prove or show

Brighter days are on the way
and I can hardly wait
With twice the sun as those before
I can't predict the date

Smoother days are on my path
goodbye to all the stress
A month, a year or by tonight
no clue, I must confess

I know it for the simple fact
that life's a ball they say
Sometimes it rolls to others and
sometimes it rolls my way!

Bigger Days
Walt's Life Rhyme #178

"I share what I know,
so that others may grow!"
www.LifeRhymes.com

Walt's Life Rhyme #177: Can I Wait That Far?

It's plain as day to those who see it
but hidden in the dust from some
The thing I'm seeing in the distance
my eyes tell me will soon come

But those who lack the vision
will think me psychic or seer
My only trick is how I pass time
until the thing I see draws near

Step by step the thing approaches
and lest you think it comes too late:
Image comes first and then thing follows
and good things come to those who wait

Yes, those with vision must have patience
it's just the way things are
The only question that needs your asking
is "Can I wait that far?"

Can I Wait That Far?
Walt's Life Rhyme #177

"I share what I know,
so that others may grow!"
www.LifeRhymes.com

Commentary:

Think about it. In the real world, as you travel along a path, you can usually see a thing approaching long before you are close enough to touch it. And the better your eyesight, the longer you may have to wait between the time you first see it, and the time it reaches you. And so it is in the realization of your dreams. The image of the thing you seek will usually be evident long before the thing itself. So, the question is, do you have the patience to wait until reality catches up to your vision?

Walt's Life Rhyme #176: Whoops!

Watch where you step for the ground is real slippery
watch where you sit for the paint's not yet dry
When there's trouble in Eden every move brings you danger
you just can't avoid it as hard as you try

Watch what you say for every topic is loaded
look but don't touch for the wound may be sore
And don't ever point for everyone is a suspect
beyond what eyes see you can bet there's much more

The best thing to do to avoid sure disaster:
keep thoughts to yourself so there's no cause for strife
Some battles are best fought by the ones who declared it
so back away slowly, and then run for your life!!

Whoops!
Walt's Life Rhyme #176

"I share what I know,
so that others may grow!"
www.LifeRhymes.com

Commentary:

Have you ever found yourself in the middle of a war you didn't declare? Have you ever walked into an already charged situation, said something innocent, then wished you could just hit rewind and walk back through time? Well, there's no way back, but there's always a way out! Don't walk, RUN, before it's too late!

Walt's Life Rhyme #175: The New Year Promises

Now what can I do different
in this new year that arrives?
What habits might make impact
in my own and other lives?

I promise that I'll smile more
at the people who I meet
I promise to remember names
of all those who I greet

I promise in my days
that I'll spend more time socializing
I promise in my thoughts
that I'll spend less time criticizing

I promise to remember
that life is not just about money
I promise to relax each day
and find at least one thing funny

I promise to forgive
at least one person every day
I promise compromise
and let one person have their way

I promise that I'll pay my debts
and never incur more
I promise to start saving
and keep it up, unlike before

I promise that I'll view the world
with love not out of fear
I promise that I'll treat myself
in ways that show I care

I promise that these promises
won't be just idle show
I think, therefore, I'm ready
on my mark now, get set, GO!

The New Year Promises
Walt's Life Rhyme #175

*"I share what I know,
so that others may grow!"*
www.LifeRhymes.com

Walt's Life Rhyme #174: Guess Who's Coming To The Rescue?

They say you've reached adulthood
when you come to terms with this:
If you don't come to rescue you
your knight will not exist

No armor-plated savior
riding in to save the day
No cavalry with guns ablaze
to chase your foes away

Don't think the world's indifferent
or can't see that you're in need
But history shows the passive
are the last ones to be freed

Help finds those who help themselves
so choose to right your plight
Wait for the world to come to you
and you might just wait all night

Who better than you to plan the escape?
who's more equipped to be the star?
Only you can find you in the fortress
for only you know where you are!

Guess Who's Coming To The Rescue? Part I
Walt's Life Rhyme #174

"I share what I know,
so that others may grow!"
www.LifeRhymes.com

Walt's Life Rhyme #173: Nourished From Within

The fish you catch when hungry
are a sad and sorry breed
You'll think the thief your savior
when you're in a state of need

You'll sell your soul for pennies
when resources are depleted
Your cause will go unchampioned
when you think yourself defeated

With hand outstretched and eyes cast low
what treasures can you gain?
When all that you project
is just a sad picture of pain

No, life rewards the one
who shows a constant will to win
Who knows through feast or famine
that she's nourished from within!

Nourished From Within
Walt's Life Rhyme #173

"I share what I know,
so that others may grow!"
www.LifeRhymes.com

Walt's Life Rhyme #172: Ok, But Is It Getting You What You Want? (time for a new refrain)

Put away the ego and act like you want it
put away the microscope and go with the flow
Put away the crutches and walk like a champion
stop being a critic and be part of the show

Drop the dead weight now and fly like an eagle
lean off your neighbor and stand like you're grown
No one brings gifts to a friend's pity party
the guests are just there to find guests for their own

Don't wait for perfection to show your commitment
don't wait to take action 'cause no one showed how
There'll always be flaws and a cause for excuses
so close the back door so there's one way out now

It's true that old ways give a good deal of comfort
and when you feel stressed yes they come back to haunt
And I know you have more than a short list of reasons
that's all well and good, but is it getting you what you want?

Ok, But Is It Getting You What You Want?
Walt's Life Rhyme #172

"I share what I know,
so that others may grow!"
www.LifeRhymes.com

Commentary:

"I won't do THIS until THAT happens."
"I've been hurt before, so I don't trust too easily."
"I need to know everything up front before I take a chance."
"What do you think he/she meant by that?"
"This is what you need to do in order for me to consider you."
"If only someone would help me, I could do this."

Do any of these refrains sound familiar? They, along with many other things we tell ourselves when faced with new opportunities to trust, risk, and step forth on faith, are the crutches we use to feel comfortable and safe in our decisions NOT to do the thing that needs to be done. They are the "liner notes" with the lyrics of our lives that we've gotten used to hearing ourselves recite. Now listen. I understand your history, your fears and your concerns completely. But is that way of thinking and way of being getting you what you want? If not, then "put away the ego and act like you want it...." (repeat and fade to end)

Inspired by Dorothy P.

Walt's Life Rhyme #171: A Club Called Me

In a crowded room I stand
with members only just like me
I look at who's invited
and I'm surprised at what I see

For every word of sorrow spoken
someone there says, "Me too"
The jealous meet the hateful
and share the selfsame point of view

But in the very room we gather
seems other clubs meet here as well
The bright and cheerful find their members
we're all mixed in, how can they tell?

You'd expect just mass confusion
when all these clubs at once do meet
The truth is that we find our peers
whether in clubs or on the street

For ski clubs don't draw golfers
and humble clubs repel the vain
The miserable and their company
attract the ones who think the same

So if I look at how I'm living
and don't like the things I see
I can't throw blame on those around
they're just members of a club called me!

Commentary:

I can always count on Gary Zukav (author of *Seat of The Soul*) to give me something interesting to think about. I'm now reading his *Soul Stories* and happened upon his analogy of life being like a club you join. I won't give away much more than that (you'll have to pick up a copy for yourself) except to say:

"In a club called whatever you're wishing for, you'll find others who wish for it too. But you only get to join the club with people who think like you."

A Club Called Me
Walt's Life Rhyme #171
© Walt F.J. Goodridge
"I share what I know,
so that others may grow!"
www.LifeRhymes.com

Walt's Life Rhyme #170: You Can't Get It Back

No refunds, no cash back
no two for one split
It's a one ticket journey
no u-turns, that's it

No recounts, no rewind
no instant replay
No chance to do over
or re-live this day

No recalls, no upgrades
no trade-in for you
Take care of the rental
you can't ask for two

One shuffle, one deal
and one throw of the dice
Play your hand like a winner
you can't play it twice

Time passes and heeds not
the choices you make
By choice make the most
of the time that you take!

You Can't Get It Back
Walt's Life Rhyme #170

"I share what I know,
so that others may grow!"
www.LifeRhymes.com

Commentary:

Arguments for reincarnation notwithstanding, it's generally agreed upon that this journey is not a practice run, but a one-time chance to get things right. So while you may have the time to review, rethink, revise, react, and remake your life from one day to the next, you don't have the option of getting back the time you lose in doing so! *Dedicated to Christine S.*

Walt's Life Rhyme #169: Undecided
For US Election 2000

What if each vote was like a thought in the mind of a single individual facing the challenge of making a decision. What would a conversation between one's two selves sound like when one is undecided?

I'm leaning more towards the left
The right's inviting too
But what of this vote over here?
Now what on earth are we to do?

Ok, let's start this thing again
Here's one for you and one for me
Let's get this done once and for all
And keep your thoughts where I can see

No compromise, no halfway point
No suspect shades of gray
Each thought to go this way or that
casts one vote into the fray

When pros and cons are tallied
the course I choose will then be clear
My destiny awaits
I step forth bold and have no fear

I'll thank the stars when this is done
to end this hesitation
A confused mind remains at rest
and claims no destination.

Undecided
Walt's Life Rhyme #169

"I share what I know, so that others may grow!"
www.LifeRhymes.com

Commentary

....now was that two million and seven or two million and seventy???......
oh, heck...>sigh<......one for me.....one for you.......two for me....two for you.....three.....

Walt's Life Rhyme #168: Interested? I Must Have Missed That Day

Interested?

I need to know who's interested
so I can make a move
If I only knew the cues and tips
successes might improve

I've noticed when there's interest
that they sometimes make the call
But then they'll stop and wait for days
so I can't use that at all

So then I thought I'd make the call
and see who calls me back
"Pursuer makes the calls", I'm told
"don't rail against this fact"

I've learned that if they're open
that I'll be allowed to touch
But then they'll pull back
claiming that they're not inclined to such

Some tell me that in dating
that the man should always pay
Trade dollars for affection?
hmmm...is that the game we play?

Then, even if they SAY "I am",
minds change one day to next
Consistency is not the norm
I end up feeling vexed

So tell me once again, dear friend
(it doesn't have to rhyme)
How do I know who's interested
so I don't waste my time?

"I Must Have Missed That Day"

I missed that day the teacher said
"Ok, class, settle down!
Today you learn your roles in life,
so please now gather 'round

The dating game is easy
once you know just what's expected
If not, you'll just keep striking out
and risk feeling rejected

Your roles as boys and girls are these:
pursuer and pursued
He opens doors, he pays the bill
she cleans and cooks the food

He'll be the one to ask her out
she'll be demure and shy
You listening you there in the back?
No Johnny, don't ask why."

It seems most learned the dos and don'ts
much earlier in life
Well on their way to find and be
that nice husband or wife

But those of us who missed that day
quite often feel like fools
How thrilling it must be to know
the game and all its rules

Interested? I Must Have Missed That Day
Walt's Life Rhyme #168

"I share what I know,
so that others may grow!"
www.LifeRhymes.com

Walt's Life Rhyme #167: Still Keeping Score?

There was a time
not long ago
I kept a mental list
of all I spent
and all I got
so nothing would be missed

Who paid for what?
how much is mine?
make sure it evens out
In time I learned
the tally's not
what this is all about

While keeping score
I missed the things
no ledger can record
like love and trust
and friendly hearts
that can't be saved or stored

So now I give
straight from the heart
no invoice, notes or pad
and find this life
and times with friends
the best I've ever had!

Still Keeping Score?
Walt's Life Rhyme #167

"I share what I know,
so that others may grow!"
www.LifeRhymes.com

Commentary:

The more you love, the more you give
the less you will keep score.
The more you give, the more you get
you'll never end up poor!

Walt's Life Rhyme #166: What Will It Take?

What will it take to raise the bar
and give it all you've got?
Will habits keep you stagnant
'til the fire gets too hot?

Or will it take the loss
of everything that you hold dear
To push you into action now
despite that inner fear?

Or will you wait until your back
is up against the wall
To finally say, "You know what,
I can do this after all!"?

Perhaps you'll have to look back
on a life filled with regrets
Before you break the cycle
and no longer hedge your bets

Or, maybe in the morning
when you see the world anew
You'll just decide to do it
and show yourself what you can do!

What Will It Take?
Walt's Life Rhyme #166:

"I share what I know,
so that others may grow!"
www.LifeRhymes.com

Walt's Life Rhyme #165: The Short List

There's a real short list of friends I call
to be my helping hand
For help must be condition-free
and this few understand

There's yet a shorter list of those
I tell my troubles to
Who share new ways of thinking
and enlightened points of view

The list is even shorter still
of those I really trust
What pain it is to find your values
trampled in the dust

You enter on this list of mine
to find your rank and station
Not via public thoroughfare
but special invitation

Choose NOT your love or friend
from just the free, fine, fit and able
But ask of who would be with you
"What do YOU bring to the table?"

The Short List
Walt's Life Rhyme #165
© Walt F.J. Goodridge
"I share what I know,
so that others may grow!"
www.LifeRhymes.com

Commentary:

Of course, in fairness, you too should have a clear idea of what YOU bring to the table. What do YOU have to offer those who would have you in THEIR lives. It's not enough to simply want the right person. It's often more critical to BE the right person.

Walt's Life Rhyme #164: The Elephant Under The Rug

Perhaps we can avoid it
and it just might go away
Perhaps you'll read my mind
and hear the words I want to say

We wouldn't be the first to use
this tried and true technique
It's often easier to avoid
assume rather than speak

It's like there is this elephant
we're pretending isn't there
We talk and walk around it
treading lightly and with care

You'd think it near impossible
to ignore something so huge
That's begging for attention
and has taken up refuge

We trip and fall and stumble
as intentions meet with doom
For no real progress can be made
while this "thing" is in the room

A misread cue or act, perhaps
an unmet expectation
Requires some word or deed now
in defense or explanation

(Or maybe it's the fire
of a strong physical attraction
You say it's just a friendship
but you feel the mounting tension)

This thing's too real and heavy
to dismiss with just a shrug
So speak the words and dare to face
the elephant under the rug!

The Elephant Under The Rug
Walt's Life Rhyme #164

*"I share what I know,
so that others may grow!"*
www.LifeRhymes.com

Commentary:

Closure. Resolution. Intention. Revelation. Clarification. The "elephant under the rug" takes on many forms in our lives. There's something in your life that has gone unsaid and unaddressed for too long that is casting a shadow of doubt and uncertainty, and leaving itself open to misinterpretation. Stop avoiding it. The only way to move it out from under the rug is to put it in plain view so it can be addressed, discussed, seen for what it is, and ultimately resolved. Give it a try. Words are the best way to move the mighty elephant. It might be heavy at first, but if everyone involved does some lifting, you'll make it work!

Walt's Life Rhyme #163: What If?

What if that sense of emptiness
is not based on fact at all
And help and love are waiting
and all you have to do is call?

What if the rejection
is just all in your own mind
And folks are not all evil
but are mostly good and kind?

What if all their actions
are not really out of hate
But caused by thoughts arising
from a confused and fearful state?

What if all the doors that slammed
were just not yours yet to explore
And opportunities await you
with more abundance yet in store?

What if all the barriers
are really there for your own good
And someone's keeping you safe and sound
like a guardian angel should?

What if the delays
are no real reason for alarm
But interventions from above
that keep you free from harm?

What if all the pain you feel
is just a passing thing
And makes you that much stronger
and has lessons it could bring?

What if that winding gauntlet
were really fans lined up for miles
Who wait the chance to cheer you on
and shower you with smiles?

And what if your perspective
is what decides your every day
What changes could you make
if you just see things a different way?

What if?
Walt's Life Rhyme #163
© Walt F.J. Goodridge
"I share what I know,
so that others may grow!"
www.LifeRhymes.com

Commentary:

Choosing to accept the "what if" of our dreams is the universal challenge. In the acceptance of what might be, we must give up the comfort of who we are, and face the uncertainty and vulnerability of who we wish to become. At other times, we battle with negative "what ifs" and ask ourselves, "But what if I lose?" "What if they're really rejecting me?" "What if there's really no one there for me?" Well, there's no right or wrong. There are simply choices to make. Some choices will be easy. Some will be hard. Make the choice of which "what if" will rule your every day by choosing the "what if" that empowers YOU and those you love.

Walt's Life Rhyme #162: A Private Conversation

Of course I value your opinions,
I have to, 'cause mine don't seem to work
My views of how and why things are
cause me too much pain and hurt

Each time I think I have a handle
turns out I really hold the blade
And cut after cut my heart reveals
the fragile stuff of which I'm made

But before you start to pity me
or throw me a rescue rope
Rest assured I'll always bounce back
for one thing I always have is hope

And know that even in the darkness
when things don't seem to go my way
I know my future isn't tied to my past
so I start fresh with each new day!

A Private Conversation
Walt's Life Rhyme #162

"I share what I know,
so that others may grow!"
www.LifeRhymes.com

Walt's Life Rhyme #161: The Benefit of Change

I tell myself and others
I'm just too set in my ways
They say that I can change
and live life free these later days

But what of the excuses
that have kept me safe from fault?
The comfort of my failures
that brought dreaming to a halt?

For how would I then manage
with no designated foes?
No "them" or "they" oppressors
I can blame for all my woes

These tried and true beliefs
are like my friends I love and know
They comfort me by telling me
"That's just the way things go."

But have I crafted for myself
a world of my own choice?
Are all the fears and pain I know
just echoes of MY voice?

I need to see the benefits first
before I let it go
Perhaps this final verse reveals
the words I need to grow:

Don't ask to see the benefit
as if incentive, bribe or fee
The benefit is you now can choose
the way you wish your world to be!

The Benefit of Change
Walt's Life Rhyme #161

"I share what I know,
so that others may grow!"
www.LifeRhymes.com

OUTTAKE: ALTERNATE VERSE 5
But have I crafted for myself
a world of my own choosing?
Are all the fears and pain I know
just me intent on losing?

Commentary:

The benefit of change is not something you search for to justify the decision to change. The benefit of change is that by changing you get to create the world of your choice.

Dedicated to J. C.

Walt's Life Rhyme #160: But That's What I Heard

What I meant and said was this, my dear
too bad you didn't hear it
It's not what you now think at all
I'd never say that, I swear it

I thought I said it plain as day
perhaps I wasn't clear
Or perhaps you simply heard again
the thing that you most fear

I'll tell it to you once again
don't let your ears deceive
But listen without bias now
and try hard to believe

I said that I would never leave
until the end of time
You heard that I was bound to go
it's just a matter of time

I said I think you're special
and that others can't compete
You heard that there are others
and already fear defeat

It's funny how you heard the words
despite their best intentions
To fit the world you've always known
the world of your invention

No words of mine are ever meant
to limit, harm or slay
But know what it may say of YOU
if YOU hear them that way!

Commentary:

It happens quite often that I'll get a compliment or some words of praise from friends or strangers, and then hours later can't remember what they actually said. Seems I turn a deaf ear to compliments since I never learned how to accept them as true. Or sometimes during a conversation, I'll interpret something someone says in one (negative) way, only to find out that they meant it in an entirely different (often complimentary) way. Are you the same way? Do you brush off, act undeserving of, or nullify good tidings? If you hear a statement that might have a dual interpretation, or if you miss a few words in a conversation, do you often fill in the blanks the way you think things are, or have always been for you?

Well, from now on (especially in your close relationships), learn to REALLY hear, accept and believe the compliments and praise people offer you, and learn how to REALLY listen to what that special person is saying so that you won't have to say:

But That's What I Heard
Walt's Life Rhyme #160:

*"I share what I know,
so that others may grow!"*
www.LifeRhymes.com

Walt's Life Rhyme #159: On Fire (A Dream)

I was awakened this morning by a dream I'd like to share with you.

I saw a homeless man on fire
by that I mean he was ablaze
Oblivious to his condition
asleep he was and in a daze

I rushed to offer my assistance
and used his clothes to out the flame
Then splashed him full and whole with water
lest heat from it should scorch or maim

Now drenched and soaked and fully wakened
none wiser to his almost fate
Mistook my act of human kindness
to be an act of callous hate

He chased and cursed me through the streets
now pelting me with rock and word
For so intent on retribution
my explanations went unheard

But to my protests he soon listened
then saw his charred and smoldered clothes
The dream ends there without conclusion
what does this mean do you suppose?

On Fire
Walt's Life Rhyme #159

"I share what I know,
so that others may grow!"
www.LifeRhymes.com

Commentary:

Remember: you can't effectively help another, or expect their full cooperation or appreciation for pulling them out of misery unless they feel the fire of their condition and in fact WANT to be helped.

Walt's Life Rhyme #158: In The Interest of Time

In the interest of time
I'll cut right to the chase
Please don't sleep on your dreams
now's the time to make haste

Yes, each day is a stride
every year like a lap
Don't choose the final stretch
to start closing the gap

(You're not competing with others
let's get that clear from the start
But for how much you live
within the beats of your heart)

It's no fun playing catch up
to make up for lost time
Seize the day and the moment
the waste of life is a crime

My best advice then is this,
as you dash through this race:
Don't wait for the final bell
before you step up the pace!

In The Interest of Time
Walt's Life Rhyme #158

*"I share what I know,
so that others may grow!"*
www.LifeRhymes.com

Commentary:

The reason more people change careers and/or start their own business later in life has more to do with a sense of urgency than anything else. As years progress, many people start to evaluate their accomplishments, their sense of fulfillment and the purpose of their lives here on our little planet. And just like in a long distance race when that last bell rings signaling the final lap, many people hear their own internal bell reminding them that they'd better get going, or else. Don't wait for the last bell!

Walt's Life Rhyme #157: freshwater yearnings
aka The Little Fish That Tried

I'm swimming in saltwater
and I'm choking on the brine
Immersed in an environment
that's poison to my kind

The waves may shine and glitter
and the eye the lake doth soothe
But thick it is with obstacles
that slow my every move

I long to live in waters
that support fishes like me
And swim unbound in schools of thought
that lift and set me free

I know that I will get there
for I've made that silent vow
Freshwater is my destiny
someday, someway, somehow

I fight an upstream battle
and yes, I swim against the tide
But freedom waits I'm sure
for I'm the little fish that tried!

freshwater yearnings
Walt's Life Rhyme #157
© Walt F.J. Goodridge
"I share what I know,
so that others may grow!"
www.LifeRhymes.com

Commentary:

Sometimes being in certain relationships can feel like you're drowning in an ocean that's getting saltier and more toxic every day. If you need fresh water to survive, but your "other" is a deep sea dweller that thrives on salt water, can the two species cohabitate successfully? Or must one or the other seek their natural habitat? What's a fish to do?

Walt's Life Rhyme #156: O "Circles And Lines" |

Some people walk in circles
every day the same old track
Some people walk in lines
from A to B and don't look back

Some people talk in circles
their points far between and few
And others' lines of reason
block all other thoughts from view

Some people live in circles
much too small to let life in
And some draw lines to tell you
where you end and they begin

Well if those circles stretch a bit
their reach they might extend
And lives distraught may turn to joy
if rigid lines would bend!

Commentary:

Circle of influence. Circle of friends.
Line of thought. Boundary line.
All have the capacity to imprison or free.
Success comes from knowing when to widen the circles and bend the lines that govern your life.

Please share this with someone you love who needs to widen and bend. And if that person is you, then simply take heed.

Circles and Lines
Walt's Life Rhyme #156

*"I share what I know,
so that others may grow!"*
www.LifeRhymes.com

Walt's Life Rhyme #155: Casting Spells

For all our lives unconscious
now it's time to take control
No such thing as magic?
Just forget what you've been told

Casting spells is easy,
let the lesson now begin
To have all that you wish for
it must first exist within

Choose your best obsession
or one you think stands in your way
What words would make your dreams come true?
or love to hear them say?

Next script the words exactly
As a playwright writes a play
Then feel the way that you would feel
And practice what you'd say

Now do this often every day
at day's dawn and at the close
In time the words will find their home
expressed by whom you chose

The secret's that your thoughts
awaken thoughts in others too
(So who's to say your actions
are not another's thoughts of you?)

And know that this will always work
in no uncertain terms
For every word that's spoken
will create what it affirms

No magic wand, enchanted brew
or potions you need sell
Just focused thoughts with feeling
casts the world under your spell!

Casting Spells
Walt's Life Rhyme #155

"I share what I know,
so that others may grow!"
www.LifeRhymes.com

Commentary:

The laws of the universe apply to all things. So whether for a business conquest, more customers, artistic recognition, investors, or for true romantic love, create the words that reflect your success, hear them being spoken in the voice of your partner, investor, customer, or other intended, and respond to them just as if you were engaged in a real conversation. Once these words are sent into the ether, know that they must, by law find their physical counterpart and objectify to the degree that your subject can see the same for themselves and to the degree that you in fact are convinced of their reality.

Spiritual author, Neville, likens this to a radio transmission which starts as words, are transformed into radio waves, finds a receiver tuned to the same frequency, and are then transformed back into the same words but now emanating from the receiver. So cast a spell by writing the script for your desired scene, and while you're at it, send this Life Rhyme to that one person or to as many people as you want to enchant!

Walt's Life Rhyme #154: I Ain't Goin' Out Like That!

HOW are you going out?
with a whimper or a roar?
Basking in the light of your best
or always knowing you could have been more?

How ARE you going out?
With a flicker or a flame?
A has-been that never was
or as the Tiger of your game?

How are YOU going out?
Dressed to impress or to spread gloom?
Will others be brightened or will they frown
when you walk into the room?

How are you going out?
Intent to conquer or set to bow?
Living the life of your dreams
or never making that silent vow?

I say go OUT the way you came in
a gift expected, celebrated and wished
Rise to the heights of your you-ness
And live your life so you'll be missed!

Commentary:

"I ain't goin' out like that!"

When I first heard a friend utter those words in response to a challenge in his life, I realized that—despite its offensiveness to students of proper English, it summed up in a unique way my own feelings towards success, failure, accomplishments, fate, my work ethic, and my ability to control my outcomes.

Since then, it's been my silent mantra whenever faced with a situation or challenges that threaten to keep me back, or an event that seeks to write a chapter in my story that I don't want written.

"I ain't goin' out like that!" says that when the final chapter is indeed written, that *"That's NOT the way I want my story to go! That's NOT what I want people to say about me! That's NOT how I want to be remembered! That's not what I will allow to take me out of the game!"*

And when faced with a challenge that is poised to relegate me to obscurity or to second place, those six words give me the energy to dig deep inside and pull out the necessary energy, stamina, thoughts, words and deeds to do what must be done, and then I do it. 'Cause I mean it, I AIN'T GOIN' OUT LIKE THAT!!!! (Ah, if my High School English teacher, Mr. Arcari, could hear me now!)

"I Ain't Goin' Out Like That!"
Walt's Life Rhyme #154

*"I share what I know,
so that others may grow!"*
www.LifeRhymes.com

Walt's Life Rhyme #153: Mental Coup d'etat
(An Allegory for Revolution)

Charge the hill and take it
while the sentry is asleep
The time to launch attacks is when
the world's in slumber deep

The guard is down and weakened
and the doors are opened wide
When walls are left unwatched
then is the time to shift the tide

By day the troops are active
but by night when all do rest
You'll catch the world off guard
and win the day without protest

Like soldiers habits linger
intent to keep you down and low
But a single dream empowered
is all it takes to overthrow!

Mental Coup d'etat
Walt's Life Rhyme #153

*"I share what I know,
so that others may grow!"*
www.LifeRhymes.com

Commentary:

The Key to the allegory:

The "world" is you. The "soldiers" are your old thoughts you've empowered to keep watch and maintain things as they are. They are the appointed sentries of self-imposed limitations, standing ever watchful to block your uprising. The "rebels" are your dreams and desires intent on overthrowing the established order. The rebels seek a moment when your own guard is down to successfully stage the mental coup that will set you free.

The "night" represents such a time of lowered defenses. A time brought about by pleasant experiences, uplifting conversation, positive associations, or simply the silence of your own meditation. Give your dreams the "cover" they need to work in your favor. Make the most of those days when you feel like you can take on the world. Make the most of your time with those who strengthen and empower you. Your rebel dreams will recognize that the sentries are "asleep" and the coast is clear to win control! Now read the allegory again and go onward to your personal mental victory!

Walt's Life Rhyme #152: Sellers Market

When markets close and scores are tallied
"sellers" always win the day
The ones who hawk their wares eternal
always know just what to say

But "buyers" meanwhile wonder
if what they're getting is pure gold
No matter how the purchase pleases
they only choose from what they're sold

What's true for stocks and bonds and products
holds true for love, ideas and thought
Yes, any thing you have of value
was sold FIRST, and THEN bought

So set a worth that makes you priceless
then make your pitch and make it count
And every part of you that's selling
endears you by the same amount

(So you can wait and then be sold to,
or you can be the one to sell.
They'll never know your wit and wonder
unless it shows or 'til you tell)

Commentary:

How will they know just how valuable, and lovable, and wonderful, and witty, and caring, and loving and likeable you are, unless you sell it or tell it? Don't be above selling. You do it every day, and in every way. You sell your skills to an employer, you sell your product to the world, you sell "the joy of getting to know you" to the one you fancy.

It's been shown that most businesses fail, and most hearts go untouched, because their owners don't know how to sell, or somehow they feel they shouldn't have to sell. Don't make that mistake. Sell! Sell! Sell! (Note: Not to be confused with "selling out" or "selling yourself short" or "selling your soul.")

Sellers Market
Walt's Life Rhyme #152

*"I share what I know,
so that others may grow!"*
www.LifeRhymes.com

Walt's Life Rhyme #151: In Final Preparation

If Success today knocked at your door
would you be ready to let it in?
If the life you want said, "Come let's go!"
would you know where to begin?

If the journey you prayed and hoped for
was yours to take with ease
Would your bags be packed and waiting
or would you say, "Just hold on please?"

Well don't wait for invitations
to write your ticket to the ball
Prepare for good in all its guises
so you'll be ready for the call

Make room for all the visitors
buy the clothes that you will wear
And if you dream of fame and fortune,
then write the words you want to hear

Between hope and preparation
There's a difference by design:
One's the light you'll use to guide you
one's the switch that makes it shine!

Commentary:

It's often been said that it's better to be prepared and not have an opportunity, than to have an opportunity and not be prepared. The act of preparing for your dreams can often be the single step necessary that brings them to reality. So have your ticket waiting!

In Final Preparation
Walt's Life Rhyme #151

"I share what I know,
so that others may grow!"
www.LifeRhymes.com

Walt's Life Rhyme #150: The River And The Rock

What would happen if you placed a wall
in the middle of a river? Try to block it
and the river will stop, rise to the level of
the obstruction and flow easily over it.

Would that I too were just like a river
rising surely to the level of the rocks
I would meet any challenge before me in life
and then surpass any and all of the blocks

For whatever terrain I encounter
whether canyon or rocks bent on wrath
They would never affect the way to my goal
but would mean I just alter my path

Nor would I fear any precipice
nor any cliff no matter how tall
But leap self-assured that the best is to come
for water shows much beauty when it falls

And in the process of seeking my level
eventually I would reach the sea
And reunited with the source from whence I have
come
I'd become the very thing I seek to be!

The River And The Rock
[Excerpt from The River And The Rock by
Walt Goodridge, an unpublished manuscript]

"I share what I know,
so that others may grow!"
www.LifeRhymes.com

The Moral Of The Story:

The river rises to the level of any obstruction.

The terrain only affects the river's path, not its progress.

The river is not afraid to fall.

The river seeks the path of least resistance.

The river eventually becomes the thing it seeks.

Walt's Life Rhyme #149: What Are You Rehearsing?

What scenes do you rehearse each day
when idle thoughts prevail?
The power scenes in which you win
or ones in which you fail?

Is your mind wrapped up in "what if" thoughts
in practice for a fight?
Do butterflies abound inside
when you go to bed at night?

"Oh boy, I just can't wait 'til then,
Show her a thing or two!
And this is what I'll say to that!
and this is what I'll do!"

Rehashing scenes that have since passed
and what you should have said?
Or pining for a rematch
though the moment's gone and dead?

Instead of "no", "not", "never", "can't"
let's play a different game
Affirm "I have", "I will", "I can"
"I love you just the same"

The funny thing 'bout life is this
(and please take this to heart)
When you practice roles first in your mind
you often get to play the part!

What Are You Rehearsing?
Walt's Life Rhyme #149

"I share what I know,
so that others may grow!"
www.LifeRhymes.com

Commentary:

So whether it's that expected call from a creditor, or that impending showdown with your boss or coworker, or the ugly upcoming scene between you and your significant other, think about how much time you spend affirming, reinforcing and practicing your lines for undesirable scenes. Consider how much strength you lose when you mentally "show up for the showdown", instead of putting your thoughts to better use.

Think about how much more productive and empowered you would be if you used the same energy instead to affirm the positive. It takes about the same amount of energy, you know, but will make your days much less stressful! Try it!

But, if you feel you really need to be prepared for that scene, then here's a tip: plan what you'll say, and write it down so you won't forget. THEN spend the rest of the time rehearsing the *ideal* desirable scene; the one in which you have the money, the one where all goes well, the one where all is healed and everyone is happy. Steep your thoughts in *that* reality and notice how you feel today.

You may find that when you practice the success script in your mind, that you never have to use any other in real life.

Walt's Life Rhyme #148: The Game

Caught up, wrapped up, blocked and barred
in a desperate bid for the ball
It's easy to forget sometimes
it's just a game now after all

Bruised and battered, tossed and turned
feels like persecution of some sort
But you're no more victim of this life
than a player is victim of sport

You chose the game now play it well
opposing teams will do what they must
So dodge and leap and overcome
with some teammates you know you can trust

Spectator and player both you must be
step back and watch yourself score
Your mortal trappings are yours to transcend
Yep, that's really what it's for

The strategy then is play to win
aim to do more than just simply survive
The goal is to recover your greatness in life
the final objective is to learn how to thrive!

The Game
Walt's Life Rhyme #148

*"I share what I know,
so that others may grow!"*
www.LifeRhymes.com

Commentary:

Here's a quote from *Do Less, Achieve More* by Chin-Ning Chu:
*"The rules of business, life and sports are
all about overcoming strong oppositional forces.
The ball game becomes a metaphor for life.
Problems occur when we forget that stress is
an inevitable part of the human condition. Have
fun playing the game of your life."*

Walt's Life Rhyme #147: Your Right

You have the right to freedom, yes
and all that means to you
You have the right to be yourself
let none choose you for you

You have the right to speak your mind
let none suppress your voice
You have the right too NOT to hear
and exercise that choice

You have the right to disconnect
if someone holds you back
You have the right to prosper now
despite a past of lack

You have the right to keep your toys
away from harm or theft
(But sometimes in this world of things
your right is all that's left!)

And anything you say or do
can be used to bind or free
So use these rights to live your dreams
make them your new decree!

Your Right
Walt's Life Rhyme #147

"I share what I know,
so that others may grow!"
www.LifeRhymes.com

Walt's Life Rhyme #146: The Right Question

Your life is the answer to a question
you'll find responding is not the real task
No, the trick to living life with purpose you see
is knowing which question to ask

Some ask "Why me?" in frustration
and respond with a life filled with pain
Some ask "What's next?" with elation
and on happiness they seem to make gain

"What's in it for me?" others query
and seem forever on a self-centered quest
"What more can I be?" a small few wonder
and show others their personal best

"What's wrong with the world? Oh, how tragic!"
Some see with eyes of woe and despair
"What's wrong with the world? Let me fix it!"
And those strive always to heal and repair

So all in all it's a question of answers
that determines if you win or you lose
For when life is an answer to a question
your life depends on which question you choose!

The Right Question
Walt's Life Rhyme #146

"I share what I know,
so that others may grow!"
www.LifeRhymes.com

Commentary for Walt's Life Rhyme #146

As an expert in five business categories on several popular expert websites, I receive dozens of questions from people wanting to know the answers to various business concerns. Yesterday morning, I received a question from "Stromie." I'm not sure whether Stromie was a child asking an innocent question, or an older person in a prankster's mood, but I took the time to answer seriously.

stromie asked:
"what will i be when i grow up???"
"how much money will i make??? "

Stromie's questions arrived in my inbox a full day after I had completed what is now today's Life Rhyme #146. Although it arrived a day after the fact, it seemed the perfect question to the Life Rhyme I had written! So here then, is my answer to Stromie, along with today's Life Rhyme which was already prepared and waiting for him/her to ask just the right question.

Hi Stromie,

That's an EXCELLENT question! Whether you're a child or adult, remember you're always growing, and what you will be from one moment to the next is completely under your control. It's great that you're asking these sorts of questions, because many people never start to really ask the right questions until they're quite unhappy in life. But instead of asking ME what you will be when you grow up, ask yourself instead "what do I love to do?" "What is it that excites me and how do I want to spend my days?" Those questions will lead you in the direction of your passion, which as you may know, is where I always direct people.

How much money you will make is not as important as "what sort of difference can you make." It's been said that you should "Do what you love and the money will follow." I sincerely believe that and I am also a living testament to that philosophy. Keep asking the right questions, my friend!

Walt's Life Rhyme #145: If Only For A Moment

No sugar coats, no candy wraps
no lens of rosy hue
What mountains could you move my friend
what magic would you do?

If things were seen for what they are
without the smoke and mirrors
Transparent would the takers be
revealed would be the givers

And lies would shrink in light of day
and truth would not retire
And eyes that could decipher
would spot wolves in sheeps' attire

The distance between who you'll be
and who you think you are
Once seen as but a single step
just wouldn't seem that far

Just for a moment work with me
allow yourself to see
And know in all its shapes and forms
the truth DOES set you free!

Commentary:

The truth of your situation, the truth of another's intentions towards you, the truth of what you've been allowing people to get away with, the truth of what you could really accomplish if you accepted the truth of your greatness--recognizing the truth in all its manifestations in your life is the key to responding in your own best interests and moving forward in love instead of fear! Don't you see it?

If Only For A Moment
Walt's Life Rhyme #145

"I share what I know,
so that others may grow!"
www.LifeRhymes.com

Walt's Life Rhyme #144: Ask The Inspirer
Restless

Dear Walt,
I am a 27 year old female with a Master's in counseling education. I am restless! My interests include traveling, watching sports, writing, and sleeping. Yes, sleeping!! I am an avid football fan, and I love working with teen-agers. Because I don't like my job and I don't possess as much money as I desire in order to do the things I like, I find myself unmotivated and caught in the monotony of work. Sometimes people ask me what it is I want to do, and my response is "I don't know." To be honest, if I had my way, I'd have enough money and influence that I would not need to work for money, but instead travel, have fun, sleep, and volunteer my time to nonprofit organizations that really serve in the best interest of children, especially teen-agers. Several people have encouraged me to go back to school and get a Ph. D. I have no desire to add another degree to my resume. Right now, I just want to have fun and enjoy life; I don't see going back to school factoring into that equation. Please help me make sense of what I am feeling! Thanks - Restless

Hi Restless,

Personally, I think you're a quite normal human being. You're simply feeling the tug of a quite healthy realization that there must be more to life than this. I felt the same way for years when I was caught up in the corporate day-to-day. It wasn't until I decided to pursue my passion and walk away from my job that life, with all its ups and downs, started to take on a new thrill.

I'm sure the sleeping is just a reaction to the absence of passion in your life. It's quite tiring to keep up the facade, don't you think? And sleep is a great way to escape from having to face the frustration. I agree with you that a PhD may not be the way to go. The pursuit of higher degrees is often just a way for frightened folks to delay the inevitability of facing the reality of a life of quiet desperation.

When I ask passion seekers "what do you want to do?", I'm not asking "Who do you want to work for?" I'm asking "What adds passion to your life? If you didn't have to work for money, what would you rather be doing?" Your letter reveals some clues as to what that might be. You've already said that what moves you to action is to do something in the "best interest of children." I suggest you head in that direction. You've got to start living life from the feeling of the wish fulfilled. I followed my passion for music, and was first a radio deejay, then I managed artists, then started a record label, which eventually led me to start writing books to share my music industry knowledge with others, which has now led me to sharing my insights online and in workshops to help others find their passion. I believe I'm on the right track now, but I wouldn't have gotten here had I not taken that FIRST step in the direction of my passion, and been willing to change course as required. So take a step towards your passion. It may not be the final answer, but it may be your first direction.

Eventually you'll discover things about yourself you never knew. You'll get to know your motivation, your mission, and the underlying feeling that you seek to have in your life. You'll be able to harness your talents to devise a passion-centered life that brings you the fulfillment you seek. Now it may not be that you'll start a business around your passion, though I believe you could easily do so. But an end to the restlessness you feel starts with taking that first step.

Walt's Life Rhyme #144: Restless

Living a life of false pretense
can make you feel so tired
You've got to find a passion, friend
to make you feel inspired

Some people think the answer
lies in higher education
But that may simply be a way
to hide one's true frustration

So ask yourself: With all needs met
what would I rather do?
What value can I add to life
that may help others too?

Don't think in terms of profit first
for money's not the thing
What matters is the journey
and the growth that it will bring

The restlessness you feel
is your desire to be more
Decide then to jump into life
and all it has in store!

Restless
Walt's Life Rhyme #144

"I share what I know,
so that others may grow!"
www.LifeRhymes.com

Walt's Life Rhyme #143: What If I Shine Too Bright?

I have a friend whose greatness shows
who holds herself in doubt
When others give her praise
prefers they whisper but not shout

Afraid she just won't measure up
the way that others see her
She shrinks from praise and accolades
the consummate self-deceiver

Genius concealed, greatness denied
her power held at bay
Her greater self: a lesser self
afraid of what they'll say

In fearing that our flaws
will much too soon be brought to light
We douse our flame, and dim our beam
and dare not shine too bright

But heed not words, both good and bad
(we fear both first and latter)
Embrace the truth of who you are
so others' words won't matter

What If I Shine Too Bright?
Walt's Life Rhyme #143

"I share what I know,
so that others may grow!"
www.LifeRhymes.com

Commentary:

I told her that it's not the responsibility of others to downplay their admiration for her because she is afraid to burst their bubble by being human. The key is to center herself in the single truth of who she is so that neither others' good nor bad opinions will displace her core, and to know that, in the words of George Clinton, "everybody's got a little light, under the sun!" So let it shine for others to see!

Inspired by and Dedicated to Denise C., Z.O., & O.F.

Walt's Life Rhyme #142: The Hidden Whole

It might seem paranormal, yes
to those who don't believe
But those who see beyond the veil
create what they conceive

If all minds are connected
then no thought can stand apart
Your dreams and mine are really one
we share a common heart

We see ourselves as separate
when we miss the hidden whole
The place where we're just faces
of a single seeking soul

Impossible is real
for those who hold them to be true
When you see the whole in every part
these and greater will you do!

EXTRA CREDIT-BONUS VERSES:
Most people paint with brushes
dipped in palettes of self-doubt
Illusions of their weakness
block their secret powers out

What is and was is everywhere
and everything is everything
Repeat these magic words
and watch the power that they bring!

The Hidden Whole
Walt's Life Rhyme #142

"I share what I know,
so that others may grow!"
www.LifeRhymes.com

Walt's Life Rhyme #141: A Tale of Time For The Tardy

She said she needed a system
but I had none I could offer
no tried and true way to make passing time bend to her will

I said the answer's much deeper
than any pilot or planner
it's about self-expectation I'm afraid there's no magic pill

"I try so hard to be on time
for each appointment", she added.
"But I keep missing the boat, so tell me what should I do?"

When YOU see yourself as a winner
you'll act in line with that self-image
and do all that you can to make that vision of you be true

For those who don't show up on time
are not their own first priority
they've devalued themselves and placed something else up above

For you will notice in life
people make time for what they value
and they never need a system to be on time for what they love

Time it's true is just illusion
but can be servant or master
It can come when you beckon or it can flee and ignore

It seeks out those with a purpose
and favors those who are focused
Time even seems to pass slower for those who love themselves more!

A Tale of Time For The Tardy
Walt's Life Rhyme #141

"I share what I know,
so that others may grow!"
www.LifeRhymes.com

Walt's Life Rhyme #140: New Words To Live By

We choose to live our lives each day
by rules that we've been taught
And put our trust in dos and don'ts
that often come to naught

It's by such rules we live life
choosing safety over sorrow
We lose control of each today
and doom each new tomorrow

New ways, new rules, new people too
are yours to pick and choose
So keep the ones that serve you well
and others you refuse

The life lived in the present
comes from choices in your past
Each moment brings the chance to make
new choices that will last

So find new words to live by
yes, new thoughts that come from you
When free to choose another view
there's no telling what you'll do!

A New Words To Live By
Walt's Life Rhyme #140

"I share what I know,
so that others may grow!"
www.LifeRhymes.com

Walt's Life Rhyme #139: You Didn't Know?

You must not know just who I am
to try to keep me back
I'm not the one who shrinks in fear
or runs from an attack

Apparently you hadn't heard
I've not come here to bow
I've come this way to conquer
and show others their way how

Fear not the man who digs a pit
it's the digger who falls in
But blessed is he who sets his sail
then makes his very own wind!

(BONUS VERSE):
For no man exists that by himself
holds the keys to all your doors
Proceed with faith and have no doubt
you'll ALWAYS get what's truly yours!!!

Dedicated to Terrie Williams

You Didn't Know?
Walt's Life Rhyme #139

"I share what I know,
so that others may grow!"
www.LifeRhymes.com

Walt's Life Rhyme #138: The Rules

Be clear on what you want
then take the time to set some rules
You'll build a life of dreams
if you will use these rules as tools

Don't make the rules then break them
then commence your daily whine
When others through their actions say
"These rules are yours not mine"

No, don't expect the rules to change
the things that people do
The rules are there for just one soul:
They're made for guiding YOU!

Commentary:

Decide what's acceptable and not in your life. Set your boundaries. Then let others know your rules. But know, most of all, that the most important person who needs to respect them is you!

The Rules
Walt's Life Rhyme #138

"I share what I know,
so that others may grow!"
www.LifeRhymes.com

Walt's Life Rhyme #137: All Of Me

Some will love your beauty
and will crave you for the view
Some are wooed well by your ways
and little things you do

Some want you for reasons
based entirely on lust
Some you'll win through honesty
you're someone they can trust

Inner charm, intelligence
your elegance and grace
Express themselves in outer ways
like features, form and face

And though you think these parts
are not in fact the real true you
All parts are part and parcel
of the you that's shining through

So fault not men for looking
shrink not guilty from the light
Say, "this I am and more "
And say it proud, with all your might!

For diamonds show all colors
when they're offered to the light
Each looker sees it differently
and everyone sees right!

Dedicated to O.F.

All Of Me
Walt's Life Rhyme #137

"I share what I know,
so that others may grow!"
www.LifeRhymes.com

Walt's Life Rhyme #136: Interview With An Inspirer

Transcribing words the truth is
that I merely hold the pen
And what I write are often truths
that help my own life mend

Is it because of who you are
you do the things you do?
Or is it through the things you do
you're molded into you?

From choices made it's said
that we too are made in turn
You always teach the best
the thing that you most need to learn!

Interview With An Inspirer
Walt's Life Rhyme #136

"I share what I know,
so that others may grow!"
www.LifeRhymes.com

Commentary: Interview With An Inspirer

[an online interview conducted by an Life Rhyme reader]

D: Walt, do you write a new inspirational poem every Friday?
WALT: Yep. Usually Thursday night, but lately they've been coming Friday mornings.
D: (they've been coming)...I take it that means the thoughts right?
WALT: Yes, I sometimes get knocked out of my sleep early Friday morning with an idea that I need to communicate. If I want to create one on demand, I can do that too, but the more effective and poignant ones are the ones that create ME.
D: Interesting. How does that work?
WALT: The Life Rhymes are lessons that I need to learn in my own journey. I find that as I go through a particular challenge in my life, there's a Life Rhyme that guides me towards a new way of thinking and being. They're often cathartic, and instructional in addition to being inspirational. So, in effect, they are creating me. They are my becoming—my path to becoming more and more of who I am. I simply move the pen.

Walt's Life Rhyme #135: The Missing Ingredient

In love it seems I'm wanting
though I wait with hopes held high
Still nothing seems to come my way
and I've got to find out why

I expect the best in all I do
so why does love elude?
What change should I enact then
in my current attitude?

I'm happy in my business life
yes, that's where I have more
I expect, then GIVE, then wait and then
the sales come to my door

Perhaps the fact that love's not there
reflects on how I'm living
Perhaps in love I'm hoarding me
and am not truly giving

For when it seems you still don't get
the dreams for which you're meant
Consistent acts of kindness
might be the missing ingredient!

Commentary:

Often, when I would compare my business life and my social life, there would be a great disparity and imbalance between the two. What was I doing wrong? In both these areas of my life I have great expectations. (And I knew that expecting the best was the key to success!)

In both it seems I often wait
for the appearance of my good.
In one rewards come every day,
while in another not as they should.

It then became clear to me that in my business ventures, I was constantly creating and giving of myself in ways that bent the universe in my direction. In my personal relationships, however, I wasn't creating (giving) with the same energy. At first the recipes seemed similar (expect, act and wait). But upon closer examination, I noticed there was a little extra ingredient (expect, act, GIVE and wait).

So, in which area of your life do you seem to waiting in vain? Perhaps you should try giving more to prime the universal pump!

The Missing Ingredient
Walt's Life Rhyme #135

"I share what I know,
so that others may grow!"
www.LifeRhymes.com

Walt's Life Rhyme #134: Running On Empty

Just enough time to get where I'm going
Just enough gas to reach there and back
Just enough water to put out the fire
Just enough money to solve this new lack

Seems I live just at the border of barely
moving from one dire need to the next
With nothing left over to save for tomorrow
with nothing to give others and that makes me vex

Wouldn't it be nice to live always in extra
tasting the froth and cream of my cup
Living life full on the other side of having
sharing earth's wealth now before time is up?

So why do I keep all my cups as half-empty?
It's always been so and I've searched to find why
My concept of love became how I viewed money
an endangered resource in limited supply

But others have taught me like air for the breathing
that love is abundant and never is spent
There's always a place to return and refill
so drink and be merry to the full heart's content

Life's gifts are abundant and there for the having
around you is more than enough so don't fear
But know first that how you view love and it's giving
determines if you'll have your extra to spare!

Running On Empty
Walt's Life Rhyme #134

"I share what I know,
so that others may grow!"
www.LifeRhymes.com

Walt's Life Rhyme #133: Lemonade

Sail high and wide where others fumble
remain safe and sound above the fray
The road is sometimes rife with thorns
that others cast right in your way

For when you're three feet high and rising
others may try to make you trip
Fear not the traps that may beset you
but go now forward with this tip:

"Use their arrows to fight your battles
use their cloud-filled thoughts as shade
When they try to sour you with lemons
use their gifts to make lemonade."

Arm in arm with competition?
it's often the best place you can hide
For they can't wage war successfully
with their opponent by their side!

Lemonade
Walt's Life Rhyme #133

"I share what I know,
so that others may grow!"
www.LifeRhymes.com

Walt's Life Rhyme #132: You First

From the moment that I saw you
I felt my heart starting to reel
But if I let you see me look
you'll know too soon just how I feel

I'm aching to approach you
with some words to break the ice
But if I make the first move now
you may respond just to be nice

I'm thinking I should call you
and put my ego to the side
But if I throw my mask away
I leave myself no place to hide

I'm feeling that I love you
and that those words I too will hear
But if I'm bold and say them first
I'll never know if you do care

But if I go on waiting
never risking 'til "you first"
I'll be safe that's true, but so alone
and I don't know which one is worse

Well I've decided to be happy
and live within this simple truth:
"Never be afraid to go out on a limb,
that's where you'll find the sweetest fruit."

You First
Walt's Life Rhyme #132

"I share what I know,
so that others may grow!"
www.LifeRhymes.com

Walt's Life Rhyme #131: Who Wants To Marry A Million Fears?

If all that you think about is silver and gold
then happiness for you is a thing bought and sold

If the dreams of your life simply stop with the buck
then your quest for fulfillment is based purely on luck

Is it any surprise those you attract feel the same
and will ransom your beauty for fortune and fame?

For to them life and love is a game to be played
and their fear they could lose is what makes them afraid

For on opposite sides of the same coin of tears
are the people who marry based on self-doubt and fears

So seek first to be rich in your view of yourself
and be more than a prize to be picked off the shelf!

Inspired by the "reality" game show Who Wants To Marry a Millionaire?

Who Wants To Marry A Million Fears?
Walt's Life Rhyme #131

*"I share what I know,
so that others may grow!"*
www.LifeRhymes.com

Walt's Life Rhyme #130: The Currency Of Your Life

Pay with money for the lessons
if that's the thing you hold most dear
Pay with time now gone forever
and maybe now your ears will hear

Pay with happiness and laughter
and then you'll choose a different way
Each day's experience holds a lesson
and every time you'll have to pay

But when your own deep inner value
exceeds the world's beyond a doubt
Your currency will be a different kind
and you'll never do without

The Currency of Your Life
Walt's Life Rhyme #130

"I share what I know,
so that others may grow!"
www.LifeRhymes.com

Commentary:

You always pay for what you learn. The marketplace of life is such that you trade the thing of most value to you for the lessons you need to learn. So what do you most value? Is it your reputation, your money, your time? If time is your most valuable asset, then the lessons you learn will almost always rob you of time. If money is your most valued possession then *your* particular life lessons will always be quite expensive. The currency of your life buys you experience and wisdom. But you can get all you need for free if you simply value the right thing!

Walt's Life Rhyme #129: A New Way To Relate

It takes some getting used to, yes
this new way to relate
For years we've known things as they were
what now shall we create?

It means new definitions
and a shift to new from old
A chance to be a different me
and play another role

Sometimes we see things as they were
and fear there's more in store
Sometimes we see things that might be
which scares us even more

It takes new eyes to see the world
beyond the past you know
With open mind the task will ease
What better way to grow?

A New Way To Relate
Walt's Life Rhyme #129

"I share what I know,
so that others may grow!"
www.LifeRhymes.com

Commentary:

The past does not equal the present nor the present the future. Who you were or who someone else was just a minute before can change in an instant. Keep an open mind to life's miracles of change that can help you move into the future. Give it a chance to become what it could be. Things are only as real as your faith in their reality.

Walt's Life Rhyme #128: Solutions

It makes no sense to speak your woes
and not want to overcome
Some people wear the troubled brow
for company when glum

They seek advice from "never wills"
who just don't have a clue
While others look for "shoulda dones"
and ask them what to do

The best advice is "what I did"
combined with "follow me"
For those you ask for guidance
should be where you wish to be!

Solutions
Walt's Life Rhyme #128

"I share what I know,
so that others may grow!"
www.LifeRhymes.com

Commentary:

Too often, we seek advice *not* from people who know, but simply people we know. We take direction not from people who've done it and now know what to do, but from people who failed and don't really have a clue. For the best teacher is experience, and the best advice is "follow me." Learn your lessons from others who are now where you wish to be. --Excerpt from *Turn Your Passion Into Profit* by Walt Goodridge

Walt's Life Rhyme #127: The Return Of What Never Was

Sometimes you get a chance to revisit the past
with the opportunity to close or to clear
We all grow beyond who we once thought we were
and should share it with those once held dear

You may find new chances to reconcile
open chapters you once left unread
You can finally close doors that you once left ajar
and say words that you once left unsaid

Your unresolved past often lingers and looms
and casts shadows on any path that you see
The point of power in life is right here with you now
so accept, learn, forgive and be free

Yes, paths that diverged can unite once again
that's the way it seems life often does
Life gives you a chance to recreate in the now
the longed for past that never quite was

The Return Of What Never Was
Walt's Life Rhyme #127

"I share what I know,
so that others may grow!"
www.LifeRhymes.com

Commentary:

Achieving the future you dream of often depends on first letting go of something or someone in your past. At other times, you may find that the people you just weren't ready for back then are back again to give you another chance! Look out for these golden opportunities to grow!

Dedicated to RJ, CTGII, MS, CS, MR

Walt's Life Rhyme #126: Not Destined To Repeat

I think I used to know what it was like to feel true love
when who and what I was became perfection in their eyes
But then I came to think that I was just not good enough
and hid myself from view within a cold dark world of lies

I saw that those around me lived for years without a touch
and smiles and hugs and kisses too need not be part of life
These images affect me still and haunt me just as much
and make me fear commitment and result in days of strife

But someone told me recently some words I've longed to hear
that other people in my life are really loving *me*
And just because some chose to live entrapped in loveless fear
that doesn't mean that I will too and thus I can be free!

Not Destined To Repeat
Walt's Life Rhyme #126

"I share what I know,
so that others may grow!"
www.LifeRhymes.com

Walt's Life Rhyme #125: The Next Soul Step

Is it time for me to move on?
Is that what this is all about?
For it seems the clues I'm getting
have gone from whisper to a shout

Should I explore some other options?
See what lies out there ahead?
Or should I give this one more chance
work on reviving it instead?

Maybe I've learned all I can learn here
seen all that there is to see
Elevated my mind's awareness
took a soul step from A to B

For when the journey seems too stressful
beyond the normal ups and downs
The path of least resistance
is where your next step can be found

The Next Soul Step
Walt's Life Rhyme #125

*"I share what I know,
so that others may grow!"*
www.LifeRhymes.com

Commentary:

What are the clues you're getting about the journey you're on with your job, your home, your friendships or your partner? Is the business interaction strained? Are you always at odds with each other? Are you being constantly disappointed? Is it getting harder and harder to do what used to be so easy? Sometimes when the hill gets steeper, you might be nearing a plateau of personal growth, or you might be wise to seek another path to get to the top.

There's a difference between struggle and stress.

The struggle of necessary growth feels different from the unnecessary stress of people and processes you've outgrown. You tell the difference by asking yourself: Is there another way to reach my goal without the stress? Is this struggle helping or hindering me? Is this person supporting or sabotaging? Is the experience making me a better person in any way? Or is it a sign I need to find a better path? Ask. Answer. Act.

Walt's Life Rhyme #124: Echoes From Within

Is it the same relationship
but just a different face?
Do you feel the view's not changing
'cause you're just running in place?

Take some time to grow
so you don't make the same decisions
You're where you are by what you know
so make needed revisions

When the questions feel like deja vu
and you get the same replies
See what need is filled
and ask again with different eyes

Until you move beyond
and let true love of self begin
Everything you meet without
will remain echoes of within

Echoes From Within
Walt's Life Rhyme #125

"I share what I know,
so that others may grow!"
www.LifeRhymes.com

Commentary:

There is nothing that you encounter in your life that is not simply a reflection of something within you. Until you discover the reasons why you keep creating the same reality over and over again, it might be wise to hold off on making choices until you're sure that your actions are based on self-love and not further expressions of self sabotage.

The only way to be sure that you're moving in the right direction is to ask the right questions and answer them honestly.

Assume you are writing the scripts of your day to day experiences, and ask yourself why would you create the scenes you do? What purpose or plot is being served by the drama you allow yourself to experience?

Walt's Life Rhyme #123: Countdown To Perfection

It's the countdown to perfection
the dawning of a new age
A chance to make a new beginning
the chance to turn a brand new page

It's the season of adulthood
a focus shift you must begin
No longer guided by the outer
seek now your guidance from within

It's the flowering of your potential
set higher goals and raise the bar
No longer bound by your excuses
free to become all that you are

It's the harvest of abundance
fret not thyself no need for tears
All that you need will be provided
so don't give in to all the fears

It's the milestone you've awaited
t minus 3... 2... 1... and then?
After this calendar moment passes
why not just simply start again?

For what of days beyond tomorrow?
Will each be viewed with equal weight?
When you see each moment as perfection
you become the master of your fate!

Countdown To Perfection
Walt's Life Rhyme #123

"I share what I know,
so that others may grow!"
www.LifeRhymes.com

Walt's Life Rhyme #122: Keeping Perspective

In the heat of the moment
your vision can often get blurred
Responses miss what was said
and instead hit what's heard

In the maze of inner anger
you get lost with no way out
Actions lead you nowhere quickly
love gets cast in shades of doubt

So step away to gain perspective
to see anew when you return
When time is used to wait for answers
you'll be surprised at what you learn

Keeping Perspective
Walt's Life Rhyme #122

"I share what I know,
so that others may grow!"
www.LifeRhymes.com

Walt's Life Rhyme #121: The Life Tide

Against the tide at times in life
it seems that you will swim
When nothing seems to go quite right
and prospects start to dim

But know that days will soon be bright
it won't be always thus
So curse not the departing tide
try not to make a fuss

Like oceans life flows high and low
you'll never know just when
The tide of life will roll back in
and good times come again!

The Life Tide
Walt's Life Rhyme #121

*"I share what I know,
so that others may grow!"*
www.LifeRhymes.com

Walt's Life Rhyme #120: The Inspirer's Dream

Live it up hold nothing back
throw caution to the wind
In life and love that perfect chance
may never come again

Say what you mean, mean what you say
live life with no regrets
This game is one you play but once
no time to hedge your bets

I shared my dreams with one
and said don't let the secret out
But truth to tell my wish is that
the rooftops hear me shout

For some will wish and want and wail
while some will wait on fate
But the future that becomes your life
is the one that you create!

Dedicated to Khadijah

The Inspirer's Dream
Walt's Life Rhyme #120

*"I share what I know,
so that others may grow!"*
www.LifeRhymes.com

Walt's Life Rhyme #119: How To Let It Go

Insults are observations
that our ego's vested in
We strive to be what we are not
and cast ourselves in sin

There's struggle in opposing truth
For what's denied will last
Resist it and it pushes back
Accept and it will pass

It's what you say does not exist
that lingers on for years
What's railed against is given life
What's seen then disappears

The man who sees things as they are
can then be free to grow
For 'til you hold a thing in hand
you cannot let it go

How To Let It Go
Walt's Life Rhyme #120

"I share what I know,
so that others may grow!"
www.LifeRhymes.com

Walt's Life Rhyme #118: The Magical Moment Of Truth

In the magical moment of truth
the risks rewards outweigh
You often find that what you want's
already on its way

In the magical moment of truth
provided you're listening well
You might hear words of love from those
you thought would never tell

In the magical moment of truth
all the illusions disappear
For lies are walls that block our view
with truth we see things clear

Commentary:

Our daily lives are filled with big
steps towards happiness that come
as little magical moments of truth.

The Magical Moment Of Truth
Walt's Life Rhyme #118

"I share what I know,
so that others may grow!"
www.LifeRhymes.com

Walt's Life Rhyme #117: Judge Not

It's the same life lesson once again
I'm learning not to judge
But habits can be mules sometimes
they just refuse to budge

When preconceptions take control
I don't accept all as I should
But everyone deserves a chance
so I'll focus on their good

I'm prone to discount others' worth
and judge by what I see
Since other's worth mirrors my own
I'm really judging me

My world is made by gifts of thought
I get that which I give
I'll judge not lest I too be judged
and learn well how to live

Judge Not
Walt's Life Rhyme #117

"I share what I know,
so that others may grow!"
www.LifeRhymes.com

Walt's Life Rhyme #116: Challenges of Scale

To walk a thousand miles just take
one step after another
For some will freeze in awe
and with the trip they just won't bother

A river weaves around a rock
through paths which least resist
And leaves a canyon in its wake
which always will exist

There's nothing made that can't be seen
the sum of smaller parts
From projects large, to daily chores
to wishes of our hearts

And we who dream big dreams should know
that we can never fail
Once success is viewed as just
a doable challenge of scale

Challenges of Scale
Walt's Life Rhyme #116

"I share what I know,
so that others may grow!"
www.LifeRhymes.com

Commentary:

Amassing a savings, losing weight, writing a book, managing a project, even cleaning a messy kitchen (my personal nightmare), are all doable tasks if you see them for what they are: the end result of a series of individual actions. Don't be intimidated by the sheer size of them, or the distance to the goal, or you may lose the will to venture forth. Similarly, long term dreams of who and what we want to be already exist within us on a smaller scale, and we just need to build on them step by step until they come true!

Walt's Life Rhyme #115: Keep It Simple

Someone asked me recently why the Life Rhymes are often so similar in ideology, and why they sometimes aren't more complex. Well, you see

Most of us don't notice
the news we hear each day is sad
That someone's made a choice
to harp and focus on the bad

A Life Rhyme's meant to counter
the flood of negatives each day
From people who don't realize
the power of what they say

Our lives, our jobs, our children
could use a boost and that's a fact
And like a single smile or hug
there's great power in simple acts

See, the solution is really simple:
we need to focus on the good
And few places can you hear
good words repeated as they should

As your situation changes
a new life-challenge is brought to bear
And that determines what it means
and interprets what you hear

So my mission here is simple
I'm simply sharing what I know
Giving thoughts of hope
that some may choose to use to grow

Keep It Simple
Walt's Life Rhyme #115
© Walt F.J. Goodridge
"I share what I know,
so that others may grow!"
www.LifeRhymes.com

Commentary:

Consider the Life Rhymes your weekly smile in the face of adversity. A hug in a world that's been pushed too far apart. And remember, keep it simple! Don't confuse simplicity with shallowness.

Walt's Life Rhyme #114: The Art Of Creation

Life's all about creation
that's all we ever do
Even amidst destruction
we're simply creating something new

Don't let appearance fool you
the cycle's not as it may seem
The sequence we accept
is simply that which we deem

Relationships that come and go
and businesses that fail
Effects of one creative force
when seen behind the veil

Through actions or the lack
you're always building in some way
It's impossible to be non-creative
as sure as night will follow day

One creation follows another
and there's no one else to blame
For behind each carefully crafted scene
stands a builder with your name

The Art Of Creation
Walt's Life Rhyme #114

"I share what I know,
so that others may grow!"
www.LifeRhymes.com

Walt's Life Rhyme #113: Restaurant of Wishes

Welcome to the world of wishes
I AM your waiter and your guide
So much exists here on the menu
it's sometimes tricky to decide

First dream at night to place your order
ask yourself how would it feel
What ways would I be living
if what I wished for was now real?

I'll take peace of mind for starters
with self-acceptance on the side
I've heard the love here is like heaven
and so I'd like to say I've tried

Bring success in 3 large helpings
for body, spirit and my mind
Prepared in love (my favorite dressing)
with lots of cash if you'd be so kind

A cup of wealth that runneth over
enough for those who aren't here
Success for all here at my table
and don't forget to hold the fear

And for dessert a bowl of memories
with wisdom sprinkled on the top
And experience to share with others
with refills of patience that don't stop

(And if it's not too late to ask it
a bit of tolerance wrapped to go
So others know that I've been through here
and as my souvenir to show)

For in this restaurant of wishes
just know that all who ask are served
Your order's taken as you thinketh
and brought to you when it's deserved!

The Restaurant Of Wishes
Walt's Life Rhyme #113

"I share what I know,
so that others may grow!"
www.LifeRhymes.com

Walt's Life Rhyme #112: The Evidence Of Truth

Until there are actions
that show you are kind
Your claims of your charity
are just thoughts held in mind

Until there is beingness
to express what you know
Then your knowledge is naught
but an unperformed show

And until you become
what you say that you are
Then the world is deprived
of one special bright star

For in physical form
do our selves manifest
And through experience alone
do we share of our best!

The Evidence Of Truth
Walt's Life Rhyme #112

*"I share what I know,
so that others may grow!"*
www.LifeRhymes.com

Commentary:

Inspired by author Neale Donald Walsch who says, "You can know yourself to be generous, but unless you do something which displays generosity, you have nothing but a concept. You can know yourself to be kind, but unless you do someone a kindness, you have nothing but an idea about yourself.. Until concept becomes experience, all there is is speculation."

Walt's Life Rhyme #111: Never Again

Today it came real close to me
but I paused and let it go
Tomorrow if it comes again
I will act and make it so

I thought it was for someone else
so I watched it slip away
And kicked myself in harsh regret
over what I did not say

But from now on I'll recognize
the chances as they near
And never shall my fire of wants
be dowsed by waves of fear

I vow before the week is done
I'll make a dream come true
And come the time when next we meet
good news I'll share with you!

Never Again
Walt's Life Rhyme #111

"I share what I know,
so that others may grow!"
www.LifeRhymes.com*!"*

Walt's Life Rhyme #110: The Real Me

and my appearance
no that's not me
that's just the me
that others see

my personality
no that's not me
that's just the me
I'm trained to be

and my decisions
could they be me?
or just the me
I choose to be

what of my thoughts
are they of me?
or someone else
I cannot see?

is my awareness then
the real true me?
that sense of self
that none can see?

Perhaps we're waves
within the sea
simply expressions
of a single ME

The Real Me
Walt's Life Rhyme #110

"I share what I know,
so that others may grow!"
www.LifeRhymes.com

Walt's Life Rhyme #109: What's Luck Got To Do With It?

And for the man who lacks direction
no sign can ever show the way
And in the life which has no purpose
then random chance doth seem at play

For if they ask me how I did it
what quirk of fate on me did smile
It's naught but faith and preparation
that makes my dreams come true in style

What's Luck Got To Do With It?
Walt's Life Rhyme #109

"I share what I know,
so that others may grow!"
www.LifeRhymes.com

Walt's Life Rhyme #108: In Relation To All This

In circumstances life presents
clear moments not to miss
The chance to ask whom shall I be
in relation to all this?

Will I be left to this right?
Will I be up for this down?
Will I be good to this bad?
Will I be smile to this frown?

For I can never really know the cold
if things have never been hot
To know myself as what I am
I must first know what I am not!

In Relation To All This
Walt's Life Rhyme #108

"I share what I know,
so that others may grow!"
www.LifeRhymes.com

Commentary:

The nature of life is that we are defined physically, mentally and spiritually in relationship to others. We only know who we are in our interactions with other people. Our chances to learn about ourselves, and to choose who we will become only exist when we interact with others.

We can define ourselves as happy only if there is something we call sad. We can define ourselves as positive only if there is such a thing called negative. We can choose who we wish to be only if there are those we know who are where we wish to be, and those who are not.

So embrace the opportunities that interacting with others offers you. Accept the role that people and circumstances play in your life simply by being who they are, and instead of crying "foul!", simply ask yourself, "Who do I wish to be in relation to this?" The answer you find will determine your reaction to life.

Walt's Life Rhyme #107: In The Comfort Of Our Own Creations

In the comfort of our own creations
we often find ourselves at rest
Content to laze away our lives
without the urge to do what's best

In circumstances of our choosing
or as they say "the bed we've made"
We dread the days and damn the drama
and often wonder why we've stayed

This life we live is like a picture
with scenes we brush from head and heart
When once you recognize the painter
your days become like works of art!

In The Comfort Of Our Own Creations
Walt's Life Rhyme #107

"I share what I know,
so that others may grow!"
www.LifeRhymes.com

Commentary:

The world you live in is like a picture. A canvas upon which you have held the creator's brush all these years. Despite appearances to the contrary, it's not a tacky "B" movie into which you've been cast against your will. Who you are and the scenes that unfold are a direct outcome of decisions you've made given who you were at those moments.

Denying your part in the drama that unfolds and refusing to move to safer more nurturing quarters is the recipe for continued heartache.

Here's how it usually works: You choose from a place of awareness and then move forward to another scene. Soon, the choices you made in Act 1 no longer serve you in Act 2. Since life won't allow you to go back and re-shoot the first act. Your only option is to make new decisions based on who you are NOW in Act 2. However, many of us get trapped forever living out our Act 1 choices fearing to make new decisions simply because of the comfort factor. We hate the place we are, but are fearful of change simply because we've gotten comfortable.

Even if we're in pain, it's such a familiar pain that we often choose to remain in the "comfort of our own creations" even when it ceases to support us in our growth.

The trick, therefore, is first to acknowledge your part in the drama, see yourself as the painter/director, forgive yourself for our earlier choices, then make new decisions from a now (hopefully) healthier mental space. Don't get trapped in the comfort.

Walt's Life Rhyme #106: With New Eyes

With old eyes I see what's normal
and act out my tried and true
With new eyes I see what's natural
and forever choose to see anew

With New Eyes
Walt's Life Rhyme #106

"I share what I know,
so that others may grow!"
www.LifeRhymes.com

Commentary:

Often when I'm in the midst of a negative emotion and am beset with fear, anger, resentment or other feelings of pity, victimization or self-recrimination, it helps to remember that the path to happiness begins with stepping out of what's normal and moving towards what's natural. If it's normal for you to feel unhappy, are you open to feeling differently? Many of us say we are, but often choose to replay the old mental recordings of self-doubt and fear rather than the more natural ones of love, peace forgiveness, and acceptance.

Are you willing to move to a new place from which to view the world? Or, are you a major shareholder and investor in the stock club of unhappiness--waiting for a return on years of regular investments?

If you're ready for change, simply affirm: "I am willing to see things differently." And don't worry if you don't have any idea just how a given situation can be viewed differently. Have faith that the answers will arrive in time. Sometimes the willingness to see things differently can bring a calm to an otherwise stressful set of circumstances in your life, that makes new sight possible. And it's from this place that all things can be seen anew.

Walt's Life Rhyme #105: Let It Be

The floods that consume
make the dormant seeds grow
Life's turbulence can propel
if you go with the flow

Winds that shudder and shake
also work with your sail
Missed attempts only sadden
if you see them as failed

And the fire that burns
also strengthens the clay
Know that one man's dark night
is another's bright day

Falls that batter and bruise
make us pause for a rest
And from the healing come answers
to help us pass the next test!

Ride it out
Dedicated to David O.

Let It Be
Walt's Life Rhyme #105

"I share what I know,
so that others may grow!"
www.LifeRhymes.com

Walt's Life Rhyme #104: Turning Points

The people who affect us most
are those who make us think
For growth comes from the gusts of thought
that push us to the brink

In thought is where we find ourselves
if lost or on a quest
From thought is where the visions come
that make us act our best

Think long and hard on who you are
and what you've come to be
And trace it back I'm sure you will
to ones who helped you see

They made you think in different terms
your tide through them did shift
They changed your thoughts of you
and new direction was their gift

These people were your signposts
offering what can't be bought
Life's turning points were people
who changed the level of your thoughts!

Dedicated to A Morrison and ERT
and to Isolene, Christie, Reina, Gurdeep,
Xino, Tony, Carlton & Zelda,

Turning Points
Walt's Life Rhyme #104

"I share what I know,
so that others may grow!"
www.LifeRhymes.com

Walt's Life Rhyme #103: Like Minds

Like minds can move mountains
and fists from fingers are made
Real power's what results
when we come to each other's aid

When a shared goal is our mission
the whole becomes stronger than the parts
But commitment to each one's success
is the mindset from which it all starts

Like Minds
Walt's Life Rhyme #103

"I share what I know,
so that others may grow!"
www.LifeRhymes.com

Commentary:

Poetsniche.com is a website I created where artists, poets, writers and other creative folk can come not only to meet others who share their interests, but launch their careers as well. It exemplifies what the power of a unified whole can accomplish! This group of online members pooled their creative and financial resources to publish the Internet's first compilation of poetry from a web-based community, and host a successful offline event! Now all the members are feeling the effects of what they set in motion, giving each other not only camaraderie and support, but a practical way to earn money as well! It just goes to prove, you can get anything you want in life if you simply help enough other people get what they want!

Walt's Life Rhyme #102: 6 Billion To 1

The odds are one in 6 billion
that you'd be just who you are
Lost in a world filled with struggle
feeling not quite up to par

The odds are one in 6 billion
you'd get the hand you were dealt
Working with fears and frustrations
that countless others have felt

But because you're 1 in six billion
the game is stacked on your side
Your unique skills and talents
will be a marked source of pride

Yes, because you're 1 in six billion
you're like a star up to bat
And with none other quite like you
odds don't get much better than that!

6 Billion To 1
Walt's Life Rhyme #102

*"I share what I know,
so that others may grow!"*
www.LifeRhymes.com

Commentary:

With 6 billion people on planet earth at this time, some of us feel like overwhelmed, lost and insignificant souls struggling to make a difference. Always remember, however, that each and every one of us has the potential for greatness just by virtue of being here. Of the 6 billion now and the billions before you, none have ever been quite like you. And that, my friend, is the real overwhelming wonder of it all!

Walt's Life Rhyme #101: My Soul Intention

I'm here to learn a lesson
that's the mission, that's the goal
A choice was made, a journey chosen
the part was cast to play my role

These circumstances that befall me
not random happenings I'm told
But carefully constructed chances
to fulfill intentions of my soul

My Soul Intention
Walt's Life Rhyme #101

"I share what I know,
so that others may grow!"
www.LifeRhymes.com

Commentary:

Some spiritualists say that we are here because we made a choice to be here from on the other side; that we're here in order to learn lessons that help our souls grow. While here, some of us choose to learn the lessons, while some doom themselves to repeat the classes over and over. The challenges you habitually encounter in search of these soul lessons fall primarily into one of 7 areas of growth I call your soul intentions. They are

1. health,
2. career,
3. spirituality,
4. love,
5. finance
6. social life and
7. family

Once you know what your "sole intention" is for being here, the journey makes more sense, and life becomes easier. You stop fighting against the tide and instead look for the opportunities to move with the flow to new levels of awareness, understanding, thought and action when it comes to matters in your area of growth. You recognize that the challenges are not a "just your bad luck" but ingeniously devised and disguised events you've attracted to use for your personal development. So what's YOUR soul's intention?

Walt's Life Rhyme #100: The Inspirer

There seems to be some interest
in these thoughts I have to share
It's nothing but encouraging words
we all do need to hear

From the universe to you my friends
the messages get sent
I have no part in what they say
or know for whom they're meant

Some say that I speak just to them
with words they need to hear
When woes are glimpsed through Life Rhyme eyes
the path gets crystal clear

Some say my words cause higher thoughts
when life looks much too bleak
The truth is that your soul attracts
the words your teachers speak

When someone in your life appears
as friend, foe, mate or mother
They bring a daily lesson to you
one way or another

It's not FROM us no, but THROUGH us
that other people's lives we bless
When once we choose to share the wealth
through talents we possess

Your smile, your touch, your words a laugh
even your email as my admirer
In turn you too will play the role
of someone else's INSPIRER!

Dedicated to all the Inspirers in the world, and to Adrienne H. whose email sparked the thoughts! In turn you too will play the role.

The Inspirer
Walt's Life Rhyme #100

*"I share what I know,
so that others may grow!"*
www.LifeRhymes.com

Walt's Life Rhyme #99: Quandary

When your interest and desires
are quite obvious to view
You fear a big rejection
is what lies in store for you

You know and feel inside
he might be way out of your league
But thoughts of possibilities
spark yearning and intrigue

You feel your chances slim
that he too might feel the same way
You want to get to know him more
but don't know what to say

Just follow with your heart, friend
but don't marry expectations
When wedded to an outcome
that's what leads to great frustration

What he offers might be friendship
what he offers might be bliss
You've got to strike it now
or this great chance you'll surely miss

And know above all else my friend
the odds are really with you
It's often true the thing you seek
is also seeking you too!

Quandary
Walt's Life Rhyme #99

"I share what I know,
so that others may grow!"
www.LifeRhymes.com

Commentary for Walt's Life Rhyme #99

Dear Walt,
There's a guy who came to my church last fall to instruct a musical workshop. I've never really met him, but he's constantly on my mind. He really impressed me with his singing, his demeanor, and his sense of humor. I know and I feel like he might be out of my league, but as stated earlier he is constantly on my mind. What should I do? I've prayed and asked the Lord to reveal to me why I keep thinking about him. I know the Lord, if he hasn't already, will answer me. Perhaps the answer is not what I want to hear, but I'm in a quandary right now and would love some printed answer or something I think is concrete. Thank you for listening! –In a Quandary

Dear Quandary

Nothing ventured, nothing gained. It's better to have loved and lost, than never to have loved at all. Not knowing is the hardest part. There are a host of proverbs I could offer you as to why it's in your best interest to initiate some sort of interaction with this fellow. I know, however, that this can be quite a scary thing. Check out Life Rhyme #97 ("Lights, Camera, Action") to read more advice on taking action.

Now, the most telling part of your letter is the phrase "I know and I feel like he might be out of my league." That little bit of self-depreciation is what's holding you back. Remember this: When it comes to your fears, it's NEVER really about the other person. It's really ONLY about you. No one else really exists but you. *("I live in a world filled with fears, foes and fancy. But there's no one else here but me.")*

Your gut feeling of a connection with this person might not be at all what you think. Maybe he has a message for you that has nothing to do with love and romance. Perhaps he is the missing link to an experience that might put you on a different career path. Don't think that just because you can't identify what you're feeling that it's an attraction for which you risk rejection. Fear not! Go forth boldly in search of your good!

Walt's Life Rhyme #98: Finals

"Under pressure to perform", he said
"and then the time runs out.
Prepared was I or so I thought,
but then I fill with doubt."

"It's just a game, my son", I said
"a sport that all can master.
A race that's won before it's run
no need to run much faster."

"The what and how and why of it
are basic rules you know
For life won't test on what you've learned
but IF you've learned to grow."

"Believe you can, and know you can
for this you've done before!"
"Just make yourself the problem solved
and final grades will soar!"

Finals
Walt's Life Rhyme #98

"I share what I know,
so that others may grow!"
www.LifeRhymes.com

Commentary:

Every week, for a few hours each day, I tutor students online in Math. Gerroll, an eighth-grader who came to my online classroom to get a head start on 9th grade Algebra, mentioned that he understood the material, but always seemed to perform below his abilities because he always gets nervous, doesn't believe he'll do well, and consequently does poorly.

In the few minutes we spoke, I explained to him that achieving higher grades had nothing to do with studying harder, or longer since I could tell he knew what, how and why he was doing things. It had to do with making *himself* the problem to be solved, and getting an "A plus" in a subject called "Gerroll" first, and that Algebra would take care of itself. I found out that there were times when he scored as high as 96% on his tests. So we reviewed those times when he did do well, we talked about why he felt nervous, and we solved problems of emotional expressions rather than algebraic ones.

I asked him if he would have to think twice about his ability to get up and go to the kitchen. He said no because he knows he can, he believes he can, and he's done it before. So we talked about believing in his ability to get 96% or better again with that same conviction and in those same terms. And though the final answer to this equation is yet to be written, I suspect Gerroll now has a little advantage that most of us wish we had at 13 years old.

Walt's Life Rhyme #97: Lights, Camera, Action!

What bold thing would I do today
if I knew I could not fail?
If it mattered not what people thought
would I let my heart prevail?

What secret wish would I act upon
if success were guaranteed?
Which actions would I then give life
with all mental shackles freed?

Would I speak my mind and then some
say the words I should have said
Become the person I've always wanted
but acted out fears instead

If my days were caught on camera
for the world to watch and view
Would my role inspire others
who wish that they could too

Well I'll never know from wishing
for the thought alone won't do
The life I crave is brought to bear
by the things I choose to do

Like cast without lead actor
your dreams await director's cue
The results you seek wait in the wings
but won't ACT until you do!

Lights, Camera, Action!
Walt's Life Rhyme #97

"I share what I know,
so that others may grow!"
www.LifeRhymes.com

Commentary:

[Inspired by *The Psychology of Achievement* by Brian Tracy] Perhaps it's starting your business, quitting a dead-end job, approaching a prospect, or maybe it's simply asking that cute teller at the bank on a date. Maybe it's just saying "I Love You" to someone who needs to hear it. Whatever it is, you've beat yourself up long enough worrying about the consequences. You become more of you each time you conquer you. Don't put it off anymore. As you rise each day, ask yourself "What would I attempt today if I know I could not fail? You might be surprised how empowering that single thought is. Keep asking it right up until you do the thing you fear to do, and greet the new you on the other side!

Walt's Life Rhyme #96: Ask the Inspirer
Undecided

Dear Walt, I want to make a living as a DJ. But I don't like the idea of selling my product or playing for others, since I find it very personal. Should I go to school for electronics, (for which I have a slight interest)? Would this be considered being untrue to myself? [Being a DJ] is the only thing I've had a passion for, but an electronics education might [be the wisest thing to do]. What do you think? –Undecided

Dear Undecided,
"...whether it was the record label, or my writing, I always followed my dreams. I started doing the radio show while I was studying engineering in college. I was running my record label while I was designing roadways and bridges as a civil engineer. I wrote my first and second books while I was working in corporate America, and it was that passion that freed me to jump out on my own. Now I earn money on my own terms through exploring ever-evolving aspects of my creativity.

My advice: Continue to do what you love. Even if you don't do it as a business, make the time and the room to do it. Never let it die. That fire you have inside of you must not be given up for something "more practical." What would be your perfect life? Would getting up each day running to the electronics lab be part of your ideal life, or would knowing you're the best DJ in the land make you excited to jump out of bed each day? Only you know the answer. What is it that gives you your greatest feeling of power, satisfaction, fulfillment and purpose? Find that thing and pursue it. You've got but one life. How will you spend it?"–Walt

Sometimes our dreams will lie in state
like lost loved ones at a wake
We never dare to take a chance
to eat and have our cake

So ask yourself when called to choose
the role that you must play
Is this the path my heart doth crave
or someone else's way?

With time as cash your dreams are bought
through fair and even trade
Your spend your time and in return
in memories you're paid

Your precious days are dollars
that in time will all be spent
So purchase things that please
and own the life for which you're meant!

Undecided
Walt's Life Rhyme #96

"I share what I know,
so that others may grow!"
ww.LifeRhymes.com

Walt's Life Rhyme #95: An Out Of Box Experience

Beyond what eyes perceive
exists a world of different rules
Apart from what the mind believes
that's formed with different tools

When searching for solutions
used to tackle any task
Quite simply the response you get
depends on what you ask

The masses watch their worlds collapse
and never find the cause
Unhappy with their answers
but the questions hide the flaws

With thoughts like eagles ever sure
but never seen in flocks
Success belongs to those brave souls
who dare to think out the box!

An Out Of Box Experience
Walt's Life Rhyme #95

"I share what I know,
so that others may grow!"
www.LifeRhymes.com

Commentary:

Are you caught in the trap of poorly framed questions? Every question has certain assumptions implied in how you ask it. Are you asking questions that condemn you to the same old answers? Are you asking questions that limit your growth and experiences? When you need more money, for example, do you automatically ask, "What kind of job can I get? or "How many more hours do I need to work to make more?" trapping yourself in the assumption that you need to trade your time for it?

Many successful men and women think "outside the box", framing their questions in entirely new and empowering ways! Here are some suggestions:

1. In business: Instead of "How come my mean boss won't give me a raise?" ask "How can I share the talents and skills I possess to provide value that people need at a profit?"
2. In love: Instead of "Why can't I find the right man/woman?" ask How can I create happiness within me first so that I'm not dependent on someone else to make me feel special?"
3. At home: Instead of "Where did this kid/husband/wife/mother-in-law from hell come from!?" ask "How can I provide a family environment that nurtures love and respect?"

Walt's Life Rhyme #94: A New Reflection

Someone showed me a different picture
of a me I'd never seen
That made me see my daily actions
for what they've always really been

Someone asked me different questions
which forced some answers to be said
And left new echoes of reality
forever spinning in my head

Someone gave me a new perspective
to change beliefs I once held dear
And helped me sort through all the conflict
and told me things I need to hear

And in that gift was a new beginning
a pool of thought from which to see
And from these crystal clear calm waters
come reflections of a brand new me

A New Reflection
Walt's Life Rhyme #94

"I share what I know,
so that others may grow!"
www.LifeRhymes.com

Commentary:

The reason we're not alone on the planet is so we can share in the wisdom, ideas, and dreams of others who are traveling the same roads we are. In a simple conversation, in a new book, or even in a weekly inspiration, you might find the answers you've always been looking for, hear a thought that changes your thinking, and sends you on your way changed forever. Let the people in your life and the messages from beyond affect you as they were meant to, and strive to derive the meaning, message and mission of all who cross your path!

Walt's Life Rhyme #93: On The Level

My life has been a pattern
etched in place since very young
I've looked at life as if a ladder
and each victory as a rung

Collecting prizes, winning favor
I never stopped to savor the view
Always "taking it to the next level"
and finding a new challenge to pursue

So with each task that I accomplished
I pushed myself to go much higher
But of this endless restless journey
it seems in time I soon would tire

And then I looked around and saw
that I was blinded to my good
For the level I sought and envied
was here exactly where I stood!

So when the time comes in your journey
you find the thrill to climb is gone
Seek not to find new levels
seek more the level that you're on!

On The Level
Walt's Life Rhyme #93

"I share what I know,
so that others may grow!"
www.LifeRhymes.com

Commentary:

Has the climb lost its thrill? Maybe what's need is not a new mountain to climb, but to spend some time enjoying the view on the mountain you're on. Stop and smell the roses along the way.

Walt's Life Rhyme #92: Move It Up & Motive And Means

Move it Up

Promote this wish to captain
make it yes beyond all doubt
Move it to the top of your list
that's what commitment's all about

Motive and Means

They say "how" is none of your business
that where there's a will there's a way
For means always follows motive
as sure as night chases day

Move It Up/Motive and Means
Walt's Life Rhyme #92

"I share what I know,
so that others may grow!"
www.LifeRhymes.com

Commentary:

Suppose you got a call from a millionaire who said, "In exactly one year from today, I need you to meet me on the corner of Broadway and West 43rd Street in New York City at 5:00pm sharp. I'll have a briefcase with one million tax-free dollars for you, but only if you're on time." Would you be there? Many of us can say, with unwavering certainty, an absolute, and emphatic "YES! I will!"

I learned many years ago that, regardless of what we perceive as life's hindrances, we all have the ability to commit to a course of action and stick to it and make it happen. Many of us, however, in our day-to-day lives have trouble keeping appointments, following through on promises and honoring our word. We've given our power away to uncertainty and doubt and feel at ease with answers like "I'll have to see," or "I'll try," or "I can't tell you right now" rather than "It's done," "I'm there," or "YES! I will!" The truth is, your ability to respond to life's requests is a matter of deciding in advance what's important enough to commit to. You, and you alone, have the ability to assign "million-dollar" importance to anything in your life.

You'll find that all YOU really need is the "will to." Once that is in place, the "how to" often takes care of itself.

Walt's Life Rhyme #91: How the Universe Speaks To You

coincidence?
a dejavu?
perhaps that's how
it speaks to you

slip of the tongue?
a TV ad?
could be advice
you'll wish you had

a stranger's words?
lyrics in song?
might be a hint
of right and wrong

a nagging hunch?
a random thought?
a signal sent
a lesson taught

a misdialed call?
perhaps more true:
"Universe calling"
and it's for you!
So pay attention

How The Universe Speaks to You
Walt's Life Rhyme #91

"I share what I know,
so that others may grow!"
www.LifeRhymes.com

Commentary:

Have you ever made a decision, acted on a feeling, set a goal or embarked on a journey, and felt certain that the universe was dropping clues in your path to let you know you made the right choice? Maybe it's just me, but I believe that there are no accidents. I believe that EVERY event, from a headline on a newspaper being read by someone in front of me, to the words I hear in a passing conversation, to the page my book falls open to provides messages for me. I receive validation of ideas and encouragement towards my goals from the strangest places. Sometimes even the typographical errors in what I write are giving me clues! Was that really a wrong number? Maybe it was a chance to learn some valuable information or make a friend I just might need. So when I see or hear echoes of my life on the news, on the radio, or in a song, I know that it's the universe telling me I'm on the right track! Don't miss the messages.

Walt's Life Rhyme #90: e-Turn

e-turn: a path which traces the path of the letter e--starting out
like a circle or "o" and then, at the critical
moment, hooking a right toward the center (your goal)

Set a goal and launched my mission
constant motion. Yes, I'm nearing it!
Round and round though never reaching
for in truth just really fearing it....

....So take a look at how you're moving
as if in orbit 'round the sun
But the power's in the middle
hook a right and then you're done!

e-Turn
Walt's Life Rhyme #90
© Walt F.J. Goodridge
"I share what I know,
so that others may grow!"
www.LifeRhymes.com

Commentary:

There are certain thoughts and actions which, instead of taking your life from a to b to c, move you instead, as if by magic, directly from a to z. The essence of happiness and success is being able to identify and implement those specific actions, in the midst of all other choices, upon which success truly hinges.

In project management, those key actions are called the "critical path." While there may be hundreds of tasks involved in completing a project, there are some that are the backbone of the project, actions which set the pace of the project and which MUST be done as they are essential for the timely completion of the project. In your own life, there's a critical path that leads to success! Once you find and follow it, your life can take an e-turn! So, today, resolve to eliminate the unnecessary steps and take a turn towards center.

Walt's Life Rhyme #89: Keep Deciding

Some decisions are sharper
and cut through the mire
And the fog of bad habits
that we find ourselves in

Some decisions are like rulers
that preside over our lives
And like statesmen for office
always campaigning to win

Some decisions are straighter
and like a path through the thicket
Lead us headlong to wishes
so we don't wander blind

Some decisions are older
collect years' worth of wisdom
But then wait to express it
as if biding their time

And if your decisions are found wanting, take heart:

They will grow sharp with the grind
they'll achieve power in time
Will too become a straight line
and will mature like fine wine, so..

...Keep deciding to do the thing,
reset your goals and be bold
For today might be the day
that your decision takes hold!

Keep Deciding
Walt's Life Rhyme #89

*"I share what I know,
so that others may grow!"*
www.LifeRhymes.com

Commentary:

Personal growth is a process that may take years, and which you might never truly perfect. Don't be too hard on yourself if it seems that you're still making the same decisions over and over. There's much that you have to do. There are habits to change, beliefs to replace, past experiences to overcome, fears to eliminate, and new ways of being to adopt. As long as you are committed to the journey, give yourself some time to make it happen, and you'll meet with the success you desire. Keep growing.

Walt's Life Rhyme #88: My List

What good are all the treasures of life
without people to share them with?

I made a list just yesterday
of things I plan to do
Activities that hold life's joy
come far between and few

And though I wrote with eager heart
an emptiness descended
It seems that what I really miss
are friendships that have ended

For when I think of joyous times
what stands out more than places
More than the where and what of it
are others' smiling faces

So now my list includes much more
than things and trips and gifts
Beside them all are special names
of friends to share them with!

dedicated to Dawn Greenidge

My List
Walt's Life Rhyme #88

"I share what I know,
so that others may grow!"
www.LifeRhymes.com

Walt's Life Rhyme #87: The Big Picture

one will paint it
few will see it
most will pass it by

all could have it
most won't bid it
few will actually try

one will own it
take it home and live it
why not more?
who knows why?

The Big Picture
Walt's Life Rhyme #87

*"I share what I know,
so that others may grow!"*
www.LifeRhymes.com

Commentary:

Do you know someone who's missing the big picture? Health, happiness, love, companionship, friendship, fulfillment, and peace of mind are all part of the big picture that we sometimes miss because we're focusing on life's minutiae–live in the masterpiece called life!

Walt's Life Rhyme #86: What's Your Recipe?

If you want to bake a cake
there are some things you have to do
If you want to make a life
well it's a similar process too

Our feelings are the outcome
of this life it seems we make
Whether loved, depressed, or mad or glad
there are steps you have to take

Beliefs and expectations
are ingredients at the start
Choose the best and measure well
combine in equal parts

Mix and blend with action
if you want to be a winner
Desire sets the temperature
be it chill, boil or slow simmer

Reactions add the flavor
so if sweet or bland or sour
Add seasonings you like
life's final taste's within your power!

What's Your Recipe?
Walt's Life Rhyme #86

*"I share what I know,
so that others may grow!"*
www.LifeRhymes.com

Commentary:

We all have certain patterns and habits we've fallen into which, like a recipe, always create the feelings we find ourselves experiencing regularly. Once you know your own "recipe"–the actions and thoughts that cause the recurring results in your life–you can reprogram yourself for success. The unique thing about this recipe of life is that it allows you to change the final taste even after all the cooking's been done! Whatever ingredients have already put into the recipe, you can always change the final taste simply by changing your reactions to what life serves you.

Walt's Life Rhyme #85: Now That I've Made It!

Now that I've made it
there's so much that must be done
I'll call up all my friends
and finally start to have some fun

Now that I've made it
time to make room in my heart
I want to gaze into the eyes
of one whose life I am a part

Now that I've made it
I know what the other half does
I can share wealth from my riches
give from my heart now just because

Yes, what I made was a decision
a simple choice to finally live
Not to wait for future fortune
before I laugh, and share and give

And the moment that I made it
oh! the weight I felt was lifted
And I can finally see and grasp
this golden chance ALWAYS existed!

Now That I've Made It!
Walt's Life Rhyme #85

"I share what I know,
so that others may grow!"
www.LifeRhymes.com

Commentary:

You really don't have to wait until some future fortune to start enjoying life. What your children really want is your time. What your partner wants is your attention. What you'll remember most about them all are the moments spent laughing together. And the best part is, you don't need money to experience any of these things with them. So go ahead and make it. Make the decision! Share this with someone you know who might be putting off enjoying life until some great milestone or achievement is reached

Walt's Life Rhyme #84: Passengers

the first to thought
controls the dream
decides the ways
and sets the means

through mind alone
the forms we know
sustained by all
who think it so

we're passengers
of a chosen few
who tell us how
and what to do

on trains of thought
this world does ride
in search of tracks
that lie inside

Passengers
Walt's Life Rhyme #84

"I share what I know,
so that others may grow!"
www.LifeRhymes.com

Commentary:

The truth is: reality is just a shared idea, a collection of beliefs that remain intact simply because we all think them true. The rules of life, love, business, birth, death, how we age, what we eat, and everything we perceive to be, all started from one idea. And like train tracks that are already laid for us to use, most of us are simply along for the ride never realizing that we can lay new tracks with the speed of thought! The world is ready for a new route! Share this with someone who doubts his or her power to set a new course in life.

Walt's Life Rhyme #83: The Feeling That You Seek

Money, power, fortune, fame
each one a worthy prize
But often fail to give relief
when seen through older eyes

For cash alone can't buy a smile
or change a bankrupt heart
And playing king with inner shame
makes life a dull bit part

And world acclaim and things won't match
a mom's adoring gaze
We fill this void called peace of mind
in often futile ways

So chase the carrot knowing that
there's more for which we're meant
And take the time to spend the time
or you'll wonder where it went

When loved, secure, and self-assured
you'll laugh when things look bleak
You'll know it's not the thing at all
but the feeling that you seek

The Feeling That You Seek
Walt's Life Rhyme #83

*"I share what I know,
so that others may grow!"*
www.LifeRhymes.com

Commentary:

All of our earthly pursuits for wealth, attention, and material things are really about creating a certain feeling. Whether that feeling is security, safety, self worth, beauty or desirability, keep in mind that you already have the power to create the very feeling you're seeking. Are you still looking out there without doing the inner pursuit that ensures happiness?

Walt's Life Rhyme #82: Live Up!

They say that when you mess up
the key is not to give up
When you're down if you can look up
it's easier to get up

Face challenges and rise up
commit and never let up
To standards you must live up
and always send the praise up

So no matter where you wind up
you're sure to always end... UP!
Live UP!

Are you looking in the right direction?

Live Up
Walt's Life Rhyme #82

"I share what I know,
so that others may grow!"
www.LifeRhymes.com

Walt's Life Rhyme #81: So Why Worry?

I used to spend time fretting
over things I would not choose
Constructing plans to build
huge homes of fear I'd never use

Like flowers, your life needs tending
and events are like lovers you woo
They respond to time you're spending
and what you're giving attention to

'Cause the stats are 50-50
that this or that thing will come true
But sway in favor of the choice of which thoughts
your daily thoughts pursue

So Why Worry?
Walt's Life Rhyme #81

"I share what I know,
so that others may grow!"
www.LifeRhymes.com

Commentary:

So you're worried that he'll show up uninvited, and cause drama at your event? But if you look at his history, you'll notice that even when you *did* invite him, and even when he promised to attend, that he rarely showed up anyway. So, it seems to me that based on past performance, there's a greater probability that he won't show up.

Sometimes the things we worry about aren't likely to happen even in the worst-case scenario. So why worry? Don't get trapped in needless worry about a possibility that likely won't come true.

Walt's Life Rhyme #80: See You At The Finish Line *(The MLM Mantra)*

Yes we're in this for the duration
proving beyond all sense of doubt
That commitment is the key to it all
and what it's really all about

Some dropped out along the way
bright faces filled with hope
Who let impatience steal their dreams
convinced they couldn't cope

Many with us at the beginning
have disappeared without a hint
Some we thought were distance runners
were in it just to sprint

But like I said though we're still here
we know the score, we know the deal
In a race where runners falter
this simple secret I shall reveal:

See if 9 out of 10 stop running
and give up hope and lose the race
The only thing you need do to win
Is commit to keep up the pace!

See You At The Finish Line
Walt's Life Rhyme #80

"I share what I know,
so that others may grow!"
www.LifeRhymes.com

Commentary:

Success is indeed a journey, or as some have said, "the progressive realization of a worthy ideal."

It's a fact of life and particularly of business that 9 out of 10 people will not stick with something once they've started. That being the case, achieving success is like running a race with 9 other runners who are destined to drop out before the race is ended. All you have to do therefore is just decide to keep going, no matter what, and you're guaranteed to win! Sometimes overcoming is simply about staying with it UNTIL you get to the finish line. Whether in business, marriage, friendship, or family, many who don't get that point will never stick around long enough to experience the joy of the journey. Failure is nothing more than stopping and allowing the race to go on without you.

Walt's Life Rhyme #79: A Roadmap For Success

Let the fire deep inside you
be your guidance on your road
Let the fear of mediocrity
give you strength to bear your load

Let the power of creation
find an outlet through your being
Let the faith in a bright future
be the sun that aids your seeing

Let the desire to be more
drive you to do what you must do
And remember above all else
to yourself you must stay true

For life's a journey of successes
your dreams are fuel and force
Accept, adapt, combine with action
that's all you need to stay on course!

A Roadmap For Success
Walt's Life Rhyme #79

"I share what I know,
so that others may grow!"

www.LifeRhymes.com

Walt's Life Rhyme #78: Which One Rules You?

Everything we do in life
and every thought we voice
it's love or fear and nothing else
from which we make our choice
Which one rules you?

Which One Rules You?
Walt's Life Rhyme #78

"I share what I know,
so that others may grow!"
www.LifeRhymes.com

Commentary:

The truth of reality is that there are only two causal emotions: fear and love. These two represent the cosmic dichotomy, and all spiritual awakening is based on the realization of this truth. This is important because once you accept that there are only these two causal emotions, it becomes easier to assess the motives behind everything you are doing or plan to do. If you can honestly say that the reason you are doing something stems from love of yourself or others, then by all means go ahead and do it. If, however, it is plainly evident that you are acting out of fear, then you may wish to change your motives. Actions done out of love will invariably create a better life for you. Actions done out fear usually just perpetuate fear.

Fear of not having enough makes you pursue professions for money but for which you have no passion. Fear of ridicule, embarrassment, and shame prevents you from attempting to earn a living in nontraditional, and more satisfying ways. Fear of failure is what cripples you from even trying. Fear of success is what keeps you living a life of mediocrity rather than confronting the greatness within.

Love, on the other hand, is the palate you dip into when you begin to paint a life worth living. In any relationship, the more you love someone, the more committed you are to not hurt them. The same should be true in your relationship with yourself. Unfortunately, many people don't exercise the same standards when it comes to how they treat themselves. If they did, their day-to-day decisions would be a lot different. Love of yourself decides that you're worth more and that no sacrifice is too great for you. In fact, it's impossible for any act of love to be a sacrifice. Love of the gift of life you've been given is what makes you want to experience it to it's fullest by being and doing all that you can, regardless of what others think." [EXCERPT FROM *Turn Your Passion Into Profit* by Walt Goodridge]

Walt's Life Rhyme #77: Out of The Blue

Out of the blue you might say
that they always come back
At the most crucial times
guess they just have that knack

Out of nowhere it seems
that they always appear
When you're not even looking
when you say you don't care

Out of the woodwork you'll notice
they come to reside
No way to escape
no you never can hide

For the blue that they come from
is the sky of your mind
Whether clear, blocked or open
thoughts returning in kind

And your nowhere's a road
on which actions do steer
And events in your life
are the signs that appear

And the woodwork's your home
built from thought, word and deed
That decides how you live
whether captive or freed!

Out Of The Blue
Walt's Life Rhyme #77

"I share what I know,
so that others may grow!"
www.LifeRhymes.com

Commentary:

Though you may think that the circumstances, people and events of your life are random, the truth is that they are the result of the thoughts you think, the words you speak, the choices you make and actions you take. Nothing in your life is really out of the blue. Make the connections between your thoughts and the world you're living in.

Walt's Life Rhyme #76: Script Or Heart

Don't play the part of villain
or you might get cast in stone
A life lived in a world of foes
is a life lived all alone

Don't play the helpless victim
in supporting role or lead
A starring role as scapegoat
is a role they'll always need

Avoid the frequent battle scenes
you might succumb to rage
No hero rises free of scars
from wars that others wage

Don't play the village idiot
though there are always roles to fill
Once cast as clown to jeer or mock
then mock they always will

The world's a stage as someone said
and each must play a part
But choose your own and each day ask:
have I followed script or heart?

Script Or Heart
Walt's Life Rhyme #76

"I share what I know,
so that others may grow!"
www.LifeRhymes.com

Commentary:

It's very easy to get caught up playing a role that others have chosen for you. It's easy to be the victim, to be the good child, the perfect spouse or a host of other roles at the expense of denying who you'd really like to be. Your parents, families, and society are quick to assign certain roles to those who will play them. Your job, however, is to listen to your heart and play only those roles that support you in the fullest expression of the you that you were meant to be!

Walt's Life Rhyme #75: Stay On Track

What would I be doing now
if things were going right?
Well I wouldn't be sitting here glum and blue
in panic o'er my plight!

Who would I be calling now
if the pressures were taken away?
I'd be planning some new goal to reach
and rehearsing what to say!

What would I be thinking of
if these roadblocks were not there?
Most likely deep in thoughts of love
and not in thoughts of fear!

So that's what I should be doing, then
from now on despite what seems
For obstacles are what you'll invariably see
with eyes taken off of your dreams!

Stay On Track
Walt's Life Rhyme #75

"I share what I know,
so that others may grow!"
www.LifeRhymes.com

Commentary:

Have you lost focus because of the chaos, or is there now chaos because you have lost focus? Are you unhappy because of the rejection? Or, did you get rejected because you were unhappy? Hmmm. The trick to success is learning how to stay calm and focused despite the chaos; learning how to keep your head up even in the face of adversity, disappointment, rejection and what others call failure. Stay on track.

Walt's Life Rhyme #74: Damage Control

Some said, "Cool, no problem, stuff happens"
others said, "Off with his head!"
Some showed themselves to be fair-weather friends
and off into the sunset they sped

And when turbulence hits and threatens the ship
and flash storms churn a once even keel
Some will jump ship and others will bail out
to live their lives in an unforgiving sea

But the journey goes on unaffected
and the port is still firmly in sight
And neither hook nor crook nor absence of light
can ever knock us out of this fight!

Damage Control
Walt's Life Rhyme #74

"I share what I know,
so that others may grow!"
www.LifeRhymes.com

Commentary:

Inspired by my own experience with a computer glitch that resulted in hundreds (perhaps thousands) of duplicate emails being sent to my subscribers, this Life Rhyme is a reminder that things may often go terribly wrong, that there'll be crises that threaten your credibility, damage your reputation, offset your goals, and test your resolve. But, this is often par for the course for anyone charting his or her own course in life. Welcome these crises, for there are naught but tests of your commitment.

Walt's Life Rhyme #73: Keep It Open

Keep open the road.
For blocked you'll find your path
unless you

keep open your choices.
For limited you'll find your options
unless you

keep open your eyes.
For barren will be your view
unless you

keep open your mind.
For you'll want for inspiration
unless you

keep open your heart

For nothing good can fill your cup
enough to quench your inner thirst
Unless you empty to receive
and give a drink to others first!

Keep It Open
Walt's Life Rhyme #73

*"I share what I know,
so that others may grow!"*
www.LifeRhymes.com

Commentary:

What do your heart, your eyes, your options, and the road all have in common? Answer: They all increase the good that can bless our lives when we keep them open. Keep the flow of good coming into your life and create a flow of good for others by giving of what you have. Remember, no more can be poured into a cup that is full. Keep it open.

Walt's Life Rhyme #72: Insight

The floodgates are open
and the downpour begins
The same words again spoken
among strangers now friends

And the gifts fall like raindrops
on a parched desert soul
And now move me to question
much of what I've been told

For often in life's great puzzle
we're forcing pieces in the dark
Not knowing what we're building
so we mostly miss the mark

But right knowledge aids vision
and remembering sheds light
And knowing the shapes of the pieces
makes all things fit right!

Insight
Walt's Life Rhyme #72
© Walt F.J. Goodridge
"I share what I know,
so that others may grow!"
www.LifeRhymes.com

Commentary:

The more you know about yourself, the better equipped you'll be to put the pieces of your life together. The more in tuned you are with your history and your own personal past, the more the pieces of the present day person you can fit into a coherent picture. Sometimes you'll find that dispelling the misconceptions of your past frees you to experience the world in vastly different and empowering ways. Turn on the lights. You'll miss some of the pieces if you're in the dark.

Walt's Life Rhyme #71: Happy New You

It's here again just better now
don't get tired of the fight
Another day to set new goals
365 more to get it right

It's here again just stronger now
renewed commitment to the race
On your mark, get set, get ready, go!
the perfect time to set a new pace

It's year again, just brighter now
create is what you'll do
Construct the pieces of your world
and don't forget: have a happy new you!

Insight
Walt's Life Rhyme #71

"I share what I know,
so that others may grow!"
www.LifeRhymes.com

Commentary:

It's been said, "today is the first day of the rest of your life!" Regardless of what the calendar shows, every day represents an opportunity to set some resolutions and start the rest of your life anew.

Walt's Life Rhyme #70: Out From Under

I'm getting out from under
and quite anxious to see
What bright shiny future
is in store now for me

I'm getting out from under
and it's really about time
For it's been too long I've carried
this heavy load of mine

Getting out from under
with the dawn of a new year
No more delaying my dreams
time to switch to high gear

Getting out from standing under
and I'm getting to understand
That the power to change my world
is here in my own hand!

Out From Under
Walt's Life Rhyme #70
© Walt F.J. Goodridge
"I share what I know,
so that others may grow!"
www.LifeRhymes.com

Commentary:

[From a letter from a fan] "*...I was trapped inside an illusion...a toxic, dead-end relationship, disguised as some sort of whirlwind romance, at least in my imagination. For years I was caught in this web of (self) deception. Though a part of me knew this wasn't meant to be - a bigger part refused to admit defeat. Soon the battle of mind and emotion ensued and I tried everything I could to mold, mend, mesh (manipulate) this situation to gel with the vision in my mind.*

I volunteered for Project Torment, enlisting with every intention of going above and beyond in my fruitless attempts at proving myself worthy (although worthy of what I was never sure) Settling for less than what I knowingly wanted and far less then what I deserved!

Intellectually I knew that I couldn't afford to tolerate this ritualistic emotional assault, but unable to explain this logic to my heart, I held on... I suffered through silently, striving to believe love really would concur all. My denial led to desperation and my commitment turned into contempt for self. His fury had infected my spirit and I didn't know what to do. so I prayed

Out of the blue one Friday I get this email from some guy named Walt. Who was this man, was he talking to me? As if he were sent to answer my prayers - whoever he was, he was right on time and his message crystal clear: Get up !! You've been down long enough – it's time to let this go. You've done your best and you'll be blessed - but you need not stop your growth! Thanks, Walt .. (for letting God use you) I'm UP ...and I'm getting out from under! Peace & Blessings - Respectfully Submitted"– **Ms. L.P.**

Walt's Life Rhyme #69: Am I In It To Win It?

Am I in this to win it
or just here for the show?
Content with life's sameness
or committed to grow?

Am I in this to win it
here to put forth my best?
Blazing trails others follow
or in line with the rest?

Every day every minute
this decision I make
And my thoughts, words and deeds
show the path that I take!

Am I In It To Win It?
Walt's Life Rhyme #69

"I share what I know,
so that others may grow!"
www.LifeRhymes.com

Commentary:

Are you committed to the dream? Are you serious about success? Do you really want what you say you do? If the answer to these questions is yes, are your actions consistent with your professed level of commitment?

Walt's Life Rhyme #68: The Wake Up Call

Some hear the bell signal it's time to arise
but roll out of bed still too late
And miss their appointment with fortune and fame
yet still seek to blame it on fate

Some snooze while trains bound for their good start to board
and wake a bit too late to pack
And watch in despair while countless others go on
pulling out well on time and on track

And of those living lives deep in restless dark slumber
who retire each night asking why?
Hear the ticking of time turn their goals to alarms
yet through comfort and fear just don't try

The truth is the life lived each day you create
through your actions your dreams you allow
And whether nightmare or daydream or fantasy wild
you're living your dream life right now.

The Wake Up Call
Walt's Life Rhyme #68

"I share what I know,
so that others may grow!"
www.LifeRhymes.com

Commentary:

It might be a sobering thought, but the truth is that you are right now living your dream life. Your life right now is the real result of the dreams you keep and the dreams that you really believe you deserve. Our dreams become the days and our actions provide the ways. So, if you don't like the life you're living, wake up! Take action! For if you don't take actions to make your dreams come true, you'll still be living a dream life, it'll just be someone else's! So, whose dream are you living? Don't allow procrastination and self-destructive habits to sabotage success.

Walt's Life Rhyme #67: On My Own Terms

Beyond the ken of average men
my vision of life lives on
I strive and yearn for the moment when
these shackles of want are long gone

I refuse to live life in installments
just on weekends doled out like good will
I opt for my prize in the always and now
with my cup running over and filled

For life's no screen test for the future
nor rehearsal for opening night bow
I'll take success in life as it should be
with dreams paid fully with interest right now!

On My Own Terms
Walt's Life Rhyme #67

"I share what I know,
so that others may grow!"
www.LifeRhymes.com

Commentary:

Don't delay! You can wait for some future time to start enjoying life, or you can make the decision to start living it on your own terms right now.

Walt's Life Rhyme #66: The Pivotal Moment

There comes a single moment
of which all great winners speak
When you know beyond all doubt
you will achieve the goal you seek

This magic milestone moment
brings and end to all your fear
The question now's not "if"
but simply "when" will you get there

Your dreams become your destiny
you've changed the way you see
You answer yes instead of no
to life's possibilities

But if you try to find it
this hard truth you'll realize
It comes when it's expected least
revealed to heart not eyes

But when it comes you'll know it
it's a line as plain as day
For between past dark and present dawn
there are no shades of gray

The Pivotal Moment
Walt's Life Rhyme #66

"I share what I know,
so that others may grow!"
www.LifeRhymes.com

Commentary:

The moment that your concept of yourself matches your belief in your abilities to achieve it, the world changes. Night becomes day. But this will be no gradual dawn. It will be a moment of clarity that comes in a blinding flash of insight and awareness. When this moment occurs, there'll be no reason to wait, no need to seek approval or anyone's advice. You will simply act, because you will know.

Walt's Life Rhyme #65: It's Only Make Believe

What you expect to make
believing it's true
well, that's what you'll be paid

And the ills that befall you
are usually those
of which you are afraid

And mountains will move
of this be quite sure
believing just a seedfull

And doubt not for once
that more can be yours
if ever you are needful

The fairy tale life
to make it your own
be childlike and naïve

The truth is that dreams
come true for you if
yourself you can make believe!

It's Only Make Believe
Walt's Life Rhyme #65

"I share what I know,
so that others may grow!"
www.LifeRhymes.com

Commentary:

Much of what you'll ever accomplish and experience in life comes as a result of mastering the game called "make believe." Whether it's how much money you can earn or whether you'll meet the person of your dreams, you live in a creative universe that returns to you that which you dwell upon with the conviction of your deepest belief.

Walt's Life Rhyme #64: The Ladder of Success

The ladder of success
is not something you search for
placed in secret by others
found leaning defiant
on some far and distant great wall

No….
It's a part of your toolbox
yours to carry since birth
plant and hoist where you choose
there to scale any hindrance
yes, indeed, no matter how tall!

The Ladder of Success
Walt's Life Rhyme #64

"I share what I know,
so that others may grow!"
www.LifeRhymes.com

Commentary:

You can achieve anything you desire, because everything that you will ever need to find happiness was given to you at birth. Even as you pursue success in our society, remember that you do not need anyone's permission or the validation of titles, degrees, or even diplomas in order to climb the ladder. The ladder is yours to place against whatever mountain you choose to climb. You've already got what it takes!

Walt's Life Rhyme #63: Humbly

I don't have to feel that I'm better than any
to do things better than most
I don't have to flaunt all my wealth to the penny
to prove I've got riches to boast

The core of esteem comes with wisdom expressed
in actions that most never see
And matters the most when all others are blessed
as I take the main focus off me

Humbly
Walt's Life Rhyme #63

"I share what I know,
so that others may grow!"
www.LifeRhymes.com

Commentary:

It's not always about you. It's been said that if you help enough people get what they want in life, that you automatically get what you want!

Walt's Life Rhyme #62: A Challenge For Discovery
(For the Shuttle Discovery)

FRONT PAGE IN THE NEWS

An exploration of sorts and a metaphor for life
has made the front page of news here today
It starts with the countdown then liftoff with man's
search for answers up up and away

While below here on earth another frontier remains
with equally infinite worlds to explore
And the challenge for us is to blast off within
for solutions that few will search for

Yes our own *inner* space doth remain twice as vast
the mental journey extends twice as far
But it's not just a search to see who's out there as such
but one to find out for sure who we are

A Challenge For Discovery
Walt's Life Rhyme #62

"I share what I know,
so that others may grow!"
www.LifeRhymes.com

Commentary:

"Inner Space: the final frontier. These are the voyages of this self-growth exercise. To seek out new worlds and remove limitations. To boldly go where few of us have gone before…"

Perhaps, this should be the mantra of our own personal space exploration program. Perhaps the keys to understanding life on this planet can actually be found within the vastness of potential of our own thoughts rather than out there. You think? Share it with someone who is seeking answers and happiness out there rather than within.

Walt's Life Rhyme #61: Compensation Is Appreciation

Compensation is appreciation, my friend
that's the first thing you should know
When others love you and the things that you do
that's one way for them to show

Fear not that others think it true
that a sale means that all good will is lost
Devalued worth brings low regard
in that which has no cost

Our world is such that money is thought
the child of evil spawned
Yet rules our lives through absence 'til
truth's light from darkness dawns

See, money does good and also does bad
whether crook, king, villain or star
The wealth you earn won't make you bad
it just makes you more of what you are!

Compensation Is Appreciation
Walt's Life Rhyme #61

*"I share what I know,
so that others may grow!"*
www.LifeRhymes.com

Commentary:

As a career coach who helps people turn their passion into profit, I always encounter people who feel guilty, and that it is somehow wrong for them to be paid money for the creative things they do. I like to encourage those individuals to realize that money is just one way for people to show their appreciation for the value, beauty or information you add to their lives. We live in a society in which it's already been decided that money will be a standard medium of exchange. Your talents are a gift from God. Your creator knows you live in a capitalistic society, and has equipped you with the means to sustain yourself. Honor that gift by allowing it to enrich others' lives and yours at the same time. The money itself is not evil; it's what you choose to do with it that defines you. And for those who feel more comfortable working for someone else, I say, your time is the most valuable thing you own. Do you feel just as guilty for trading your time for money, as you do in a job?

Walt's Life Rhyme #60: Ask the Inspirer
Interrupted

When others cross your line
it's up to you to let them know
Yes, confrontation's hard
but if not done your life is woe

The rules of common courtesy
should never be transgressed
They state that all are due respect
from birth 'til laid to rest

Don't compromise this basic right
or turn the other cheek
For none will know they've erred
if you never choose to speak

The principles you stand behind
your world they will create
The self respect that others see
is what they duplicate

Interrupted
Walt's Life Rhyme #60

*"I share what I know,
so that others may grow!"*
www.LifeRhymes.com

Commentary:

"Dear Walt, I need inspirations like yours everyday! Is it just me or are there some rude people in this world? Every time I'm on the phone here at work, people interrupt and start talking as if they don't get it...when someone is on the phone, common sense tells me not to disturb them until they're off. Am I alone on this one? A friend said I'm here to serve and I should let it go. What do you think?"–Interrupted

Dear Interrupted, I know how you feel about being interrupted. It's a simple courtesy that many people just don't practice. I felt the same way for a long time. What I found, however, is that there are thousands of people like that. The answer, therefore, lies not in changing THEM, but in changing myself to be able to let them be who they are, but WITHOUT letting them walk all over me. You've got to be able to let people know what your boundaries are without fear of reprisal. I know you feel you'll jeopardize your job if you tell someone what you're really thinking, but trust me, people will come to respect you for setting limits. Why not just say, very politely, "Could you give me a minute please? I'll be off in a bit, thanks" (big smile, no venom), then turn your head and finish your conversation. Then when you're done, say, "Now you were saying?" Stay strong, don't get upset and realize that while you should live on a higher plane of maturity, you don't have to compromise your values either. Interruption IS inconsiderate, and if it bothers you, YOU need to assert that. "Service" does not mean you allow *slavery* or *disrespect*.

Walt's Life Rhyme #59: Just Because I Am

A voice just declared I'm entitled to love
just because I am
No taxes, no charge just like rain from above
just because I am

I never knew that I could live without pain
that others would help me with nothing to gain
just because I am

I know now as well it's alright to want more
that heaven is not the birthright of the poor
just because I am

I learned on my own it's ok to have fun
that happiness is never depleted or done
And more can be mine still with each rising sun
just because I am

No reason is needed, don't have to justify
The biggest of dreams can be mine if I try
Just stand up and claim it and boldly state why
just because I am

It's already mine this much I should trust
It's fair and it's right and in life it's a must
To have all I want and to know that it's just
....because I am!

Just Because I Am
Walt's Life Rhyme #59

"I share what I know,
so that others may grow!"
www.LifeRhymes.com

Commentary:

If, as a child, you were loved only when you behaved according to the plan, then you may now feel that you have to earn everything that is given to you. You may feel that life's enjoyment is rationed in finite portions. You may resent others you meet who are "just too happy." You may walk on eggshells for fear of reprisal and punishment just as you did when you were younger. You may feel guilty just for being, never feeling that you can be loved and rewarded just for being who you are.

Well, it doesn't have to be that way! Remind yourself: "I am a creative expression of an abundant universe. We all come from the same place, and there is no order of value on any of us. What exists can be mine to use because I am of it and it is of me. I deserve to share in the expression of abundance of which I am a part! There is freedom, peace and abundance that I am entitled to pursue, and accept without feeling guilty, and without feeling that someone else will be deprived in the process! I can dream it, want it, create it, enjoy it and feel I deserve it...just because I am!"

Walt's Life Rhyme #58: Words of Praise

If more of us had heard
words of praise and not just punishment
Then less would live in fear
of another shoe about to drop

If only we had gotten
support and heartfelt adoration
Then more would have the skills
it really takes to be on top

And though your life once performed
is a thing you can't replay
It's now well within your power
to hear the words *they* didn't say

So give *yourself* words of support
insert your own love right here
Accept, grieve, forgive
and make today a brand new day!

Words of Praise
Walt's Life Rhyme #58

"I share what I know,
so that others may grow!"
www.LifeRhymes.com

Commentary:

In a memorable episode of *Oprah*, author John Gray, III, talks of the importance of hearing words of positive reinforcement, unconditional love and acceptance early in our development. Such words of praise form the basis of our self-esteem that carries into adulthood and determines how worthy, capable and deserving we feel of having the best in our lives. The good news is that though not possible to relive life, it is possible in a way to revise the effects that the absence of such words may be having in our lives. Personal development hinges on the underlying belief that change is indeed possible, and that the point of power is in the present, not the past. Share this with someone who needs to let go of the debilitating effects of an unhappy past and create new possibilities for themselves. They need to know it can be done!

Inspired by John Gray, III and Oprah Winfrey

Walt's Life Rhyme #57: A Titanic Discovery

Like Titanic was sunk
my belief in life's luxuries
Submerged like a wreck
under my own fearful sea

In the quest for lost treasure
I dive deep down inside
And untangle the thoughts
that will soon set them free

Priceless truths that I find
coins of wealth, health or freedom
Now can rise from their prison
and take their place around me

I AM meant to have more
and my internal adventure
Reunites me again
with all things that can be!

A Titanic Discovery
Walt's Life Rhyme #57

"I share what I know,
so that others may grow!"
www.LifeRhymes.com

Commentary:

In her book, *9 Steps to Financial Freedom,* Suze Orman suggests that our present financial situations are connected to our earliest memories of money and how we were first introduced to it. Once we resolve, remove and reframe our concepts of what money means in our lives, we can start to create new associations. When you make the connections that are keeping you in lack, it can like finding hidden treasure--a discovery of titanic proportions!

Walt's Life Rhyme #56: The Promptings Come In Whispers

I'm learning how to hear it
thought it's faint and gets drowned out
A guide who tells me where to go
but chooses not to shout

It sends me signals from another plane
shows me things I might not see
Who to avoid, who to embrace
it clears my path and sets me free

At times I might feign deafness
and vainly choose another course
But usually look back in regret
when the road I take gets worse

So now I practice getting silent
to hear the falling of a pin
Yes, I'm learning how to listen well
to the still small voice within

The Promptings Come In Whispers
Walt's Life Rhyme #56

"I share what I know,
so that others may grow!"
www.LifeRhymes.com

Commentary:

Learn to trust your intuition. That still, small voice within often provides you with the best course of action when faced with life's challenges. Before you can hear it, however, it will be necessary to clear the clutter and calm the chaos of a clouded mind. Whether through meditation, prayer, yoga or silent introspection, you can achieve clarity of thought and a connection to the divine when there is less distracting you. Spend time in silence. Share this with someone whose chaotic, unhealthy lifestyle is clouding his or her perceptions and is leading to self-destructive habits that sabotage success.

Walt's Life Rhyme #55: In The Flow & Just Do It

In the Flow

And if it turns into gold simply from your touch
and things happen on time without the usual rush
If your life starts to resemble the dreams you once had
and you're passing the tests that once made you sad

If your words calm the wretched and give strength to the weary
and the things that you do help the poor and the hungry
It's a sure sign your vision is now touching a great many
like a beacon of hope for those who might not have any

For when you live life ensuring that others achieve too
whatsoever you want is always granted to you!

Just Do It

Down many different paths at once
this private journey's led
To the many me's I've met
each time I face the deeds I dread

With each new fear I tackle
is revealed a brand new me
With brand new gifts to give
like priceless fruits from a secret tree

But none can know when greatness
dormant from our hearts will spring
For it's hiding in our fears
'til we resolve to do the thing

In The Flow & Just Do It
Walt's Life Rhyme #55

"I share what I know,
so that others may grow!"
www.LifeRhymes.com

Commentary:

You'll know when you are engaged in your life's work doing the thing that is your passion, because things fall into place and you enter that timeless realm of reality known as "the flow." And of course, the way to enter that sublime state of existence is to face your fears and just do it! It's the secret of happiness.

Walt's Life Rhyme #54: What It's Really Worth

Until I learn to respect my own time
the world will always impose
Until I value my talent some more
my masterpieces will go unsold

Until my best means as much to me
as I wish that others feel
Then no one else will come to trade
or be uplifted by the deal

The terms of sale are simple then
for you always get what's due
If who you are has worth to you
it will for others too!

What It's Really Worth
Walt's Life Rhyme #54

"I share what I know,
so that others may grow!"
www.LifeRhymes.com

Commentary:

At the core of all of our challenges is the issue of self-worth. If more of us valued ourselves, then we would create situations in our lives that reflect that value. All success, whether in business, personal life or romance, starts from an inner conviction that you are worth more, that you matter, and that you deserve to have more! People will respect your time and your talents to the degree that you do. If you are in business, you must learn to charge appropriately for your goods and services if you are to run a profitable venture. Do not allow your own feelings of inadequacy to undermine the value of the things you create. In relationships, you must set and maintain your value so that others will pay you the respect and attention you deserve.

Walt's Life Rhyme #53: In Your Master's Voice

When there's no good reason not to
and you feel like choosing not
It's the opposing team of failure
trying hard to block your shot

When you lose the fire of forward
and choose to stay in bed and sleep
You'll be sure it's the clutch of never will
that's grasping at your feet

The familiar face of failure
visits often as a friend
It's up to you to send it off
and choose victory in the end

So how to tell, how best to see
the habits that keep you back?
It's your thoughts from others' views of you
that's keeping you in lack

So ask the stars what road to take
what move to make your choice
Your guide towards the prize you seek
speaks in your master's voice

In Your Master's Voice
Walt's Life Rhyme #53

*"I share what I know,
so that others may grow!"*
www.LifeRhymes.com

Commentary:

The Master's Voice is about our "failure mechanism." Our failure mechanism is what keeps us doing the things that will guarantee our failure. Even though we all say that we want success, our fear of success, and our desire to stay within a familiar comfort zone are the real deciding factors in our everyday decisions.

We all hear voices that guide us throughout the day. We all have a familiar guide which consults us when any opportunity or decision presents itself. This guide often speaks to us in the voice of our fears, the voice of our self-perceptions, the voice of our beliefs and our expectations. It is what will always keep us on the outside of our dreams looking in.

Your "master" is that belief or perception which has the greatest influence over you. If your master is fear, doubt and low expectations, then that is the voice you will hear. If your master is prosperity, self-love and faith, then that is the voice you will hear. Find and choose your master and then listen well!

Walt's Life Rhyme #52: With New Resolve
The MLM Mantra

This will be the shot that hits
This will be the glove that fits
I've tried before and missed the mark
abandoned runs, aborted starts

I know the goal is mine to reach
no ifs, no buts, no more retreats
I've seen what those around me do
I've even taught and helped a few

With new resolve and force of will
this one last try myself I'll give
To cast aside the nagging doubts
create the life I've dreamt about

And sayers of nay stand back and see
the greatness freed, that now is me!

With New Resolve
Walt's Life Rhyme #52

"I share what I know,
so that others may grow!"
www.LifeRhymes.com

Commentary:

Whatever your goal is in life, all you need to do is persist, and one day it will "click" for you. Don't get discouraged if it seems that you've traveled this road before, or if others who started after you have passed you along the way. Constant motivation is required. Some days you will feel more charged than others. Sometimes, even when you get charged up, even the charge will feel familiar. You may say, "I felt excited just like this last time, and nothing different happened." Just know, however, that success is a process. And sometimes the only difference between yesterday and today will be your resolve—that simple, yet powerful inner decision that this time will be different. In fact, the only thing that separates successful individuals from the "also rans" is that the winners resolve to keep going no matter what.

(MLM = Multilevel Marketing aka Network Marketing)

Walt's Life Rhyme #51: In The Quest For Excellence

In the quest for excellence
Some will ransom respect
and claim a birthright to bounty
through righteous self pity
by pointing to the evil that others have shown

In their search for glory
some find their yardstick for greatness
is wedged in the dirt
of oppression and hindrance
and measures only the depths that they've known

But you, my friend, to be truly free, must
measure the distance to the stars
from the heights that you've flown
expect a harvest of good
from the seeds that you've sown
And trust in the outcome of actions
of none but your own

In The Quest For Excellence
Walt's Life Rhyme #51

"I share what I know,
so that others may grow!"
www.LifeRhymes.com

Commentary:

I heard a radio program recently in which two guests were in a debate over which of their respective ethnic groups was more victimized by their plight in history. It was as if whoever could prove they suffered more was more deserving of pity, and hence more favor. To me it displayed a sense of entitlement that based one's right to prosperity not on contributions to society, not on the nobility of their causes or intentions, not on obstacles overcome, but on what others have done to them.

Life Rhyme #51 is a reminder that while you may have had a rough life, and may feel entitled to compensation for being wronged by another, and that while society may indeed compensate you for the evil that others do to you, the universe rewards you for what you do in the here and now! Don't feel like the "entitled victim."

Walt's Life Rhyme #50: The Silent Performance

A silent performer's work by dawn is unveiled
delivered not on a stage but electronically mailed
With no one to see and applaud when it's done
with no cameras no lights save the rays of the sun

On the stage of your mind my performance I give
and the meaning is gleaned from the life that you live
For your life, like a melody you bring to my show
and what my words mean to you only you're meant to know

Yes, it's all done together, this our concert of thought
for my words without readers like you come to naught
Meting meaning and message midst the madness of life
while their pleasure and passion give some pause from the strife

Just a messenger still for an author on high
thoughts dispatched 'round the globe in the blink of an eye
And in each Inspiration when on Friday you wake
comes presented a gift, your own show that you make!

The Silent Performance
Walt's Life Rhyme #50

"I share what I know,
so that others may grow!"
www.LifeRhymes.com

Walt's Life Rhyme #49: Put It Out There

Put it out there so they see it
that's the only way they'll know
But soon your star to heights will rise
viewed by all from high and low

Like seeds your dreams you'll plant them deep
but give them sun once grown
The best you've borne don't keep them hidden
a tree by fruits is known

Real worth through boast and hubris deep
will get lost in what you say
But humbly placed your words are signs
that for others show the way

So reach your peak, let fear retreat
through deed and tongue you'll sell
In time the fruits themselves recite
...oh, the stories that they'll tell!

Put It Out There
Walt's Life Rhyme #49

"I share what I know,
so that others may grow!"
www.LifeRhymes.com

Commentary for Walt's Life Rhyme #49

Several years ago, while struggling through the transition from employee to entrepreneur, I found myself on a temp assignment. It was a data entry project that required a certain amount of concentration to perform. Consequently, my fellow temps and I spent more time working than talking, (which I suppose is the way our employer would have wanted it.)

During the middle of the second week, one of two young ladies with whom I was working came back from a long weekend. The other young lady began briefing her on the new guy--our new coworker--who had started working in her absence. I overheard her say, "John is very interesting, he's traveled a lot and yadda, yadda yadda." Well, to be quite honest, my ego was in a spin. At the onset of the assignment, I had chosen not to divulge much about what I did in my entrepreneurial ventures. Even though I hadn't talked much or told them some of things that I'd accomplished, I felt a little jealous that they weren't saying that I too was interesting. I thought to myself: "Oh, just you wait. Soon you'll know who you have sitting here next to you!

The truth is, I really had no one to blame but myself as they did inquire into my background. I just downplayed it in my usual humble act, and also partly because I was embarrassed to be taking odd assignments to supplement my income. After all, I thought, I'm a former radio DJ, record label executive, civil engineer, published author, inventor, poet and professional network marketer.

I wanted to tell them all the things I had done and was about to do. I wanted to have them be in awe of my accomplishments and say nice things about me too. It was an ego battle of the fourth degree. However, having perfected the art of the "ego-submersion", I remained silent and channeled the feeling into this Life Rhyme #49! The desire to tell all actually subsided as I wrote the words and I felt quite calm afterwards.

The very next day--the Friday this Life Rhyme was released-- we all had a most enlightening discussion wherein we helped one of our group really think about which direction she wanted to take her life. It was my contention that she should follow her dreams and not her father's. During the course of the conversation, I had the opportunity to share my own experiences and accomplishments and why I encourage everyone to do what they love.

So now they know almost all the things I've done including some even I had forgotten. I also got a referral for a potential customer out of it! Yep, I put it out there so they could see it. After all, it's the only way they'd know!

Walt's Life Rhyme #48: What Am I Building?

So what am I building, as I work every day?
Am I constructing my future or just temping for pay?
My efforts are bricks my foundation my dreams
My faith my supports and my prayers like beams

Is it a road of regrets that I build sure to fail?
Is it a wall of defeats with no ladder to scale?
Is it a fortress of fear to bind dreams that can't fly?
Is it a prison for hopes that then wither and die?
Is it a fence 'round my wishes with no way out, through or in?
Is it a castle for others while without I peer in?

To build bridges of victories over doubts I must choose
To build tunnels of experience that help others get through
To build towers up high from there vast lands survey
To build a temple inside and show others the way

And then built by design from a plan to be grand
my monumental life over time will still stand!

What Am I Building?
Walt's Life Rhyme #48

"I share what I know,
so that others may grow!"
www.LifeRhymes.com

Walt's Life Rhyme #47: It's All Good

I'll still stand if they steal it
for trinkets and jewels are not the real me
and things that do matter are mine to have free

I won't bawl if they break it
for my heart remains strong with a strength they can't know
and true gifts will not shatter but withstand any blow

I'll survive if they sell it
for my shelter's not brick, and if they knew my landlord
they'd know where I dwell, that no bank can afford

It's no loss if I lose it
for a pension and paycheck's a pawn's only prize
But true payment in life are one's dreams for the wise

I'll still get there without it
'cause the things that I own don't determine my fate
And I'll fly that much higher with no extra weight

It's All Good
Walt's Life Rhyme #47
© Walt F.J. Goodridge
"I share what I know,
so that others may grow!"
www.LifeRhymes.com

Commentary:

A friend and fellow entrepreneur was recently going through some rough times. He was facing a deteriorating rent situation with a mounting overdue balance, and was faced with the very real possibility of being forcibly removed from his apartment. It was a situation which required a great deal of faith. He couldn't be home to watch his possessions if indeed the sheriff did come, for he needed to be out earning money to pay the rent. As he was a very positive individual with an enviable "faith quotient", he did what many of us passionpreneurs might do, he took a chance and hoped for the best.

We'll look back one day and realize the good that came as a result, and marvel at the infinite wisdom of the universe. Until that time, however, what happened can only be described as unfortunate. My friend returned home to find that his possessions had indeed been removed from the premises and left out on the sidewalk. By the time he got home, much of his valuables had already been looted by people walking or driving by, who picked freely from the pile of articles they assumed to be discarded or abandoned. Gone were much of his clothes, stereo, papers, books, pots, pans, furniture and more. It's an experience I wouldn't wish on anyone. I wrote this Life Rhyme to soothe the loss and to focus his thoughts on where his true wealth resided.

Walt's Life Rhyme #46: Come Into My Whirl

In a lake quite still I dipped my hand
and stirred to make it spin
The motion touched a kindred soul
and someone else joined in

Caught in the swirl and pulled inside
like driftwood by the sea
A thousand hearts and minds joined in
attracted by my dream

Like wisps of breeze that father storms
and shake the world with force
My little spiral growing still
pulls mighty ships off course

This movement now on its own (r)evolves
and draws whole nations in
The ripple from a single act
that caused the world to spin

Come Into My Whirl
Walt's Life Rhyme #46

"I share what I know,
so that others may grow!"
www.LifeRhymes.com

Commentary:

In his book, *The Powers of Thought*, Omraam Mikhael Aivanhov paints the following picture : *"you are standing at the edge of the sea, twirling a stick in the water. Gradually you create a tiny whirlpool and some little straws and a few corks or pieces of paper begin to chase each other round and round. You keep twirling your stick and some little boats are caught up in the movement....you go on and on and, one after another, huge liners start whirling round...and you keep twirling your stick until the whole world is caught up in the movement! And now for the interpretation of this little story: human beings also swim in an ocean, in the etheric Cosmic Ocean, but they don't know what motions to make in order to influence their environment and obtain results. ...that is what this [spiritual] work I am talking about is: the motions you have to make to get things moving."*

The image Aivanhov painted immediately struck me as analogous to what was happening in the Poets Niche, an online community of poets which had its genesis in me, but is not of me at all. Life Rhyme #46 (one of my own personal favorites of all the Life Rhymes) is all about the other minds that are touched and sparked into action by a single vision.

Walt's Life Rhyme #45: Here's What They Say

Unless I start conforming
they say my climb will be quite brief
But my ways are all of spirit
and I rise on my beliefs

They say my loyalty is suspect
and I don't work with the team
But I'm in synch with all my muses
and I'm committed to my dream

They say I don't take well to orders
that my laziness runs deep
But I listen to my heart and soul
and build pyramids in my sleep

They say keep time with the masses
and let my rebel drum be tame
But my rhythm is inspired
and so I play a different game

But my faults will prove my virtues
when my world's seen by their eyes
And what they called reckless abandon
was really true faith in disguise

Here's What They Say
Walt's Life Rhyme #45

"I share what I know,
so that others may grow!"
www.LifeRhymes.com

Commentary for Walt's Life Rhyme #45

JOURNAL: I am determined to create my wealth entrepreneurially. While living with friends during the lean and down periods in my life, many people suggested that I go out and get a regular job in order to sustain myself. While there's nothing wrong with working a 9 to 5, for me, that won't be the way to go. What I need to learn in order to be successful in my ventures is a level of faith, commitment, confidence and experience that comes from doing. I need to learn how to swim by swimming. I need to learn how to fly by flying. I recall all the people who were fearful of leaving their secure jobs because of the uncertainty factor, and ultimately still have not left. I swore that I would never end up that way.

I did "temp" a few times. I took a three-day assignment that, after being independent for the last three years, was pure hell! It didn't do much for my self-esteem, either. So I resolved that I would use the temp route only in emergencies. I always had it in the back of my mind that if things got really bad, I would call up the temp agencies and offer myself for an assignment. Well, things got bad, and I made the call. But, there was nothing available! This unforeseen situation called for some different thinking and a new sense of urgency to get cash rolling in.

Life Rhyme #45 came from these thoughts, and is for all those who think outside the box. It's for all the mavericks who know, beyond the shadow of a doubt, that they are meant for something greater! It's for the entrepreneurs for whom freedom is more important than so-called security. It's for all the people who have heard, as I have, from bosses, best friends, family and foes alike that "it's tough out there", "you've got a good job, why do you want to give that up?", "it's not as easy as you think." It's for all those who are experiencing the deluge of doubt and derision that others dump on your dreams and dowse your flame of greatness so they they can have the company of someone else equally soaked in misery.

I don't want to believe that my good is linked to servitude and slavery--or as my friend Diamond says, to life "on the plantation." I maintain that this is a demonstration of my faith rather than mere stubbornness. Besides, stubbornness isn't necessarily a bad thing.

Walt's Life Rhyme #44: Try Another Door

I thought it was the Universe
that was holding back my good
That fate, and luck and cards and stars
against me did conspire

It made no sense to me at all
exactly why they should
It's just my plight back then in life
quite plainly seemed that dire

And then one night I clearly found
a trick that wouldn't fail
A foolproof plan I realized
I'd used at times before

When good seemed locked away in vaults
I didn't weep or wail
Instead of cursing fate
I simply tried another door

Try Another Door
Walt's Life Rhyme #44

"I share what I know,
so that others may grow!"
www.LifeRhymes.com

Commentary for Walt's Life Rhyme #44

JOURNAL: Recently, after launching a new internet site, I sent out about 25,000 emails announcing it to my subscribers. Then, I tested my ability to access the site, and to my dismay, was completely unable to access the internet. Every time I logged on and tried to access the site, I received an "unable to make connection with server" error. I tried to visit other sites, and received the same message. I panicked.

"What was going on?" I asked myself. What a catastrophe! For the entire weekend following a large mailing, NO ONE would be able to visit my site. I figured it was the Universe throwing up interference in my run toward success. But why? Was I supposed to be learning something from this? Was there something I was supposed to be focusing on instead. Was the Universe shutting down the entire internet so that Walt would not be successful just yet? Was I not prepared for fame, fortune, or at the very least, the luxury of paying my rent on time? For the next two days I battled with these thoughts. I listened for news reports confirming that the world wide web was strangely slow this weekend. Hearing no such reports, and with growing frustration over my plight, I decided to call it quits, shut down the computer and go to bed.

However, as I headed off to sleep at 3:00am that morning, something inside me clicked. I can't tell you what it was. But, I suddenly had the thought that there might be actually be another explanation, and something I could do to right this. Could it be that my phone connection was the issue? Though it was also conceivable that Father's Day traffic was jamming up the information superhighway, I wasn't one to remain passive, no matter what my beliefs about the how the Universe sends messages. I turned the computer on and tried to access the Internet by using another access telephone number.

Lo and behold! Bada bing! Bada boom! Wouldn't you know it! Kiss mi neck! I was online in a jiffy surfing and clicking with glee! Whew! Imagine that! It wasn't the Universe at all, it was me! All I had to do was simply try a different way in!

Walt's Life Rhyme #43: Out In Front

Be strong, you the leader
for your actions will seem like folly
to those who've always been led

Have faith, you the savior
for your works will cause disbelief
in the minds of those most dead

Take heart, you the visionary
for your dreams will seem pure fancy
to the masses of men who don't

Stick with it, you the victor
for the race will seem most lonely
when you're the farthest out in front

Out In Front
Walt's Life Rhyme #43

*"I share what I know,
so that others may grow!"*
www.LifeRhymes.com

Commentary:

Life Rhyme #43 contains words to be heeded by any who would aspire to greatness. Ever since I graduated from college, I've wanted to achieve success as an entrepreneur. When it came time to go into the workforce and choose between the two job offers I had, I chose the one that offered less money because they were flexible in when I could begin. I decided to take the entire summer off to pursue some business ventures. Perhaps if things went well, I thought, I'd call up my prospective employer at the end of the summer and "regretfully" inform them that I had become a millionaire and therefore wouldn't be coming in to work.

Well, things didn't quite work out as hoped, but I never gave up the dream. I toiled late into the night, early in the mornings, weekends, lunch hours, and pushed myself to extremes of endurance in order to get my first company off the ground while working a nine-to-five. Seven years later, when I walked away from a well-paying civil engineering profession (still haven't looked back yet), there were those who thought and still do think I'm crazy!

Maybe I am. But I'm also at peace with the direction that I have taken my life. It's always been more important for me to be independent. And, after following a dream that others couldn't see, after feeling so far "out there" compared to the rest of my friends and family, I've done and created in my life what I had always envisioned! For that I am proud of my strength, my faith, my heart and count that move as a personal victory.

Walt's Life Rhyme #42: Fortunes Of Thought

Why others have much while some none at all
oft my mind this question does haunt
The haves seek a world they've been told is their right
those without have memories of want

Your words and ideas about wealth will affect
like chains or wings will bind or free
To be in league with moguls and monarchs
Live from the feeling that this is for me!

For the one thing that separates rich from the poor
is not from brick, wood nor steel wrought
It's while some build worlds of lack with beliefs
others build fortunes with thought!

Fortunes Of Thought
Walt's Life Rhyme #42

"I share what I know,
so that others may grow!"
www.LifeRhymes.com

Commentary for Walt's Life Rhyme #42

Fortunes of Thought was inspired by an article in *Forbes* magazine listing the 400 richest people in America. It stated that a significant number of the fortunes in the list were made not in the traditional ways. In previous eras, wealth came by controlling the means of production of paper, steel, etc. Today, fortunes are made overnight by individuals who deal in intellectual property and control ideas (i.e. software, websites, licenses, trademarks, copyrights). The writer of the piece said something about today's wealth being "fortunes of thought." The line intrigued me and I knew right away it would make a great title for a Life Rhyme.

JOURNAL: I'm reading a book entitled *The Trick to Money is Having Some* by Stuarte Wilde. Great book which basically goes into the mindset one must have in order for money to be attracted into his or her life. Also this week, I saw an Oprah show on *The 9 Steps to Financial Freedom* by Suze Orman. All these messages are coming to me at the same time that I'm experiencing the same lack I vowed I would not repeat. My rent is late again. My telephone service has been cut off. I know beyond the shadow of a doubt that my struggle is not one to find the perfect product, or the best marketing strategy, nor the best mailing list, but simply to free myself from the thoughts that I've grown up with concerning money.

By all outward appearances, there's no reason why my pockets should be empty. I have talent by the truckload, business ideas by the bushel and inspiration into infinity. At the same time, there's a voice that reminds me of past memories of never having enough. That recording is what my life is dancing to. It's the familiar refrain that my subconscious chants in my mind at the same time that I sing my songs of freedom from debt and lack. I've got to do whatever it takes to drown out that noise and take my place among monarchs and millionaires!

My good friend, Odette, gave me some insight into providing service to people. She reminded me that in all the creating that I've been doing—from websites to business plans—that I might have been forgetting the main ingredient to success: helping others to get what they want. She said that each person's required level of service is different. And even though the things I was creating had the potential of helping others, my intent might have been more the wealth and fame than true service. And it might be more of what I wanted to create, more so than what people needed.

She might be right, for some things are happening which are indicating abundance coming from another direction. Among the great responses to my Life Rhymes, there've been two requests from people who want me to create personal Life Rhymes for them. One young lady wrote that she liked them so much that she'd like me to write something for her wedding. Another was from a young lady who was feeling a little bummed out by school and life and wanted a personal Life Rhyme to keep her motivated.

So, taking Stuart Wilde's advice, when people show up at your door because of something special that you give out to the universe....bill 'em! I enjoy writing the poems, and judging from the responses I've been getting, they are providing a valuable service to others. It should be no surprise then, that channels of support and potential income are coming from that direction. Perhaps *my* fortune will come by way of *these* thoughts.

Walt's Life Rhyme #41: Victory Is An Act Of Surrender

When you live without the freedom
that's yours by right divine
Your life becomes a prison
and your thoughts your world confine

When you live without the blessings
that come freely when you ask
Then every step you take in life
seems like the hardest task

When you live without the happiness
that a smile could easily buy
You'll always envy your brother's rise
and never know quite why

In your battle for fame, success and wealth
your prize no man can hinder
It's not a fight you win by force
Victory is an act of surrender

Victory Is An Act Of Surrender
Walt's Life Rhyme #41

"I share what I know,
so that others may grow!"
www.LifeRhymes.com

Walt's Life Rhyme #40: How I See It

Some say it's a race,
and the trick is to win it
The more people you pass
the better your finish

Some say it's a game
with players and pawns
Control the most pieces
and they'll say that you've won

Some say it's a dream
so don't get too involved
When you wake up in time
all problems are solved

Some say it's a show
you just watch, smile and sigh
Don't look for an author
don't ask yourself why

I say it's a road trip, with its left turns and rights
a flight with no limits that you take to new heights
With dreams as your tracks each event is a station
I see life as a journey, not a destination!

How I See It
Walt's Life Rhyme #40

"I share what I know,
so that others may grow!"
www.LifeRhymes.com

Walt's Life Rhyme #39: It's On

My time is right now
and I sprint at the gun
No doubt who's the winner
the race has been won

I've fought all my foes
and I've battled the best!
The prize is in hand
'cause I've passed every test

This day's photo finish
was already in mind
An image of success
Seen a thousand times

Divine flow and energy
hasn't failed me yet
I can hurdle with the swiftest
and I don't break a sweat!

It's On
Walt's Life Rhyme #39

"I share what I know,
so that others may grow!"
www.LifeRhymes.com

Walt's Life Rhyme #38: The Tables Have Turned

The tables have turned
yes the tide has now shifted
I'm now lifting others
where before I was lifted

Take someone with you
as you soar to new height
Your wings become stronger
their burden becomes light

The Tables Have Turned
Walt's Life Rhyme #38

"I share what I know,
so that others may grow!"
www.LifeRhymes.com

Walt's Life Rhyme #37: Take Time Out To Be Great

While chasing privilege, chasing power, seeking fortune and fame
there's a secret you can use at will to make others remember your name

It's what you do with cameras off and no press 'round to greet
that makes your image stick in minds and hearts of those you meet

A friendly call, a word of love, a lunch date just to talk
A caring smile, a birthday wish, a listening ear, a walk

Make a difference in the hours when the daily chase is done
You'll find greatness isn't a prize to be caught, but an honor to be won

Take Time Out To Be Great
Walt's Life Rhyme #37

"I share what I know,
so that others may grow!"
www.LifeRhymes.com

Commentary:

JOURNAL: Today I helped a dear friend put a few of the pieces of her life on the table so she could see where they all fit.

Walt's Life Rhyme #36: Jumping Into Abundance I

Standing on the edge of my today
looking out to my future
I feel like jumping but
fear the fall
It's only natural to look down when
you've never really tested your wings

My faith will be the wind
that lifts me up, up and away
The unseen force in life
that will keep gravity at bay

I take one step
What will it feel like to fly?

(…to be continued)

Jumping Into Abundance I
Walt's Life Rhyme #36

"I share what I know,
so that others may grow!"
www.LifeRhymes.com

Commentary:

This Life Rhyme is about my bid to acquire an apartment which was a bit of a step up in rent and represented a leap of faith in my ability to afford it given my situation at the time. Now living in Silver Spring, MD with a friend, I was quickly getting acclimated to life "south of New York." I'd been visiting apartments all week in search of some place to call home. I found one in particular which had a great: balcony, two bathrooms, nice exposure and priced a bit steeply.

In discussing the decision with a friend, we decided that I should "go for it!" There were, of course, all the usual fears and doubts that come with biting off a bit more than I was used to. I resolved, however, that I would indeed take the leap. If I was approved for the apartment (there's that pesky credit rating again), I'd have to follow some advice I'd heard that "If you bite of more than you can chew....then chew like crazy!"

I was prepared to do a whole lot of chewing in order to meet the obligations I was getting myself into.

Walt's Life Rhyme #35: Jumping Into Abundance II

The breeze I awaited
Came mixed with some rain
But I jumped, and I floated,
And I flew just the same!

The cloud that I aimed for
Is not one I ride
The height was all ego
The view, mere false pride

Through the sky of my life
I soar high just as free
On a cloud called grace
Abundance is all that I see

Jumping Into Abundance II
Walt's Life Rhyme #36

*"I share what I know,
so that others may grow!"*
www.LifeRhymes.com

Commentary:

JOURNAL: I didn't get approved for the expensive apartment. However, I did get a really nice one literally just across the street that, as I look at it now, is actually more to my liking!

Iyanla Van Zant says that there's someone in your life who's always taking care of you. Her name is Grace, and she always knows best! Grace knew I had no business (not yet, anyway) taking such an expensive apartment, and did what she needed to in order to save me the further heartache of realizing it the hard way!

Sometimes, we can't always be sure that the decisions we make are really in our best interest, even if they appear to be taking us higher. Sometimes, in fact, we've been so programmed for hardship and failure that we actually seek to create situations that cause more of the same in our lives. Until we know for sure (and that's about operating from a position of true self-love), there's a force that exists to keep us on the right track! Thanks, Grace!

Walt's Life Rhyme #34: On My Way Back Up

Like a prophet I rise
after bearing my cross
Resurrected from a tomb
of my own backward thoughts

Like a ball I bounce high
after hitting the ground
Reaching up to the skies
with the new strength I've found

Like a phoenix I soar
up from ashes of me
Nothing left but to do it
and be all I can be

On My Way Back Up
Walt's Life Rhyme #34
© Walt F.J. Goodridge
*"I share what I know,
so that others may grow!"*
www.LifeRhymes.com

Commentary:

This is the quintessential Life Rhyme!

Whenever I wish to give someone an idea of what Walt's Life Rhymes are all about, I'll send them this one. It is the epitome of the inspirational message. It speaks to everyone who has ever faced and is overcoming hardships. It is an anthem for every entrepreneur who keeps trying after each lesson that life throws. It is a ray of hope for those who can still see the light at the end of the tunnel even when their journey seems darkest. And it is a heartfelt validation for those who understand that unbecoming and rebirth are keys to personal growth.

Walt's Life Rhyme #33: San Diego

Sometimes the impossible happens
and you learn that dreams come true

Sometimes success will show itself
and you haven't got a clue

Sometimes your plans just fall in line
and it's not because of you

Sometimes the impossible happens
and you can only say "Thank You"

San Diego
Walt's Life Rhyme #33

"I share what I know,
so that others may grow!"
www.LifeRhymes.com

Commentary:

San Diego is about a miracle which happened in my life. The team of Network Marketing entrepreneurs of which I was a part, was holding a major event in San Diego, California. It promised to be the mother of all training events with motivation, breakthrough personal growth information, fun, as well as insights and strategies for creating a wealth mindset. I needed to be there. However, I was living in Yonkers, New York, on a friend's couch (read: penniless and practically homeless) at the time.

By all reckoning, therefore, it seemed I wouldn't make it as, in the vernacular of all true entrepreneurs, "cash flow was tight" at the time. I felt I had exhausted all the possibilities, borrowed from just about everyone I knew, and quite frankly had almost resigned myself to not going. The night before the event, I was on the phone with a friend and fellow team member discussing our similar situations. It was about 11:00 pm, and as we were in the same boat, found ourselves discussing some off-the-wall ways we could make this trip happen. She and I were having the "yeah-I-know-how-you-feel-I'm-broke-too-but-maybe-if..." conversation.

Well, right at that moment, a call came in on the other line. It was a friend who happened to know someone who had pre-purchased a bunch of airline tickets, only to have two people on her team cancel at the last minute. She wanted to know if I could use the tickets.

I got back on the line with my partner in financial straits, and told her of the situation. Now even though we are both of the mindset that God works in seemingly miraculous ways, we both hesitated as we contemplated the wisdom of actually taking the tickets. After all, they weren't free, so we'd be incurring debt. We didn't have hotel reservations in California, or any money to spend on luxuries like gum or potato chips once we got there. And then, there was that $20 admission fee to the event. Perhaps it wouldn't be wise.

But then, we put things in the perspective of those who live by faith. Here it is 11:30 pm the night before the event, we reasoned. Something is happening that appears to be an answer to what we'd been praying for. It may not be the free ticket we wished would fall out of the sky, but then, do we have enough time to wait for that to happen? It was exactly two tickets, one for a man, one for a woman. I think it would be a little ungrateful to God, an affront to the Universe, and a slap in the face of divine intervention to send it back and ask for something a little more convenient. So we decided to go for it!

Well, now to make this all happen, I needed to borrow my current roommate's jeep, drive the 25 miles to my friend's place in Queens, and have her packed and ready to roll. We also had one other stop to make. Since the tickets were pre-purchased, they were in other peoples' names, and well....(At some other time, I'll tell a story of what one can achieve with a bit of artistic license, a 24-hour copy-center, and a laminating machine.) We had to do all this, and arrive back in Yonkers in time to return my roommate's vehicle so he could leave by 3:40 am to get to work. The high-speed, action drama was under way! Miraculously, we did it all, and made it back to Yonkers by 3:35 am, which gave me about 3 minutes to shower, dress, pack and for all of us to head out the door, so my roommate could drop us at the train station on his way to work.

THEN, with luggage in hand, we settled in for the 90 minute train ride to the last station, where we would then catch a ferry boat for another half-hour trip to Staten Island. There we would meet another friend at 6:00am, and ride to the airport to meet the friend of the friend who was getting us the tickets. Confused yet?

But wait, it's not over yet! Soon we were at the airport, each with our single piece of identification in hand, talking our way past the better judgment of airline personnel, so we could use the tickets. Ultimately, it all worked out and we were on a plane on our way to sunny California!

But wait, there's more! Having just made all our plans at about 12:00 midnight, we had no hotel room, no transportation, and I might add, no money once we reached San Diego! But, the wonderful thing about being part of our team, is that we all understood the challenges that we all face in making the business work for us. One of the things we could always count on was having at least a space on the floor in someone's home or hotel room in any city where we've got team. Sure enough, we were able to do just that.

Well, as anticipated, the event was spectacular! It was another milestone in personal growth and someplace I know I needed to be in order to move to the next level of living. In fact, now that I look back, getting there was probably the first test I passed that pre-qualified me to be where I am today.

These days, both my friend and I often reflect on San Diego and what it meant to us when we talk about miracles, commitment, determination, friendship and faith! Often, when similar situations arise, I'll think to myself "another San Diego moment" and smile. It's come to symbolize a very personal miracle that enabled me to be where I needed to be in order to take the next step forward in an on-going journey!

Walt's Life Rhyme #32: The Dollar That Made Me A Millionaire

The dollar that made me a millionaire
was an ordinary sort of bill
Not very crisp, in fact quite dull
just your ordinary run of the mill

I got it at the checkout
of my favorite little store
Changed some coins into paper
so I could feel like I had more

Feeling down about my lot in life
over a success I often craved
Yet in all the years I lived and toiled
not one penny had I saved

I took it home and made a pact
for no one else to see
This wrinkled bill I'll use to build
a changed and different me

(So late that night in present tense
I made a silent vow
To reach my dreams despite my state
I had to live them now)

I imbued it with a mission then
to tithe and save and grow
A symbol of commitment
to my rise to high from low

So with this piece of paper,
depressed and almost on the dole
To spend it, though, I knew would mean
the forfeit of my goal

From that point on the tide did shift
each day I watched in awe:
I learned that wealth comes first in mind
and not by luck but law

This bill I've saved to this day still
was equal to the task
For the dollar that made me a millionaire
was the first one, not the last!

The Dollar That Made Me A Millionaire
Walt's Life Rhyme #32

"I share what I know,
so that others may grow!"
www.LifeRhymes.com

Walt's Life Rhyme #31: It's Not The Money

It's not the money it's the mindset
that keeps me striving for the prize
It's not the money it's the mindset
that has me smiling when all other eyes
are looking down in fear and lack
it lets me know I can't look back

It's not the money
it's the mindset that makes me free
It's not the money
it's the mindset that has me be
all that I want and all I see
and brings me closer to divinity

It's not the money,
it's the mindset that brings me love
It's not the money
it's the thoughts from up above
that give me strength and give me peace
that lets the joy in life increase

It's not the money,
it's the mindset that makes me healthy
It's not the money
it's the mindset that makes me wealthy
and safe from ills and fear and greed
and harm and want and lack and need

It's not the money, it's not the money
I repeat it's not the cash!
Though it would be nice to have my share
a piece, a little stash!

Money comes in droves when it's crystal clear
that the wealth life will be bestow
is a measure of the love that you let yourself show

For money is life's reward for being true
your earthly prize for being you

It falls like rain when you finally live
the truth that to get you first have to give

It's not with money that you make your dreams real
but with thoughts from above that no man can steal

The secret to success is revealed in this clue
it starts not with the money at all, but with you

It's Not The Money
Walt's Life Rhyme #31

"I share what I know,
so that others may grow!"
www.LifeRhymes.com

Walt's Life Rhyme #30: The Millionaire's View

What would I see from a millionaire's view?
How would I act if my dreams now came true?

What would I do if I simply believed?
How would I feel if my goals I achieved?

Where in the world would my happiness lead?
Who would I help up in word, thought or deed?

To make that world real here's my formula how:
the only sure path is to be that way now!

The Millionaire's View
Walt's Life Rhyme #30

"I share what I know,
so that others may grow!"
www.LifeRhymes.com

Walt's Life Rhyme #29: All Things Matter

If you think all things matter then, my friend, think again
for all things that have come shall soon pass
For all things that are matter and not spirit or soul
are just one of the things you'll outlast

Inspired by H. Walters

All Things Matter
Walt's Life Rhyme #29

*"I share what I know,
so that others may grow!"*
www.LifeRhymes.com

Walt's Life Rhyme #28: I Have a Friend

I have a friend who gives so much
it makes ME hurt inside
When others are in need of help
his heart is opened wide

He gives in ways that were it me
I'd see it as a chore
But not my friend, he gives and gives
....and then he gives some more

I asked him if he doesn't see
their inch become a mile
He said "Of course, but give I do,
and do it with a smile."

I asked what was his secret
so I could hone the skills I lack
He said, "Just give and know in time
somehow it all comes back!"

I Have A Friend
Walt's Life Rhyme #28

"I share what I know,
so that others may grow!"
www.LifeRhymes.com

Dedicate to E.J.C.

Walt's Life Rhyme #27: Save This Piece of Me

Save this piece of me
for I may need it back someday
Hold that view of me
for no one else knew me that way

Remind me who I was back then
before we grew apart
No one else can comprehend
what lives within our hearts

High and low our paths diverged
today we reunite
And childhood ways and dreams
come once again now into sight

The keeper of my secret dreams
support through ups an downs
A source of strength and friendship
when my smiles turned into frowns

Let's make a pact to reconcile
this promise I'll fulfill
To keep alive that part of me
that sees you that way still…

Save This Piece of Me
Walt's Life Rhyme #27

"I share what I know,
so that others may grow!"
www.LifeRhymes.com

To fathers, mothers, brothers, sisters, cousins, lovers and friends who've lost contact.

Walt's Life Rhyme #26: Life's Adventure Into The Unknown

Think of change as adventure
and greet chaos without fear
When challenges beset you
it means a new chapter is near

Jump into life boldly
and hang on for the ride
The ups are there to instruct you
the downs there to guide

Life may shake and break you
and build you up anew
It's the only way that really works
to make a better you

Your journey offers lessons
even sages could not teach
They prepare you for the heights
and the greatness you will reach

So try the untried way
do the thing not often done
It's the only way you'll find
to make your true good come

For it's in the unknown places
that it often seems
Life gives you the chance
to fill in your own dreams

Life's Adventure Into The Unknown
Walt's Life Rhyme #26

"I share what I know,
so that others may grow!"
www.LifeRhymes.com

Commentary:

What's the most unsettling thing you can conceive of happening to you? Is it a divorce? a breakup with that "special" someone? an eviction? being homeless? moving out of the familiarity of your "home town"? getting fired? being robbed? losing a particular possession? losing big in the stock market? the death of a loved one who has been sick for a long time? Well, sometimes what we perceive as calamities are actually the first necessary steps to the realization of our dreams.

Once we start to wish, the universe usually gives us what we want, but we're too busy looking out one window into darkness and miss the sunlight streaming through another behind us. Keep your eyes and all your windows and doors open! Opportunity may come precisely after what you perceive as tragedy, loss, chaos, destruction or disappointment. Wish for "happiness through divine order" and then know that the Universe in its wisdom knows just what has to be let go, released or destroyed from your life so that the good you desire can be let in!

Walt's Life Rhyme #25: I Can

I can do this that
and even the other thing too
There's no limit on earth
to what a focused mind can do

Every victory takes me up
and allows me to see
Down, around and beyond
to just how powerful I can be

I Can
Walt's Life Rhyme #25

"I share what I know,
so that others may grow!"
www.LifeRhymes.com

Commentary:

Every now and then, I score a victory that just puts me on cloud nine! Sometimes I feel that the only reason a particular event went my way was because I willed it to be so. It could be something as simple as a telephone call going just the way I planned, or a successful sale being made, or a successful romantic advance.

Who can say why these moments of fortune happen? Perhaps the frequency of our mental emanations are resonating at the perfect pitch needed to affect the thoughts of others. Perhaps our subtle body language communicates our desires in the perfect way. Perhaps the position of the moon and the alignment of the telecommunication and power cables beneath the ocean set up a magnetic field which creates a temporary anomaly in the space-time continuum rendering all miracles possible. Or perhaps it's these lucky shoes.

Regardless of the reason, let's use these moments as stepping stones, or wings to take us to the heights of personal power. These moments are gifts to us from a loving universe. They might be the beginning of that endless stream of blessings we've been praying for, or just a single one that trickled through to prepare us for more later! In any event, let's enjoy them and know that there are an infinite many more on the way!

Walt's Life Rhyme #24: Progress

Progress is being made.
(Sometimes it seems so slow)
Mountains are being moved
(Though it might not really seem so)

Like grass and homes and journeys long
Success and wealth will come
One inch, one brick, one step each day
Until the job is done

Progress
Walt's Life Rhyme #24
© Walt F.J. Goodridge
"I share what I know,
so that others may grow!"
www.LifeRhymes.com

Commentary:

Does your life sometimes seem like it's moving rather slowly? Do you feel as if you're forever in a state of waiting? This may be true, but often it's simply a matter of perception.

If in fact, you've been procrastinating and not working diligently and smartly towards your goals and dreams, then things might just indeed be creeping along. If, on the other hand, you're working towards your goals, yet still feel frustrated, perhaps you're choosing to focus on the wrong thing. Stop and take stock of your accomplishments and realize that as long as you are working towards the creation of your goal, you are, in fact, moving forward. It's often because we are so focused on forward that we rarely look over our shoulders to see all the ground we've traveled.

Also, it is precisely during those seemingly slow times that your good is being prepared for you. Know that there are forces at work of which you haven't a clue which are working to bring your dreams to you. People are turning left instead of right, calls are being made, romantic situations are being righted, homes are being sold, people are relocating, jobs are being given up, all in a complex but perfectly orchestrated and synchronized symphony of events which will bring your dreams to you at just the perfect time and in just the perfect way! So don't curse the slow, act like you know!

Walt's Life Rhyme #23: Which Ones To Keep

Live in the thoughts of your most treasured experience
not in the pain of your last

See from the heights of your loftiest dream
not from the depths of your past

Judge and be judged from your best creation
not from what you didn't do

Your power in life comes from which thoughts you keep
and which you let pass on through

Which Ones To Keep
Walt's Life Rhyme #23

"I share what I know,
so that others may grow!"
www.LifeRhymes.com

Commentary:

The power to determine your reality is right here. Too often we tend to see what we believe, believe in what we see, feel the way we've been programmed to feel, and then act on what we feel.

To see the good in people and in situations, we must make a conscious effort until it becomes a habit. For many who know me, when I'm asked how I'm doing, I usually reply, "FANTASTIC!" That's a choice I made a long time ago, and one that I continue to express. One of the most powerful realizations I had occurred many years ago when I learned that I could, in fact, choose how my reaction to ANY situation. If someone steps on my foot on the train, or cuts me off on the highway, I can choose to get angry, OR I can actually choose to laugh and smile. Try it!

They say that stress comes from feeling out of control. If more people broke free of their automatic responses to people and situations, and instead exercised choice in how they responded, a lot of stress would decrease as people realized that in choice there is control. Let Life Rhyme #43 be your reminder of which thoughts to make your friends and which to send on their way!

Walt's Life Rhyme #22: Do It Now

Do it now before you're ready
'cause that's what winners do
Do it now before you're ready
'cause to wait is to lose

Do it now before you're ready
'cause no one will teach you
that things are never just right
and time is always in flight
and dreams and reality forever will fight

So do it now even though you're not ready
and you'll find this much is true:
When you seek your goal with faith and do hurry
the world will bow.... and give it to you!

Do It Now
Walt's Life Rhyme #22
© Walt F.J. Goodridge
"I share what I know,
so that others may grow!"
www.LifeRhymes.com

Commentary:

Want to know the secret to achieving all that you desire? To go where you want to go, do what you want to and be whom you desire, you must take risks and jump out, sometimes often before you are sure. Success favors the risk-taker. Seems a bit of a paradox. However, the truth is, your very first step in life was taken before you really knew if you could do it. Birds are pushed from the nest and are forced to learn very quickly how to fly. In jumping out before you're ready, two things occur. First, you take a leap of faith which is often all that's required to create your reality. Second, you force yourself to grow. For it's in our "discomfort zones" that growth occurs. Forcing the outer limits of your comfort zone is the only way to expand it.

"Do it now" doesn't mean that you won't plan your actions, and it doesn't mean you won't weigh your options before you act. It's simply a reminder that often you are more qualified than you think, you are more powerful than you believe and you can often accomplish more than you expect is possible!

Walt's Life Rhyme #21: Promises

When rent is due and checks don't clear
and bills in piles hide deep
When ringing phones inspire fear
These words I hope you'll keep

Success, you see, is like a house
and lies are sinking sand
Your word, your bond, must be like rock
the strength on which it stands

A promise kept is all it takes
to keep the world at bay
Start anywhere your word is weak
And strengthen what you say

Refund the world for stock it bought
in worthless words you sold
Through faith in time your house restored
built high on solid gold

Promises
Walt's Life Rhyme #21

*"I share what I know,
so that others may grow!"*
www.LifeRhymes.com

Commentary:

Like a lot of people who are in debt, there was a point in my life when I dreaded answering the phone for fear of encountering those pesky bill collectors! For me it was akin to that old childhood fear of punishment and that scene of being scolded for something I didn't do.

In trying to figure out the message behind the events in my life, I came to realize that creditors were calling, websites were being shut down, friendships were being lost, not as punishment for some heinous act I committed, but simply to point out something I needed to change about myself: I was making promises I couldn't keep. I needed to make some changes in how I was interacting with people, and the calls were simply a reminder of this.

Walt's Life Rhyme #20: A Work In Progress

Listen to the Universe
Listen to it well
When things don't seem to go your way
There's a message it's trying to tell

Ask yourself: what can I learn?
What truth is being shown today?
For there's always good in every bad
Despite what others say....

A Work In Progress
Walt's Life Rhyme #20

"I share what I know,
so that others may grow!"
www.LifeRhymes.com

Commentary:

Life Rhyme #20 was created during a unique phase in my life. I call it the "nomad era", and it started with an originally non-consensual, but later mutually agreed upon decision between me and my landlord for me to leave my apartment (read: eviction), precipitated by mounting debt and other "fun" stuff that are almost pre-requisites for many an entrepreneurial success story!

A few things happened recently which resulted in my website being shut down, and several other things not quite working out the way I planned. What kept me going was a firm belief in the concept that there's a lesson here, that there's something being highlighted about my life and thoughts that I need to pay attention to. In fact, in a strange way, I welcome adversity for the simple reason that I know something better is coming. Since I'm not where I want to be, there must be a process, a journey, a test to get me there. So I say bring on the tests!

This Life Rhyme is special to me because it was the first one that I consciously sat down and created to be an official Life Rhyme. It also sums up my overall philosophy about life.

And, incidentally, just what is the "work in progress?" The work in progress...is me.

Walt's Life Rhyme #19: It's Not The Money (Excerpt)

Money is life's reward for being true
your earthly prize for being you
It falls like rain when you finally live
the truth that to get you first have to give

It's not with money that you make your dreams real
but with thoughts from above that no man can steal
The secret to success is revealed in this clue
it starts not with the money at all, but with you

It's Not The Money (Excerpt)
Walt's Life Rhyme #19

"I share what I know,
so that others may grow!"
www.LifeRhymes.com

Walt's Life Rhyme #18: Epictetus

No great thing is created suddenly, anymore than a bunch of grapes or a fig.
If you tell me you desire a fig, I must first answer that there must be time. Let it first blossom, then bear fruit, then ripen. --1st Century Roman Philosopher Epictetus

Epictetus
Walt's Life Rhyme #18

"I share what I know,
so that others may grow!"
www.LifeRhymes.com

Walt's Life Rhyme #17: Principles of Miracles

A Miracle is a thought. A miracle is a correction introduced into false thinking...Miracles are expressions of love, but they may not always have observable effects. A miracle is never lost. It may touch many people you have not even met, and produce undreamed of changes in situations of which you are not even aware. [The power is within--Walt.]
--Excerpts from A Course In Miracles, Chapter 1.Principles of Miracles

Principles Of Miracles
Walt's Life Rhyme #17

"I share what I know,
so that others may grow!"
www.LifeRhymes.com

Commentary:

Life Rhyme #17 is a reminder that once we understand where power in this universe is; once we accept that we are co-creators by virtue of our ability to think, then the real and true ability to do magic can be ours. It starts with our thoughts and then our actions. When we send out thoughts of love, the world is changed forever. In your actions, the good that you do is never lost. It will return to you tenfold. The words that you say, the things that you do, the life that you change causes an effect like a ripple in a lake that ventures out and reaches miles into the sea, is touched by the Sun, is pulled into the heavens and becomes part of a downpour of good that drenches you too!

In business, this chain reaction and geometric growth is what Richard Poe, in *The Wave 3 Way to Building Your Downline*, calls the "butterfly effect." It's the concept that speaking to one person who speaks to another who speaks to another creates an eventual tidal wave effect that can make you wealthy. It gets its name from the theoretical concept that the fluttering of a butterfly's wings in Brazil can have far reaching effects on weather conditions as far away as the north pole. It's also referred to as the avalanche effect, based on the idea that one snowflake has the power to start a mass movement of staggering proportions. Its effects can be seen in business, life, love, health and even on the Internet. So create your unique effect of wealth now by sending out the right thoughts!

Walt's Life Rhyme #16: Carl Waugh

"If you have water sitting on the burner at 211 degrees, it's just hot water, but when it reaches 212 degrees it's boiling water. Momentum is that one-degree difference. In your business (and your life), that one degree starts the ball rolling!"--Carl Waugh

Carl Waugh
Walt's Life Rhyme #16

"I share what I know,
so that others may grow!"
www.LifeRhymes.com

Commentary:

"That one degree starts the ball rolling." Often it's only when things get real "hot" that many of us are forced into action. For some of us, only when we get sick and tired of being sick and tired do we have the energy to make change. We get boiling mad and then things start to cook! For many, only after hitting bottom do we have the momentum to bounce back up.

Walt's Life Rhyme #15: Neville

"Life is a controllable thing. You can experience what you please once you realize that you are…what you are by virtue of the state of consciousness FROM which you think and view the world."
--Neville, Awakened Imagination

Neville
Walt's Life Rhyme #15
© Walt F.J. Goodridge
"I share what I know,
so that others may grow!"
www.LifeRhymes.com

Commentary:

The operative word here, in Life Rhyme #15, is "FROM." Neville is reminding us that thinking OF success is great, but thinking FROM success is the way to create it!

.

Walt's Life Rhyme #14: Orin Solomon

"If it feels good in your gut, go with it!"
--Orin Solomon, ACN Regional Vice President

"Pain comes from the tendency not to follow what the heart dictates"
—(paraphrase; source unknown)

Orin Solomon
Walt's Life Rhyme #14

"I share what I know,
so that others may grow!"
www.LifeRhymes.com

Commentary:

Your "gut" is that part of you that speaks to you in feelings, not words. It is the prompting you receive to do a thing or not do a thing. It is the impression you get about a person or situation that often proves more accurate and more beneficial than any advice, or observation!

Also known as gut feelings, hunches and intuition, it's the way most great inventions come about, the way many people find their soul mates, and the way many people decide what to do in a given situation.

NOT listening to that still small voice within is a sure request and recipe for more painful lessons!

Walt's Life Rhyme #13: H. Jackson Brown, Jr.

A racehorse that consistently runs just a second faster
than another horse is worth millions of dollars more.
Be willing to give that extra effort that separates
the winner from the one in second place.

--H. Jackson Brown, Jr.
Life's Little Treasure Book on Success

--H. Jackson Brown, Jr.
Walt's Life Rhyme #13

"I share what I know,
so that others may grow!"
www.LifeRhymes.com

Commentary:

It doesn't take much to be excellent. They say that in business, to be perceived as radical and innovative, you need only be about 10% different from the competition. Imagine that! Most "new" products are simply a repackaging or slight improvement on a current way of doing things. There's an old joke that says most people are getting paid just enough to keep them from quitting, and in return, they are doing just enough to keep from getting fired! With that sort of mindset as your competition, success is a "no-brainer" for that special someone willing to do just a bit more.

Walt's Life Rhyme #12: H. Jackson Brown, Jr.

When starting out, don't worry about not having enough money.
Limited funds are a blessing not a curse. Nothing encourages
creative thinking in quite the same way.

--H.Jackson Brown, Jr.
Life's Little Treasure Book on Success

--H. Jackson Brown, Jr.
Walt's Life Rhyme #12

"I share what I know,
so that others may grow!"
www.LifeRhymes.com

Commentary:

Several years ago, when I was running my independent record label, we accomplished quite a lot despite having little to no money. It was the early 1990's, and with four artists on our roster, we needed videos to launch their careers. I often brag about how we were able to produce three outstanding videos two of which got aired on Black Entertainment Television and a host of other shows nationwide, all for under $7500! That figure will mean more if you understand that at the time, the lowest cost that most people thought you had to spend for just *one* music video was between $10,000 and $20,000.

It was through the sheer creativity and planning genius of my video producer, Lance Cain, and the generous folks who donated their time, favors and expertise, as well as the patience of the artists that we were able to get it done! It brought out ideas and a drive that made the whole project as well as the finished product quite unique and outstanding. The lack of money was not an obstacle, and never will be for anyone truly committed to a dream!

Walt's Life Rhyme #11: Les Brown

"Each of us has a unique offering. No one else is going to produce your product, write your book, open your academy. And if you don't bring your gift forward, if you die with it still inside you, then we all suffer from being deprived of your particular genius."

--Les Brown "*Live Your Dreams*"

Les Brown
Walt's Life Rhyme #11

"I share what I know,
so that others may grow!"
www.LifeRhymes.com

Commentary:

Everyone is here for a reason. We are each here to make a special contribution to the collective. Every one of us has something that we do better than anyone else. Our mission while we are here is to find that one gift (or more) that we possess and do it justice by expressing it to the world. In that expression lies our genius and our unique offering to humanity.

Is there any doubt that Michael Jackson has found and perfected his art and genius. Is there any doubt that Michael Jordan is doing what he was sent here to do? How about Mother Theresa, Gandhi, Martin Luther King, Jr.? How can you tell when you've found your universal calling? It will be the thing that gives you your greatest sense of worth and importance. It will be that thing that you would do even if you weren't paid to. It will be that thing that gives meaning to your life and to the lives of others. Find it, do it, and the world will reward you in ways unimaginable just to have you continue doing it.

Find that thing and then, as Les Brown says, you too can live your dreams!

Walt's Life Rhyme #10: Louise L. Hay

"Our minds create our future. When we have something in our present that is undesirable, then we must use our minds to change the situation. ...When there is a problem, there is not something to do, there is something to know."
--excerpted from You Can Heal Your Life by Louise L. Hay

Louise L. Hay
Walt's Life Rhyme #10

"I share what I know,
so that others may grow!"
www.LifeRhymes.com

Commentary:

Most situations in life, from illness, to unhappiness, poverty to stress are actually results and consequences stemming from our lack of awareness of truth.

The truth, as I often tell people, is that we have no control over what people do, say or feel, or over situations that other people bring about. The only thing we have complete control over is how we react to those people and situations. Once we know this truth, we are freed from the feeling of obligation to change others, and the powerlessness and frustration that comes with it. If you make changing others your mission in life, then over the course of your life you'll have hundreds, maybe thousands of people to change. If you instead make your goal changing yourself to be more tolerant, you only have one person to work on.

In other words, the solution here is not to do more, just to know more. The more you know, the less you do. Knowledge is the seed of growth.

Walt's Life Rhyme #9: Paramahansa Yogananda

"The season of failure is the best time for sowing the seeds of success.
The bludgeon of circumstances may bruise you, but keep your head erect.
Always try once more, no matter how many times you have failed.
Fight when you think you can fight no longer, or when you think that you
have already done your best...or until your efforts are crowned with success!"

-- Paramahansa Yogananda
from *The Law of Success*

Paramahansa Yogananda
Walt's Life Rhyme #9

"I share what I know,
so that others may grow!"
www.LifeRhymes.com

Commentary:

All great success stories are about the overcoming of adversity. Life Rhyme # 9 is a reminder that the ability to triumph despite obstacles is the hallmark of the great leader and achiever.

If you're not overcoming, you're not achieving. If you're not achieving you're not progressing. If you're not progressing, you're standing still. If you're standing still, your journey has ended.

Walt's Life Rhyme #8: H. Jackson Brown, Jr.

"Success is getting what you want.
Happiness is liking what you get."
--H.Jackson Brown

H.Jackson Brown, Jr.
Walt's Life Rhyme #8
© Walt F.J. Goodridge
"I share what I know,
so that others may grow!"
www.LifeRhymes.com

Commentary:

No amount of success ensures happiness. And even though most of us think the two are linked, it is only if we understand the critical difference between the two, that we can begin to marry them.

Happiness is a state of being that comes from your thoughts about things. Success is a state of having all the things about which you've thought.

Success and happiness for most people are tied together by money. In other words, they say "If I made more money, I'd be successful and then I'd be happy."

However, many successful people reveal that money doesn't buy happiness. In fact, the successful ones who are also truly happy will tell you that they had the happiness *before* the money. They were able to laugh, create the desired thoughts, and feel secure despite bad breaks, and setbacks. They had peace and a sense of fulfillment which came from simply being on the journey.

Success has been referred to as "the progressive realization of a worthy goal or ideal." I like that definition because it puts the emphasis on the journey not the destination, and emphasizes loving what you do!

So make this your new idea: "I need to be happy first, develop a sense of personal success, and then the money will come!" Once you master this important difference between happiness and success you'll be on your way to achieving all you desire!

Walt's Life Rhyme #7: Big Mama

"If you let bad times stop you,
you won't be around to enjoy
the good times."

"Big Mama, "
From the movie *Soul Food*

Big Mama
Walt's Life Rhyme #7

"I share what I know,
so that others may grow!"
www.LifeRhymes.com

Commentary:

We've all asked ourselves at one time or another: Why am I here? I believe that our souls are here to learn lessons. Each stage in life is like a grade level in school. Every now and then there will be pop quizzes, tests to see if we've been paying attention. These "bad time" tests are just our Teacher's way of seeing if we're ready to move on to the next higher grade. The really ironic thing about this school we're in, is that ALL the tests are of our own choosing. In other words, we are only tested on the lessons we need to learn. By our thoughts, intentions and actions, we tell the universe what tests to send to us. If we can't pass the first grade exams, we won't be allowed to go on to second grade. We'll keep attracting first grade tests until we get them right! And if we quit school because we're frustrated with the tests, we'll never get to graduate! Graduation in life is the reward of peace, prosperity and happiness.

Oh, and by the way, Soul Food *is a great movie! Check it out!*

Walt's Life Rhyme #6: John Luther

Natural talent, intelligence, a wonderful education--none of these guarantees success. Something else is needed: the sensitivity to understand what other people want and the willingness to give it to them.

Worldly success depends on pleasing others. No one is going to win fame, recognition, or advancement just because he or she thinks it's deserved. Someone else has to think so too.

John Luther
Walt's Life Rhyme #6

"I share what I know,
so that others may grow!"
www.LifeRhymes.com

Commentary:

While it is true that your own personal sense of worth must precede any advancement in your condition, service to others is the surest way to secure your own success. To paraphrase motivational speaker, Zig Ziglar, "You can get everything you want in life, if you'll just help enough people get what they want in life!"

Walt's Life Rhyme #5: John Randolph Price

"The Universe does not compensate individuals based
on the activity of work, but on the activity of consciousness"
--John Randolph Price
The Abundance Book

John Randolph Price
Walt's Life Rhyme #5

*"I share what I know,
so that others may grow!"*
www.LifeRhymes.com

Commentary:

If there's one thought that is central to all personal growth philosophies it is this: as you think, so shall you become. Yes, your thoughts create your reality, for as a man (and woman) thinketh, so is he (or she). Our whole journey of growth, therefore, hinges on changing the nature of our thoughts—our consciousness—and allowing everything else to follow suit. The challenge, of course, is that we are dealing with thoughts that have their origins in experiences, words and feelings which impacted us when we were young, before we were even able to recognize them, name them, and filter them if necessary. We could barely speak, much less defend ourselves. Our mission, therefore, is to uproot the weed-like thoughts which have grown up in our minds as a result of the seeds of past experience and replace them with a new garden of our own choosing. Then, and only then, will the universe reward us in the manner and with the fruits we desire.

There are certain thoughts that get rewarded with stress, poverty, lack and disappointment. Similarly, there are thoughts that, just by their very nature, lead to improved health, wealth, happiness and success. The truth is, that while we may not have the practice thinking all the thoughts, I believe we intuitively know which thoughts lead to which effects.

*Through normal powers of discernment
it's not too hard to tell
Which roads will lead to heaven
and on which your soul you'll sell*

Walt's Life Rhyme #4: Gloria Copeland

"You should refuse lack
just as quickly as you
refuse illness"
--Gloria Copeland
[from Faith's Little Instruction Book for Finances]

Gloria Copeland
Walt's Life Rhyme #4

"I share what I know,
so that others may grow!"
www.LifeRhymes.com

Commentary:

Spiritualists will tell you that the way to be wealthy is to give. Blocking the flow of abundance by hoarding your money or your talents creates poverty. Giving creates a flow of good "out" of your life which in turn encourages the flow of good "into" your life.

Similarly, the key to achieving health lies in creating and maintaining flow. All illness and disease that we experience is simply a form of blocking the flow. Eating foods that are out of harmony with the natural order (processed, refined foods, dairy, meat etc) congest the system and creates a block that impairs health.

Giving, through tithing and sharing maintains the flow that keeps us wealthy. Eating foods that are natural maintains the flow that keeps us healthy.

Every process in the universe exemplifies that flow, the passage of energy from one form to another is what keeps it all going. Rainfall, food chains, ecosystems, life and death, all rely on maintaining the flow. Breathing, what keeps us alive, is a flow of air in and out. Giving of what you own, keeping money circulating is a part of the formula for wealth.

To disrupt this flow in any way is to halt a natural process and invite lack, disorder and chaos into your life. Knowledge, love, power, control, responsibility, freedom and wealth are all valuable to us as a society only as long as they are being shared and experienced by more and more people. Disparate levels of income and power is the stuff that revolutions are made of!

Yes, there's a strikingly similar parallel between maintaining health in the body, and maintaining wealth in your financial situation.

Dollars and food you'll find
to be alike in much they do
To maintain wealth and health my friend
some of it's got to pass on through!

Walt's Life Rhyme #3: Neville

You never attract what you want,
what you wish for, or what you desire.
You attract only what you believe,
what you expect, and what you are

The secret to having
all that you desire, therefore, is to
"live FROM the feeling of the wish
fulfilled."

In other words: Live, act and be
as if the thing you desire is already yours,
and the universe will have no choice
but to bend to you!

Neville by Walt Goodridge
Walt's Life Rhyme #4

"I share what I know,
so that others may grow!"
www.LifeRhymes.com

Commentary:

Life Rhyme #2 is another of the eternal truths I've uncovered in my travels. The quote in the second verse is something from the Neville text *Resurrection*. Neville is another writer for whom I have a great deal of appreciation. And, as I often say to my friends and just about everyone I meet, "This book will CHANGE YOUR LIFE!"

The premise is this—and we'll return to this thought again and again—thoughts are things. Your thoughts create your reality. And your thoughts, coupled with feeling speed the process of achieving all that you desire! It's not enough to simply want something, you must become it. Your soul and being will then pull to it the things, events and people that resonate with the vibe you have become.

You must first be the person you wish to become, own the thing you wish to have, live in the place you wish to be and feel the emotion of the experience you wish to enjoy before it will become real. [see Life Rhyme #15 and the story behind it for even more on this topic] If this all seems a bit cryptic, and paradoxical, great! It means you've got some exciting lessons in the journey ahead of you!

Walt's Life Rhyme #2: Marianne Williamson

"Thought that is unlimited, brings experience that is unlimited.
.We are not held back by the love we didn't receive in the past,
but by the love we are not extending in the present."
-Marianne Williamson (A Return To Love)
Reflections on the principles of A Course In Miracles

Marianne Williamson
Walt's Life Rhyme #2
© Walt F.J. Goodridge
"I share what I know,
so that others may grow!"
www.LifeRhymes.com

Commentary

I've come across many books in my travels that have shaped my understanding of myself, of life and that I've recommended to friends, family and customers and clients. *A Return to Love* by Marianne Williamson is one of the more profound and uplifting among them.

My whole way of thinking was radically changed thanks to my dear friend Christine, who I consider a sister, a teacher, a mentor, therapist and friend. She was my supervisor during my work-study assignment in college, and we became friends after graduation. Were it not for her, I really don't know where I'd be today. She and another good friend, Randy, were instrumental in helping me look inward for the answers to the questions and patterns I was noticing in my life. Their guidance and love put me on whole different path that made me an avid seeker of truth. It was Christie, I believe, who introduced me to *A Course In Miracles*, a profoundly spiritual book which, for those of you who are familiar with it, changes lives. Those of you who are familiar with it also know that it is such deep reading (the type that you have to re-read a dozen times for it to sink in!) that many people may need a bit of coaching to really understand it, and that's what Marianne Williamson does. Marianne is a speaker, and teacher who's written several books, and travels the world sharing her insights and interpretation of *The Course in Miracles*. Her own book is a distillation of the central themes of The Course set in everyday language.

With my friend Christie's help, I realized the connection between my past and my inability to let people inside emotionally, my fear of commitment, my often aloof and intimidating posture, my fear of intimacy, and I was then able to begin the work of remedying the situation. It was her patience and guidance that made me open to taking the inner journey towards emotional health.

Marianne's quote is a refreshing prescription for those similarly afflicted. The remedy to all of our ills exists in the present. The point of power is in the here and now. That's really all there is, actually. The past is over and the future doesn't exist. All there is is the now. And while forgiveness and healing are all necessary parts of one's personal victory in life, they both only exist and have their meaning in the now. In other words, the question is "what are you doing in the now to heal the wounds of the past?" Often, the extending of love that Marianne talks about involves extending love to ourselves first and foremost in order to repair the holes that exist in our sense of completeness, worth and value.

Walt's Life Rhyme #1: Walt Goodridge

"The road to the top is for those who gamble with life's uncertainties, and who view setbacks as opportunities to excel!"

--Walt Goodridge, (College Yearbook)

Walt's Yearbook Quote
Walt's Life Rhyme #1
© Walt F.J. Goodridge
"I share what I know,
so that others may grow!"
www.LifeRhymes.com

Commentary:

Who is praised more, the person who steps over a pebble to reach his goal, or the one who climbs Mount Everest? Your greatness in life and your place in history and in the minds of others, and your own self-satisfaction is assured by the conquest of major obstacles.

Success is a matter of risk. Every great invention, movement, revolution and even love affair is about jumping out into the unknown. If you are not risking you are not growing.

This very first Friday Inspiration was created while I was in college. I wrote it just before my number was called to have my picture taken for the college yearbook. I don't recall exactly where I picked up that mindset, but it stayed with me throughout later years and has defined how I choose to live my life and pursue my business ventures.

[Just for the record, I'm a graduate of Columbia University in Harlem, New York City. I was let loose on the world with a Bachelor of Science in Civil Engineering. And neither the world, nor Columbia, nor me, for that matter, have been quite the same since.]

About the Author

A Columbia University graduate with a Bachelor of Science degree in civil engineering, Walt Goodridge was, like many people, destined for a career in his profession of training. And while he endured the frustration of working in an unfulfilling job, it was several years until he was able to grow his sideline business in the music industry--a personal passion--and walk away from his career to become a full-time "passionpreneur." He authored several books on the music industry, created a brand of inspiration called "Life Rhymes," and launched dozens of websites.

As he honed his expertise in website development, internet marketing, creating the life of his dreams, and living true to himself, he developed a unique "Passion Profit Philosophy and Formula" and a coaching practice to help others do the same. In 1999, he published the formula in *Turn Your Passion into Profit* which, with yearly updates, has consistently sold in the top 50 in home-business books on Amazon.com.

In 2006, Walt escaped from New York to live his nomadpreneur dream on the pacific island of Saipan. Walt now writes a weekly business column for the Saipan Tribune entitled " The Saipanpreneur Project." He has written *Doing Business on Saipan* to further encourage entrepreneurial activity on the island, and, with former garment factory worker Chun Yu Wang, co-authored *Chicken Feathers and Garlic Skin: Diary of a Chinese Garment Factory Girl on Saipan* and is the founder of Destination Saipan Marketing, Inc., a tourism company.

Walt currently owns and operates over 50 websites, has written a total of 16 books, over 400 articles and almost 500 motivational poems.

Walt is originally from the island of Jamaica, and, you can read about his first year and impressions of his new island home in the book *Jamaican on Saipan*! Contact Walt at P.O. Box 503991, Saipan, MP 96950, or via email at Walt@saipanliving.com.

NEW! Living True to Your Self

Creating the Life You've Always Dreamed of
by Walt F.J. Goodridge
(author of *Turn Your Passion Into Profit*)
Living true to your self requires that you adopt a new belief system about yourself, others, and the world you live in. It requires that you identify what's true, find your purpose, develop an effective survival strategy, overcome inertia, motivate your self consistently, sustain momentum, decipher the Universe's code to recognize the opportunities and harness the power in the setbacks, evolve in the direction of life's clues, while honoring body, mind and spirit...and that's just for starters! Who better to guide you through the internal dialogue, thoughts, and actions that can make it possible for you than Walt Goodridge, passion coach, nomadpreneur, and author of 16 books, who escaped the rat race to live his personal dream on a Pacific Island? Visit www.passionprofit.com/livingtrue ;$19.95

Books and Products by Walt F.J. Goodridge

(most are available in ebook,and paperback formats)

Turn Your Passion Into Profit (ebook, paperback, 6-CD)
The Tao of Wow
The Ageless Adept
Change the Game
Hip Hop Entrepreneur Lists of Exposure
This Game of Hip Hop Artist Management
Life Rhymes for the Passion-Centered Life
Come into Our Whirl
Lessons in Success
Hip Hop Profits
The Hip Hop Record Label Business Plan
The Niche Market Report
Chicken Feathers and Garlic Skin
Jamaican on Saipan
Doing Business on Saipan
Living True to Your Self

a complete product list, along with articles, free reports and a passion personality test are available at www.passionprofit.com

The New York Rhymes

Discovering Life's Rhyme

NEW YORK—Andrew A. used them to gain a new perspective about his relationship and credits them with saving his marriage. DST22 believes they are messages from up high written just for her. Lorna P. uses them to teach values and ethics to her 7th grade students. Thomas uses them to motivate his employees, and Susan, like tens of thousands each week, looks forward to her weekly dose "to read something that resonates deeply within me that edges me to keep on towards success." They're all fans of Walt's Life Rhymes, a unique form of self-help writings created by Walt F.J. Goodridge, an entrepreneur, author and career coach known as the "Passion Prophet."

"Life Rhymes are poetic expressions of the thoughts that create success," explains Goodridge. "They are part affirmation, part advice column, part inspired observation, part proverb, part prayer and life lesson all rolled into one. They are meant to guide your thoughts so that you see the world differently, interpret situations effectively, think critically, and make the choices that help you reach your goals and highest aspirations. And like the easily-remembered lyrics of a favorite song that stay with you for years, these are literally rhymes for your life."

Life rhymes are inspired by everything from Walt's personal insights, phone conversations, headlines and current events to memorable episodes of Oprah. With well over 365 now in existence (he's consistently written a new one every week for 7 years), they offer guidance on everything from business building, relationships, marriage, divorce, child-raising, spirituality, job security and romance.

All reinforce Goodridge's personal philosophy of the pursuit of one's passion, personal accountability, and spiritual growth as the foundation for success in life, with titles like "Just Because I am", "There's Something About Money", "What if I Shine Too Bright?" and the recent #351--"Reverse Then Make a Right" which some suggest is a thinly veiled commentary on US foreign policy:

It's not a sign of weakness to admit you might be wrong
In fact some say you'll access strength that's been there all along

It's not the end of greatness to admit you might be lost
It's greater to save time than to save face at any cost

It won't invite disaster to admit when you don't know
For only to the emptied cup will wisdom ever flow

It's not the road to ruin to go back and start again
The options on the retraced path elude most average men

It's not through compensation that you heal a victim's heart
To listen and seek justice...that's the best way you can start

And it's not by way of vengeance that true justice you invite
But actions that reverse your course, and serve to make things right.

Life Rhyme fans look to Walt's weekly creations and commentary for insight and guidance when interpreting life's many "situations." They give voice to and often confirm the inner wisdom we all have access to. As one fan remarked, "If the still small voice within communicated its wisdom in rhyme, this is what it would sound like." And, as thousands of fans worldwide have attested, they always seem to show up in their inboxes at just the right time, speak just to them, and can literally change lives! But whether you credit divine inspiration, or simply a poet's insightful musings, one thing is clear: if not reason, life now at least has some rhyme to it.

Browse all 365 Life Rhymes, order *Life Rhymes in paperback* at www.liferhymes.com.

READER FEEDBACK

RE: #107: (In The Comfort Of Our Own Creations") — "THANK YOU, this came at a good time. GOD for some reason always sends me answers. Love, a friend" —BBart

Re: #141 ("A Tale Of Time For The Tardy")—"Oh now Walt, you've stepped on some toes this time. Expect a few e-mails from some folk asking to be removed from your list! I'm just kidding! You hit the nail on the head with this one!" —Millicent Kelly

Re: #130: ("The Currency of Your Life")—"This one was particularly valuable. It is manifested everyday ... but never articulated the way you have. Brilliant!!! Particularly, for friends of mine, (and I'm sure you have some too) that "know the cost of everything, but the value of nothing.""—Saleem

Re: #104: ("Turning Points") —"This is a great poem .I know for me it brings to mind people friends, loved ones both dead, and living who have changed my life my direction in one way or another for the better ,and because of them the lives of my children will be affected."—Jim Roche

RE: #124: ("Echoes From Within") —"THANK YOU AND HOW APPROPRIATE TO ME AT THIS TIME.... THANK YOU, THANK YOU, THANK YOU.... I NEED TO ASK MYSELF SOME QUESTIONS... AS I FIND MYSELF REPEATING AND GOING BACKWARDS." —P Bedow

RE: #113 ("Restaurant of Wishes") —"The statement at the bottom of "A Restaurant Of Wishes" is very appealing. It sounds like a wonderful slogan for those of us who have reached crone-hood via a lifetime of experience. I am a 79-year-old widow living on an island in Puget Sound and welcome each opportunity to share my "wisdom" with those who ask for it." —Louise G. Smith Orcas Island, Washington

RE: #115 ("Keep it Simple")—"I've never sent you a reply before but today I wanted to because I number one, have loved all of your Friday inspirations! I send them on to my family and friends every week; and, two, because I think what you wrote today in response to what someone asked you is perfect! I think it is important for us to write what we feel, especially if we're wanting to touch, hopefully just one person's heart."

RE: #106 ("With New Eyes")—"I printed out your Life Rhyme this morning to read on the train. I had to stop myself from crying after reading "With New Eyes." What was even more powerful was the information you shared after the poem. We all need to be in the habit of repeating the affirmation to ourselves . . .
…and teach our children to do the same."—Zelda

For more, visit www.LifeRhymes.com

www.ingramcontent.com/pod-product-compliance
Lightning Source LLC
LaVergne TN
LVHW081255100826
845148LV00005B/887

* 9 7 8 0 9 7 4 5 3 1 3 1 1 *